California Residential Foreclosures

The Complete Guide to Equity Purchases and the Laws Governing Distress Sales

Fifth Edition

Cutoff Dates:
Legal editing of this material was
completed December 2007

Copyright ©2008 by first tuesday

Printed in the United States of America

Editorial Staff

Legal Editor/Publisher:
Fred Crane

Managing Editor:
Ai M. Kelley

Project Editor:
David F. Crane

Contributing Editors:
Connor P. Wallmark
Giang Hoang

Senior Editorial Assistant:
Joseph Duong

Editorial Assistant:
Sylvia Rodemeyer

Published by:

Zyrus Press Inc.
PO Box 17810, Irvine, CA 92623
Tel: (888) 622-7823 / Fax: (800) 215-9694

www.zyruspress.com
ISBN 978-1-933990-23-1

Table Of Contents

Section A

Guidelines for an E.P. Investor

Section B

Equity Purchase Time Frame

Section C

Property Analysis

Section D

Title Condition

Table of Forms

Introduction

If you are interested in learning the mechanics of buying and selling homes in foreclosure from the experts, then this book is for you. **California Residential Foreclosures** takes you beyond the foreclosure hype and into the practical mechanics and legal framework required to successfully execute a sale or purchase of distressed residential property.

Buyers and sellers will learn how to confidently complete transactions with simple step-by-step examples while gaining a comprehensive understanding of the pitfalls and prevailing laws that govern such transactions.

Furthermore, this book will arm the equity purchase (EP) investor with the expertise needed to apply all EP rules, while personally handling the negotiations and documentation necessary to contract for, escrow and acquire a home during the period the property is in foreclosure.

Real estate licensees and lawyers will find a comprehensive and complete treatment of the subject matter. Whether you act as an agent to a transaction or as an attorney advisor to a client, this book provides the most current laws and covers all the relevant statutory provisions that control interactions between sellers-in-foreclosure and investors. As this book goes to print, pending legislation may even require brokers representing EP investors to be bonded.

Filled with scores of case examples that present the subject matter in an easy to understand, hands-on approach, **California Residential Foreclosures** will arm homeowners, investors, licensees and attorneys with the tools necessary to handle all aspects of the sale and acquisition of residential property in foreclosure.

SECTION A

Guidelines for an E.P. Investor

Chapter 1

Equity purchase investments

This chapter introduces the equity purchase (EP) restrictions that must be known and applied by all investors who purchase owner-occupied, one-to-four unit residential property during a foreclosure.

The home equity sales scheme

An **equity purchase (EP)** occurs when an owner-occupied, one-to-four unit residential property in foreclosure is acquired for rental, investment or dealer purposes by a buyer, called an *EP investor*. Conversely, an EP transaction does not occur and the EP rules do not apply if the buyer acquires the property as his *principal residence*.

Equity purchase statutes apply to all EP investors regardless of the number of EP transactions the investor completes. The investor does not need to be *in the business* of purchasing homes in foreclosure, or even know about the EP law, for the statutes to apply to him. [**Segura** v. **McBride** (1992) 5 CA4th 1028]

Both the EP investor and the investor's selling broker must comply with EP law, or be subject to drastic penalties — the investor under the EP law and the broker under Agency law.

Printed form and language

For example, the **EP agreement** signed by an EP investor must be printed in *bold type*, ranging from 10-point to 14-point size. Also, the printed agreement must be in the *same language* used in negotiations with the seller-in-foreclosure. [Calif. Civil Code §§1695.2, 1695.3, 1695.5]

Additionally, the EP investor and all brokers and agents involved in an EP transaction must use a written agreement containing statutory EP notices. Failure to use **correctly structured forms** subjects the EP investor and the brokers to liability for all losses incurred by the seller-in-foreclosure, plus penalties. [Segura, *supra*]

*Editor's note — **first tuesday's** Equity Purchase Form 156 complies with all statutory requirements, and properly sets forth the seller-in-foreclosure's right to cancel. [See Chapter 2]*

Cancellation within five business days

Prior to closing a sale, a seller-in-foreclosure has a statutory five-business-day **right to cancel** the EP agreement he has entered into with an EP investor and avoid the sale entirely.

When the notice of the seller-in-foreclosure's cancellation rights are properly contained in the EP agreement, the seller's **cancellation period** ends:

- midnight of the fifth business day following the day the seller enters into any type of purchase agreement with an EP investor; or

- 8:00 a.m. of the day scheduled for the trustee's sale, if it is to occur first. [CC §1695.4(a)]

The seller-in-foreclosure's five-business-day right to cancel does not begin to run until **proper notice** of the cancellation period is given to the seller. [CC §1695.5]

The first and proper time for giving the seller-in-foreclosure the notice is in the EP agreement. The buyer's failure to give notice of the seller's right to cancel allows the seller to cancel the sales agreement and escrow. Further, and more critical, the seller has the right to *rescind* the sale after closing until the notice is ultimately given by the investor and the five business days have run — without cancellation by the seller. [See **first tuesday** Form 156 §16]

A **business day** is any day except Sunday and the following business holidays: New Year's Day, Washington's Birthday, Memorial Day, Independence Day, Labor Day, Columbus Day, Veterans' Day, Thanksgiving Day and Christmas Day. Thus, Saturday is considered a business day under EP law, unless it falls on an enumerated holiday. Many state holidays are not included as holidays. [CC §1695.1(d)]

No performance until notice expires

Without the seller's receipt of the notice of right to cancel, an EP transaction may not proceed to closing, a sort of limbo until the cancellation period expires. Until expiration of the seller-in-foreclosure's right to cancel the transaction, the **EP investor** may not:

- *accept a conveyance* of any interest in the property from the seller;

- *record a conveyance* of the residence signed by the seller with the county recorder;

- *transfer an interest* in the property to a third party;

- *encumber any interest* in the residence; or

- *hand the seller* a "good faith" deposit or other consideration. [CC §1695.6(b)]

Thus, escrow may be opened on acceptance, and deeds and funds may be deposited with escrow, since the seller-in-foreclosure is not delivering a conveyance (to the buyer) and will not receive funds until the close of escrow.

In negotiations with the seller-in-foreclosure, the EP investor's or his agent's representations may not mislead the seller regarding:

- the value of the property in foreclosure;

Locating properties in foreclosure

To locate properties in foreclosure and begin an investigation of ownership, debt and value of the properties, an EP investor needs data on the recording of Notice of Defaults (NODs), Notice of Trustee's Sales (NOTS), rescission of a NOD and trustee's deed, and the content of these documents.

Services exist which gather and publish the daily recording of foreclosure related documents, their contents and ancillary information on the properties available from public records. The reporting is available primarily on the internet, and is updated daily. Title companies are also a source of the recorded information.

The foreclosure data are obtained directly from recorded documents or from providers of the data who collect and enter the data directly from the county recorder's records. One such company collecting statewide data available by subscription on their website is Real Estate Transaction Network at www.retran.net or (323) 290-7132. The present monthly fee is $119.00 for access. Other websites that provide similar services include: www.countyrecordsresearch.com; www.foreclosures.com; and www.redloc.com.

Foreclosure data from providers can be sourced and sorted in any manner, such as by address, zip code, city, county, type of property, improvements (bed/bath/lot size), recording dates of the trust deed/NOD/NOTS, original loan amount, delinquency amount, Thomas Guide coordinance, etc. Data includes plat maps and photos of some properties.

- the net proceeds the seller will receive on closing escrow; [See **first tuesday** Form 310]

- the terms of the purchase agreement or any other document the EP investor uses to induce the seller to sign; or

- the rights of the seller in the EP transaction. [CC §1695.6(d)]

Cancellation of the purchase agreement by exercise of the statutory five-business-day contingency is **effective on personal delivery** of written notice of cancellation to the EP investor's address given in the purchase agreement. [CC §1695.4(b)]

If the EP investor receives the seller-in-foreclosure's written notice of cancellation before expiration of right to cancel, he must return, *without condition*, all original contract documents, such as the EP agreement bearing the seller's signature, to the seller within 10 days following timely receipt of the cancellation notice. [CC §1695.6(c)]

Accordingly, the EP investor should not place **funds in escrow** before either expiration of the cancellation period or a call from escrow for funds, since the EP investor is prohibited from coupling the release of funds to the return of documents on cancellation.

When the cancellation period expires without receipt of a cancellation, the purchase agreement becomes enforceable and escrow may be closed — unless other conditions remain to be eliminated.

Two-year, post-closing rescission rights

After escrow closes, the EP investor's title is subject to the seller-in-foreclosure's **right of rescission** for two years. The rescission must be based on some unconscionable conduct of the EP investor and an advantage on price or terms of payment. The seller's two-year right to *rescind and recover* the property from the EP investor cannot be *waived*. [CC §§1695.10, 1695.14]

Also, any provision in an EP agreement or escrow instructions that purports to **limit the liability** of the EP investor for money losses claimed by the seller due to misrepresentations of the EP investor or his broker is void. [See **first tuesday** Form 150 §10.7]

Thus, the EP investor is liable for all losses incurred by the seller-in-foreclosure due to misrepresentations made by himself or his broker. [CC §1695.15]

The EP investor is liable for any money losses of the seller caused by the investor's failure to comply with the EP statutes. Additionally, the EP investor is subject to a statutory penalty of three times the amount of the seller's losses if he transfers or encumbers the property before the cancellation period expires. Again, the period does not begin to run until proper notice is given. [CC §1695.7; see Chapter 2]

An EP investor who violates the five-business-day cancellation period or takes *unconscionable advantage* of the seller-in-foreclosure will be subject to imprisonment for less than one year, a fine no greater than $25,000, or both imprisonment and a fine for each violation. [CC §1695.8]

Also, prior to December, 2007, any broker representing an EP investor as the buyer's agent had to provide, and most likely will have to provide in the future, the seller-in-foreclosure written proof, under **penalty of perjury**, that he is:

- a licensed real estate broker; and

- bonded by a surety insurer for any losses incurred by the seller due to the broker's conduct. [CC §1695.17(a); see Chapter 3]

Chapter 2

The equity purchase agreement

This chapter sets forth the guidelines for an equity purchase (EP) investor's acquisition of an owner's principal residence that is in foreclosure, the harsh penalties for violation of the EP laws and the preparation of an EP offer.

Requirements for all EP investors

A homeowner defaults on a note secured by a trust deed lien on his principal residence, a one-to-four unit residential property. A **Notice of Default** (NOD) is recorded as agreed under the power-of-sale provision in the trust deed, placing the property in foreclosure status.

An investor, having good credit and **no knowledge** of equity purchase (EP) laws, orally agrees to sell the use of his creditworthiness to the owner. The investor will qualify to refinance the property in exchange for receiving a fee from the owner. The owner agrees to convey title as security for the deferred payment of the extension-of-credit fee charged by the investor for the refinancing.

It is additionally agreed the owner will **remain in possession** and make monthly payments to the investor. Title will be reconveyed to the owner when he pays off the investor and assumes the refinancing placed on the property by the investor. The investor coincidentaly is a real estate licensee, but at no time acts as an agent in the transaction. He acts only as a principal for his own account.

The investor erroneously believes he is purchasing ownership to the real estate when he receives and records a grant deed conveying title into his name. He will be the vested title holder of record until title is repurchased and reconveyed to the owner.

Without a written agreement or escrow instructions to document the terms of their extension-of-credit and refinancing arrangement, the owner conveys title to the investor by handing the investor his signed grant deed. The investor immediately records the deed.

Concurrent with the conveyance, the owner enters into a written sale-leaseback agreement with the investor, calling for the payment of monthly rent. The lease agreement includes a purchase option. The option allows the owner to repurchase title to the property on payment of a fixed sum of money within three years. The amount is the fee due the investor for the investor's extension of credit for the refinancing. This reverse **lease-option sales agreement** also states the investor reserves the right to sell the property on the owner's default.

The owner receives no funds for the conveyance of his equity. On acquiring title, the investor pays off the existing trust deed loan with his own funds. The foreclosure process has advanced to a Notice of Trustee Sale (NOTS) and no sufficient time remains to process the refinancing before the date set for the trustee's sale.

The investor further transfers the property's title to himself and his spouse as requested by the lender originating the first trust deed loan to refinance the property. The loan is recorded and the investor recovers the funds he advanced to payoff the delinquent loan. All costs relating to the new loan — including title insurance premiums, escrow fees and loan charges — are paid for by including them in the new loan amount.

Later, the investor again refinances the property when interest rates drop. Thus, he increases his cash flow differential between the loan payments and the rent he receives as set by the lease-option sales agreement. Prepayment penalties are incurred on the payoff, as well as origination costs for the new loan, all of which are also added to the new loan balance.

As the real estate recession deepens, the owner defaults on the monthly payments due on the lease agreement. A 3-day notice to pay rent or quit is served on the owner. Eventually, the owner is evicted from the property.

The investor then sells the property that is not now occupied. The buyer is a *bona fide purchaser* (BFP), unaware of the owner's unrecorded option rights to repurchase the property. No sales proceeds remain after the loan payoff due to a decline in the property's value after the investor took title. The owner receives no money from the sale.

The owner now makes a demand on the investor to pay the owner the dollar value of his **equity in the property** based on its value at the time they entered into the lease-option sale, claiming the arrangements violated the state's equity purchase laws.

Is the owner entitled to recover the value of his equity from the investor?

Yes! The owner is entitled to recover money equal to four times the sum of the fair market value of his equity at the time he conveyed title to the investor, minus any funds he received from the private lender.

Recovery of the owner's lost equity is allowed since the **investor violated** the EP laws repeatedly by:

- **failing to document** in writing (a note) the terms for repayment of the funds he was owed [Calif. Civil Code §§1695.3(c),1695.3(d)];

- **acquiring recorded title** to the owner's principal residence, consisting of a one-to-four unit residential property in foreclosure, without first entering into a written purchase agreement that conforms to EP statutes [CC §1695.6(a)]; and

- further **transferring title** to the property (to the spouse and again to the resale buyer) without the written consent of the owner. [**Boquilon** v. **Beckwith** (1996) 49 CA4th 1697; CC §1695.6(e)]

Editor's note — The investor in our facts should have structured the transaction as a first trust deed loan, so his advance of payoff funds would be evidenced by a note in his favor and secured by a trust deed on the property, and then collaterally assigned or sold the note and trust deed to recover his advance. Note and trust deed documentation of the loan would have avoided compliance with EP laws and the penalties for failure to comply due to the transfer of title.

Title to real estate is not transferred when a trust deed lien is created to encumber the property. [**Monterey S.P. Partnership** v. **W.L. Bangham, Inc.** (1989) 49 C3d 454]

The equity purchase transaction

An *equity purchase* (EP) transaction occurs when a one-to-four unit residential property occupied by the owner as his principal residence is **in foreclosure** (due to an NOD, not just a delinquency) and is then acquired by a buyer for investment or dealer purposes.

Although an investor may not be *in the business* of purchasing homes in foreclosure, a financing transaction structured as a "reverse" lease-option sale is a violation of EP law since **title is acquired** by the investor without the use of equity purchase documentation. On a conveyance in violation of EP law, the seller recovers four times the value of his equity plus attorney fees. [**Segura** v. **McBride** (1992) 5 CA4th 1028; CC §1695.7]

Editor's note — The use in this chapter of the real estate jargon "seller-in-foreclosure" or "owner-occupied" will always indicate the occupancy is of a one-to-four unit residential property by the owner as his principal residence.

The Boquilon court interpreted the legislative intent behind one of the EP statutes differently than the legislature expected by denying the seller-in-foreclosure an additional award of treble damages against the equity purchaser, a private lender under a lease-option sale agreement. The court concluded the lender should not be charged with constructive knowledge of EP law, and eliminated the award of treble damages.

However, in 1997, the legislature reacted abrasively to the holding in Boquilon *by modifying the statute to mandate equity purchasers be charged with knowledge of EP law, whether or not they have actual knowledge of the law's existence, and then mandatorily penalize them with a minimum additional award to the seller of at least treble damages. Hence, the minimum recovery of four times the value of the unpaid equity. [CC §§1695.6(b)(3), 1695.7]*

Now consider an EP investor who properly documents his purchase of an owner-occupied, one-to-four unit residential property that is in foreclosure.

The property will be acquired either for the purpose of flipping it in an immediate cash resale (dealer property) or holding it as a continuing investment in real estate (rental). It will not be occupied as the investor's principal residence. The investor is not represented by a broker since no broker can be located who is willing to obtain the statutory bond that will most likely be required to act as an agent for the equity purchaser.

An EP agreement form that complies with the EP statutes is used by the EP investor to properly document the transaction in writing. [See Form 156 accompanying this chapter]

Escrow is immediately opened, conditioned on cancellation of both the EP agreement and escrow within five business days of acceptance. Deeds are deposited in escrow, but the investor will not place any funds in escrow until escrow makes a demand for funds on closing. [See Chapter 1]

The seller-in-foreclosure's five-business-day right to cancel expires without the seller exercising his right to cancel. Thus, the EP agreement is now enforceable since no contingencies remain to be eliminated. The EP investor funds escrow, which closes as agreed.

Right of rescission, recovery of residence

However, once the cancellation period runs under a properly documented EP agreement and the transfer occurs (escrow closes), the EP investor has an additional risk to be concerned with — his title is subject to the seller-in-foreclosure's **two-year right of rescission**. This right of rescission after closing is held by the seller and is separate from the five-business-day right to cancel before closing.

The two-year rescission right is based on any *unconscionable advantage* the investor-buyer may have introduced into the negotiations that brought about the transaction. The two-year right of rescission cannot be waived by the seller. [CC §§1695.10, 1695.14; see Chapter 4]

However, the seller-in-foreclosure cannot rescind his closed sale and recover the property if the EP investor has:

- resold the property to a buyer who is classified as a *bona fide purchaser (BFP)*; or

- further encumbered the property with a loan originated by a lender classified as a BFP.

A bona fide purchaser or lender is allowed to know that the investor acquired the property from a seller-in-foreclosure. That knowledge does not affect bona fide purchaser status. However, they are not a bona fide purchaser or lender if a recorded lis pendens notifies them of the seller's claim or the seller is still in possession of the property and, on inquiry, would have stated his claim of unconscionability against the EP investor and right to title to the property. [CC §1695.14(c)]

Instead, when the EP investor (or private lender) has resold the property to a BFP, the recovery by the seller-in-foreclosure is converted to a **recovery of money**.

Money recovered on an EP law violation

Although the investor in the opening scenario violated three separate aspects of EP law over an extended period of time, the date of the first violation (improperly acquiring title) is the **valuation date** of the equity for the owner's money recovery. Regardless of whether the EP investor holds title to the property, the amount of money the seller-in-foreclosure can recover as his loss is:

- the dollar value of the property on the date of the EP investor's first violation;

less

- the unpaid principal and accrued interest on the existing loan at the time of the violation;

less

- any money advances received by the seller-in-foreclosure from the EP investor.

More importantly, the seller will automatically recover punitive money damages not less than three times his money losses.

The seller-in-foreclosure is also entitled to the statutory rate of interest (10%) on the value of the equity he lost from the date of the first violation, the day he was separated from his equity.

Conversely, the EP investor is not entitled to any offsets against the dollar amount of the seller's equity. Disallowed offsets include escrow costs, prepayment penalties, carrying costs of the property, maintenance and improvement costs, or any post-violation decline in the property's value due to adverse market conditions.

However, the owner is not entitled to a refund of rental payments paid to the investor since he may not occupy property rent-free, regardless of the illegality of the circumstances.

Any recovery of money by the seller must be settled or an action filed within four years of the first violation of the EP laws, usually the conveyance of title.

One further issue: the seller, due to the conveyance in violation of EP laws, has an alternative to seeking money during the four year statute of limitations period. He may seek "equitable relief." One such equitable relief is rescission and restoration of his ownership — apart from the two-year restoration based on unconscionable advantage claims. [CC §1695.7]

Structuring the EP agreement

An individual, not intending to be an owner-occupant buyer, wants to purchase single-family residences (SFRs) for investment purposes.

Acting as an investor, the individual locates an owner-occupied SFR encumbered by a trust deed lien on which a Notice of Default (NOD) has been recorded, placing the property in foreclosure by commencing a trustee's foreclosure proceedings.

Because the seller occupies the residential property as his principal residence and an NOD has been recorded, the **investor realizes** — or one of the agents realizes and advises him — that he must comply with California's EP laws when preparing and submitting an offer to purchase the property. [See Form 156]

Terms of the purchase

The EP investor is willing to purchase the SFR on the following terms:

- **pay** $10,000 cash to the seller-in-foreclosure for his equity in the property;

- **take over** the existing loan with a total of $316,000 due the lender in unpaid principal, delinquent installments and foreclosure costs; and

EQUITY PURCHASE AGREEMENT

NOTE: For use by Buyers of one-to-four residential units which are owner-occupied and in foreclosure when the Buyer does not intend to occupy the property. [Calif. Civil Code §1695]

DATE:_____, 20_____, at _____, California.
Items left blank or unchecked are not applicable.
FACTS:

1. This agreement is for the purchase of property situated in the City of_____,
   County of _____, California, referred to as
   Real property _____
   _____

   Personal property, ☐ See attached inventory_____
   _____

2. This agreement is comprised of this six-page form and _____ pages of addenda/attachments.
   TERMS: Buyer to pay the purchase price as follows:

3. Cash payment through escrow, including deposits, in the amount of. . . . . $_____

4. ☐ Take title subject to, or ☐ Assume, an existing first trust deed note held by
   _____ with an approximate unpaid principal balance of . . . . $_____
   payable $_____ monthly, including interest not exceeding _____%,
   ☐ ARM, type _____, plus a monthly tax/insurance impound
   payment of $_____.
   4.1 The unpaid amount includes delinquent payments, late charges and
       foreclosure costs to be the responsibility of Buyer in the amount of
       $_____, including unpaid delinquent monthly payments
       beginning with the payment due _____, 20_____.
   4.2 The impound account to be transferred without charge.

5. ☐ Take title subject to, ☐ or Assume, an existing second trust deed note held by
   _____ with an approximate unpaid principal balance of. . . . . $_____
   payable $_____ monthly, including interest not exceeding _____%,
   ☐ ARM, type_____, due _____, 20_____.
   5.1 The unpaid amount includes delinquent payments, late charges and
       foreclosure costs to be the responsibility of Buyer in the amount of
       $_____, including unpaid delinquent monthly payments
       beginning with the payment due _____, 20_____.

6. At closing, loan balance differences from those stated above as disclosed by
   beneficiary statement(s) to be adjusted into the purchase price unless the
   balances exceed the amount stated, in which case the difference is to be adjusted
   into the cash payment.

7. Buyer to obtain a ☐ first, or ☐ second, trust deed loan in the amount of . . . . $_____
   payable approximately $_____ monthly for a period of _____ years.
   Interest on closing not to exceed _____%, ☐ ARM, type _____.

8. Assume a tax bond or assessment lien with an unpaid principal balance of. . . . . $_____

9. Note for the balance of the purchase price in the amount of . . . . $_____
   to be executed by Buyer in favor of Seller and secured by a trust deed on the
   property junior to any above referenced financing, payable $_____
   monthly, or more, beginning one month after closing, including interest at
   _____% per annum from closing, due _____, 20_____, after closing.
   9.1 This note and trust deed will not contain provisions for due-on-sale,
       prepayment penalty or late charges.
   9.2 A Carryback Disclosure Statement is attached as an addendum. [See ft Form
       300]

10. Total Purchase Price Is . . . . $_____

— — — — — — — — — — — — *PAGE ONE OF SIX — FORM 156* — — — — — — — — — — — — — —

11. ACCEPTANCE AND PERFORMANCE:

11.1 This offer to be deemed revoked unless accepted in writing ☐ on presentation, or ☐ within _____ days after date, and acceptance is personally delivered or faxed to Offeror or Offeror's Broker within this period.

11.2 After acceptance, Broker(s) are authorized to extend any performance date up to one month.

11.3 On failure of Buyer to obtain or assume financing as agreed by the date scheduled for closing, Buyer may terminate the agreement.

11.4 Buyer's close of escrow is conditioned on Buyer's prior or concurrent closing on a sale of other property, commonly referred to as _____.

11.5 Any termination of the agreement shall be by written Notice of Cancellation timely delivered to the other party, the other party's Broker or Escrow, with instructions to Escrow to return all instruments and funds to the parties depositing them. [See ft Form 183]

11.6 Both parties reserve their rights to assign and agree to cooperate in effecting an Internal Revenue Code §1031 exchange prior to close of Escrow on either party's written notice. [See ft Form 171 or 172]

11.7 Should Buyer breach the agreement, Buyer's monetary liability to Seller is limited to $_____.

12. PROPERTY CONDITIONS:

12.1 Seller to furnish prior to closing:

    a. ☐ a structural pest control inspection report and certification of clearance of corrective conditions.

    b. ☐ a home inspection report prepared by an insured home inspector showing the land and improvements to be free of material defects.

    c. ☐ a one-year home warranty policy:
    Insurer_____
    Coverage _____

    d. ☐ a certificate of occupancy, or other clearance or retrofitting, required by local ordinance for the transfer of possession or title.

    e. ☐ a certification by a licensed contractor stating the sewage disposal system is functioning properly, and if it contains a septic tank, is not in need of pumping.

    f. ☐ a certification by a licensed water testing lab stating the well supplying the property meets potable water standards.

    g. ☐ a certification by a licensed well-drilling contractor stating the well supplying the property produces a minimum of _____ gallon(s) per minute.

    h. ☐ _____

    i. ☐ _____

12.2 Seller's Condition of Property Disclosure —Transfer Disclosure Statement (TDS): [See ft Form 304]

    a. ☐ is attached; or

    b. ☐ is to be handed to Buyer on acceptance for Buyer's review. Within ten days after the Buyer's post-acceptance receipt of the NHD, receipt, Buyer may either cancel the transaction or deliver to Seller or Seller's Broker a written notice itemizing any material defects in the property disclosed by the statement and unknown to Buyer prior to acceptance. [See ft Form 269] Seller to repair, replace or correct noticed defects prior to closing.

    c. On Seller's failure to repair, replace or correct noticed defects under §12.2b or §12.3a, Buyer may tender the purchase price reduced by the cost to repair, replace or correct the noticed defects, or close escrow and pursue available remedies. [See ft Form 183]

12.3 Buyer to inspect the property twice:

    a. an initial property inspection is required on acceptance to confirm the property's condition is substantially the same as observed by Buyer and represented by Seller or Seller's Agents prior to acceptance, and if not substantially the same, Buyer to promptly notify Seller in writing of undisclosed material defects discovered. [See ft Form 269] Seller to repair, replace or correct noticed defects prior to closing; and

    b. a final walk-through inspection is required within five days before closing to confirm the correction of any noticed defects under §12.2b and §12.3a and maintenance under §12.11. [See ft Form 270]

12.4 Seller's Natural Hazard Disclosure (NHD) Statement [See ft Form 314] ☐ is attached, or ☐ is to be handed to Buyer on acceptance for Buyer's review. Within ten days of the Buyer's post-acceptance receipt of the NHD, Buyer may terminate the agreement based on a reasonable disapproval of hazards disclosed by the Statement and unknown to Buyer prior to acceptance. [See ft Forms 182 and 183]

12.5 Buyer acknowledges receipt of a booklet and related seller disclosures containing: ☐ *Environmental Hazards: A Guide for Homeowners, Buyers, Landlords and Tenants* (on all one-to-four units), ☐ *Protect Your Family from Lead in Your Home* (on all pre-1978 one-to-four units) [See ft Form 313], and ☐ *The Homeowner's Guide to Earthquake Safety* (on all pre-1960 one-to-four units). [See ft Form 315]

12.6 The property is located in:

☐ an industrial use area, ☐ a military ordnance area, ☐ an airport influence area, ☐ a rent control area,

☐ _____ .

12.7 On acceptance, Seller to hand Buyer the following property information for Buyer's review: ☐ Property Operating Cost Sheet [See ft Forms 352 or 562], ☐ _____

    a. Within ten days of receipt, Buyer may terminate the agreement based on a reasonable disapproval of the property information received.

12.8 If a Homeowners' Association (HOA) is involved, ☐ Buyer has received and approves, or ☐ Buyer on acceptance to be handed copies of the Association's Articles, Bylaws, CC&Rs, collection and lien enforcement policy, operating rules, operating budget, CPA's financial review, insurance policy summary and any age restriction statement.

    a. No association claims for defects or changes in regular or special assessments are pending or anticipated. Current monthly assessment is $_____ .

    b. Seller is not in violation of CC&Rs, except _____ .

    c. Seller to pay association document and transfer fees.

    d. Buyer to approve Association's statement of condition of assessments and confirm representations in §12.8a as a condition for closing escrow.

    e. Within ten days of Buyer's post-acceptance receipt of the association documents, Buyer may terminate the agreement based on a reasonable disapproval of the documents. [See ft Form 183]

12.9 Smoke detector(s) and water heater bracing exist in compliance with the law, and if not, Seller to install.

12.10 Possession of the property and keys/access codes to be delivered: ☐ on close of escrow, or ☐ as stated in the attached Occupancy Agreement. [See ft Forms 271 and 272]

12.11 Seller to maintain the property in good condition until possession is delivered.

12.12 Fixtures and fittings attached to the property include but are not limited to: window shades, blinds, light fixtures, plumbing fixtures, curtain rods, wall-to-wall carpeting, draperies, hardware, antennas, air coolers and conditioners, trees, shrubs, mailboxes and other similar items.

12.13 Notice: Pursuant to Section 290.46 of the Penal Code, information about specified registered sex offenders is made available to the public via an Internet Web site maintained by the Department of Justice at www.meganslaw.ca.gov. Depending on an offender's criminal history, this information will include either the address at which the offender resides or the community of residence and ZIP code in which he or she resides.

12.14 ☐ Criminal activity and security statement prepared by Seller setting forth criminal activity on or about the property during the past two years relevant to the security of persons and their belongings on the property, and any security arrangements undertaken or which should be undertaken in response. [See ft Form 319]

13. **CLOSING CONDITIONS:**

13.1 This transaction to be escrowed with _____ .
Parties to deliver instructions to Escrow as soon as reasonably possible after acceptance.

    a. ☐ Escrow holder is authorized and instructed to act on the provisions of this agreement as the mutual escrow instructions of the parties and to draft any additional instructions necessary to close this transaction. [See ft Form 401]

    b. ☐ Escrow instructions, prepared and signed by the parties, are attached to be handed to Escrow on acceptance. [See ft Form 401]

13.2 Escrow to be handed all instruments needed to close escrow on or before _____, 20_____, or within _____ days after acceptance. Parties to hand Escrow all documents required by the title insurer, lenders or other third parties to this transaction prior to seven days before the date scheduled for closing.

    a. Each party to pay its customary Escrow charges. [See ft Forms 310 and 311]

13.3 The amount of any taxes, liens, bonds, assessments or other encumbrances on the property not referenced are, at Buyer's option, to remain of record and be deducted first from the cash payment and then from any carryback note.

13.4 Buyer's title to be subject to covenants, conditions, restrictions, reservations and easements of record.

_____

13.5 Title to be vested in Buyer or Assignee free of encumbrances other than those set forth herein. Buyer's interest in title shall be insured by _____Title Company under a(n) ☐ Homeowner(s) policy (one-to-four units), ☐ Residential ALTA-R policy (vacant or improved residential parcel), ☐ Owner's policy (other than one-to-four units), ☐ CLTA Joint Protection policy (also naming Carryback Seller or purchase-assist lender), or ☐ Binder (to insure resale or refinance within two years).

   a. Endorsements _____

   b. ☐ Seller, or ☐ Buyer, to pay the title insurance premium.

13.6 Buyer to furnish a new fire insurance policy covering the property.

13.7 Taxes, assessments, insurance premiums, rents, interest and other expenses to be pro rated to close of Escrow, unless otherwise provided.

13.8 Bill of Sale to be executed for any personal property being acquired.

13.9 If Seller is unable to convey marketable title as agreed, or if the improvements on the property are materially damaged prior to closing, Buyer may terminate the agreement. Seller to pay all reasonable escrow cancellation charges. [See ft Form 183]

14. BROKERAGE FEE:

14.1 Parties to pay the below-mentioned Broker(s) a fee now due of _____as follows:

   a. Seller to pay the brokerage fee on the change of ownership.

   b. The party wrongfully preventing this change of ownership to pay the brokerage fee.

14.2 Buyer's Broker and Seller's Broker, respectively, to share the brokerage fee _____:_____.

14.3 Attached is the Rules-of-Agency Disclosure. [See ft Form 305]

14.4 Broker is authorized to report the sale, its price and terms for dissemination and use of participants in brokerage trade associations or listing services.

15. ☐ Buyer's Broker hereby confirms he is a licensed real estate broker and holds a bond issued by a security insurer for more than twice the property's fair market value.

16. CANCELLATION PERIOD:

16.1 Seller has the below noticed right to cancel this agreement until midnight of the fifth business day following the day Seller signs this agreement, or until 8 a.m. on the day scheduled for a trustee's foreclosure sale of the property, whichever occurs first.

NOTICE REQUIRED BY CALIFORNIA LAW:

Until your right to cancel this contract has ended,

_____(Buyer)

or anyone working for

_____(Buyer)

CANNOT ask you to sign or have you sign any deed or any other document.

You may cancel this contract for the sale of your house, without any penalty or obligation at any time before _____:_____, _____.m. on _____, 20_____.

See attached Notice of Cancellation form for an explanation of this right.
(To be filled out by Buyer)

---

17. NOTICE OF YOUR SUPPLEMENTAL PROPERTY TAX BILL:

California property tax law requires the Assessor to revalue real property at the time the ownership of the property changes. Because of this law, you may receive one or two supplemental tax bills, depending on when your loan closes.

The supplemental tax bills are not mailed to your lender. If you have arranged for your property tax payments to be paid through an impound account, the supplemental tax bills will not be paid by your lender. It is your responsibility to pay these supplemental bills directly to the Tax Collector.

If you have any questions concerning this matter, please call your local Tax Collector's Office.

Buyer's/ Selling Broker: _____	Seller's/ Listing Broker: _____
By: _____	By: _____
Is the agent of: ☐ Buyer exclusively.	Is the agent of: ☐ Seller exclusively.
☐ Both Seller and Buyer.	☐ Both Seller and Buyer.
I agree to the terms stated above.	I agree to the terms stated above.
Date: _____, 20_____	Date: _____, 20_____
Buyer: _____	Seller: _____
Buyer: _____	Seller: _____
Signature: _____	Signature: _____
Signature: _____	Signature: _____
Address: _____	Address: _____
_____	_____
Phone: _____	Phone: _____
Fax: _____	Fax: _____
Email: _____	Email: _____

— — — — — — — — — — — **NOTICE OF CANCELLATION** — — — — — — — — — — — —

(To be filled out by Buyer)

Seller signed the Equity Purchase Agreement on _____, 20_____.

You may cancel this contract for the sale of your house, without any penalty or obligation, at any time before _____:_____, _____.m. on _____, 20_____.

To cancel this transaction, personally deliver a signed and dated copy of this cancellation notice, or send a telegram to _____ (Buyer)

at _____ (Business Address)

NOT LATER THAN _____:_____, _____.m. on _____, 20_____.

I hereby cancel this transaction.

Date: _____, 20_____

Seller's Signature: _____

Seller's Signature: _____

— — — — — — — — — — NOTICE OF CANCELLATION — — — — — — — — — — —
(To be filled out by Buyer)

Seller signed the Equity Purchase Agreement on _____, 20_____.

You may cancel this contract for the sale of your house, without any penalty or obligation, at any time before _____:_____, _____.m. on _____, 20_____.

To cancel this transaction, personally deliver a signed and dated copy of this cancellation notice, or send a telegram to _____ (Buyer)

at _____ (Business Address)

NOT LATER THAN _____:_____, _____.m. on _____, 20_____.

I hereby cancel this transaction.

Date: _____, 20_____

Seller's Signature: _____

Seller's Signature: _____

FORM 156   01-06   ©2008 **first tuesday**, P.O. BOX 20069, RIVERSIDE, CA 92516 (800) 794-0494

- **pay** the delinquent installments of principal, interest, taxes and insurance (PITI) and the foreclosure costs totalling approximately $15,180 — all of which are included in the $316,000 owed the lender on the loan.

An EP agreement is then prepared, calling for a $10,000 cash down payment.

Also, the EP investor will take title to the property "subject to" the existing first trust deed note with a 28-year amortization remaining, in spite of the due-on clause in the lender's trust deed.

The conditions of the trust deed note are:

- $300,000 remaining principal on closing (after the delinquent payments have been brought current);

- 6.5% fixed rate of interest;

- $1896.00 monthly principal and interest payments;

- $360 monthly taxes/insurance (TI) impounds payments;

- five months of delinquent payments on PITI of $12,280; and

- foreclosure costs of $2,900.

The first trust deed is a loan insured by the Federal Housing Administration (FHA) subject to the Department of Housing and Urban Development (HUD) due-on-sale rules controlling investor purchases. However, only HUD, not the lender, has the right to call a HUD-insured loan. The likelihood of HUD calling any loan that is kept current is remote. Thus, the EP investor may take over the loan "subject to" with minimal interference from the lender — assumption fees and loan modification are avoided. [See Chapter 14]

Editor's note — As of the date of this text, FHA is suffering a 12% delinquency rate on its insured loans.

The seller-in-foreclosure will not be carrying back a portion of the purchase price since this is a cash-to-loan transaction. As an alternative, negotiations could have arranged for the seller to carryback paper in the EP transaction.

Taxwise, the payment of the delinquent principal and interest (PI) payments (not the TI impounds) is reported as part of the EP investor's original **costs of acquisition**. The interest paid by the investor that accrued **before acquiring** the property is an expense of the seller-in-foreclosure, not the investor. Thus, the payment of the seller's debts assumed/taken over by the investor must be capitalized as part of his *cost basis* in the property. [Internal Revenue Code §1012]

The investor's cost basis on acquisition of the property will be the purchase price of approximately $325,000, which includes the down payment, the seller's delinquent (PI) installments, foreclosure costs, the principal balance on the loan and transactional costs, less the impound account balance assigned to the investor.

A prudent EP investor will determine the total cash funds needed to close escrow before making an offer. Cash expenditures of the EP investor on closing include:

- a down payment of $10,000.00

- delinquent principal, interest, taxes and impounds of $11,280.00

- foreclosure costs of $2,900.00

- escrow fees and charges of $1000.00

- total cash investment: $25,200

Preparing the equity purchase agreement

The following instructions are for the preparation and use of the Equity Purchase Agreement, **first tuesday** Form 156. Form 156 is designed as a checklist of practical provisions so an EP investor (or his agent), when offering to purchase a homeowner's residence located in California while it is in foreclosure, can prepare an offer providing for the investor to take title subject to the existing financing, assume it or refinance.

Each instruction corresponds to the provision in the form having the same number.

*Editor's Note — **Check** and **enter** items throughout the EP agreement in each provision with boxes and blanks, unless the provision is not intended to be included as part of the final agreement, in which case it is left unchecked or blank.*

Document identification:

Enter the date and the name of the city where the offer is prepared. This date is used when referencing this document.

Facts:

1. **Enter** the name of the city and county in which the property is located.

   Enter the legal description or common address of the property, or the assessor's parcel number (APN).

   Check the box and attach an itemized list of the inventory, or **enter** the description of any personal property included in the price. [See **first tuesday** Form 250]

2. *Addenda*: **Enter** the number of pages comprising all of the addenda, disclosures, etc., that are attached to the equity purchase agreement. Addenda may include additional disclosures regarding the condition of the property, title conditions, property operating expense estimates, hazards in the area surrounding the property's location, an agency addendum and brokerage fee provisions.

Terms for payment of the purchase price:

3. *Cash down payment*: **Enter** the dollar amount of the EP investor's cash down payment toward the price. The down payment represents the amount the seller-in-foreclosure will receive on closing, less any adjustments, escrow charges and fees.

4. *Subject-to existing loan (first)*: If the EP investor is purchasing the property "subject to" an existing first trust deed

note, **enter** the lender's name, the aggregate amount of the remaining loan balance, accrued and unpaid interest and foreclosure costs. **Enter** the amount of the monthly principal and interest payment and the interest rate on the note. **Check** whether the interest is adjustable (ARM) and **enter** the index name as the type. **Enter** any monthly impound payments made in addition to the principal and interest paid.

Editor's note — For a formal loan assumption, strike the words "Take title subject to" and enter "Assume."

4.1 *Delinquencies*: **Enter** the dollar amount required to cure all defaults on this loan. **Enter** the due date for the most delinquent loan payment.

4.2 *Impound balances*: **Authorizes** the impound account to be transferred without charge to the EP investor.

5. *Subject-to existing loan (second)*: If the EP investor is to take title "subject to" an existing second trust deed note, **enter** the lender's name and the aggregate amount of the remaining loan balance, accrued and unpaid interest and foreclosure costs. **Enter** the amount of the monthly payment and the interest rate. **Check** whether the interest is adjustable (ARM) and **enter** the index name as the type. **Enter** the due date for the final/balloon payment.

Editor's note — For a formal loan assumption, strike the words "Take title subject to" and enter "Assume."

5.1 *Delinquencies*: **Enter** the dollar amount required to cure all defaults on this loan. **Enter** the due date for the most delinquent loan payment.

6. *Loan balance adjustments*: **Authorizes** any adjustments for the difference between the loan balances stated in the agreement and those actually existing at the time of closing to be made into the purchase price. Thus, the down payment amount remains the same. However, if the actual balance on the loans exceeds the amounts stated in the purchase agreement, the difference is subtracted from the cash down payment. Thus, the purchase price remains the same.

7. *New trust deed loan*: **Check** the appropriate box to indicate whether any new financing will be a first or second trust deed. **Enter** the amount of the loan, the monthly PI payment, the term of the loan and the rate of interest. **Check** the box to indicate whether the interest will be adjustable (ARM), and if so, **enter** the index name.

8. *Bond or assessment assumed*: **Enter** the amount of the principal balance remaining unpaid on bonds and special assessment liens (such as Mello-Roos or 1915 improvement bonds) that will remain unpaid and become the responsibility of the EP investor on closing.

Editor's note — Improvement bonds are obligations of the seller that are assumed by the buyer. If assumed, the bonded indebtedness becomes part of the consideration paid for the property. Some purchase agreements erroneously place these bonds under "property tax" as though they were ad valorem taxes, which they are not, and then fail to prorate and charge the unpaid amount to the seller.

9. *Seller's carryback*: **Enter** the amount of any carryback note to be executed by the EP investor as partial payment of the price. **Enter** the amount of the note's monthly PI payment, interest rate and the due date for the final/balloon payment.

9.1 *Special carryback provisions*: No transfer restrictions or charges for early payoff or late payment will be included in the carryback note and trust deed.

9.2 *Carryback disclosure*: **Fill out** and **attach** a Seller Carryback Disclosure Statement as an addendum. [See **first tuesday** Form 300]

Editor's note — Further approval of the disclosure statement in escrow triggers a statutory buyer's contingency allowing for cancellation until time of closing on any purchase of a one-to-four unit residential property.

10. *Purchase price*: **Enter** the total amount of the purchase price as the sum of lines 3, 4, 5, 7, 8 and 9.

11. **Acceptance and performance periods**:

11.1 *Delivery of acceptance*: **Check** the appropriate box to indicate the time period for acceptance of the offer. If applicable, **enter** the number of days in which the seller-in-foreclosure may accept this offer and form a binding contract. Acceptance occurs on the return delivery to the person making the offer (or counteroffer) or to his broker of a copy of the unaltered purchase agreement offer containing the signed acceptance.

*Editor's note — Under either time period for acceptance, the seller still has a statutory period of five business days after acceptance to cancel the agreement. [See **Cancellation Period** below]*

11.2 *Extension of performance dates*: **Authorizes** the broker to extend the performance dates up to one month to meet the objectives of the agreement — time being of a reasonable duration and not the essence in this agreement as a matter of policy. This extension authority does not extend to the acceptance period.

11.3 *Loan contingency*: **Authorizes** the buyer to cancel the transaction at the time scheduled for closing if the financing for payment of the price is not obtainable or assumable.

11.4 *Sale of other property*: **Enter** the address of the property to be sold by the buyer if the closing of this transaction is to be contingent on the buyer's receipt of net proceeds from a sale of other property. Should the seller want to be able to enter into a back-up offer and require the buyer to waive the sale of other property contingency or the agreement be cancelled, prepare a waiver agreement and attach it as an addendum to the purchase agreement. [See **first tuesday** Form 276]

11.5 *Cancellation of procedures*: **Provides** the method of cancellation required to terminate the agreement when the right to cancel is triggered by other provisions in the agreement, such as contingency or performance provisions.

11.6 *Exchange cooperation*: **Requires** the parties to cooperate in an IRS §1031 transaction on further written notice by either party. **Provides** for the parties to assign their interests in this agreement.

11.7 *Liability limitations*: **Provides** for a dollar limit on the buyer's liability for the buyer's breach of the agreement. **Enter** the maximum dollar amount the seller may recover from the buyer.

12. **Property conditions**:

12.1 *Seller to furnish*: **Check** the appropriate box(es) within the following subsection to indicate the items the seller is to furnish prior to closing.

a. *Pest control*: **Check** the box to indicate the seller is to furnish a structural pest control report and clearance.

b. *Home inspection report*: **Check** the box to indicate the seller is to employ a home inspection company and furnish the buyer with the company's home inspections report.

c. *Home warranty*: **Check** the box to indicate the seller is to furnish an insurance policy for home repairs. **Enter** the name of the insurer and the type of coverage, such as for the air conditioning unit, etc.

d. *Local ordinance compliance*: **Check** the box to indicate the seller is to furnish a certificate of occupancy or other clearance required by local ordinance.

e. *Sewer or septic certificate*: **Check** the box to indicate the seller is to furnish a certificate of the condition of the sewage disposal system stating it is functioning properly.

f. *Potable well water*: **Check** the box to indicate the seller is to furnish a certificate stating the well supply meets water standards.

g. *Well water capacities*: **Check** the box to indicate the seller is to furnish a certificate stating the amount of water the well supplies. **Enter** the number of gallons per minute the well is expected to produce.

h. *Other items*: **Check** the box and **enter** any other report, disclosure, certification or clearance the seller is to furnish.

i. *Other items*: **Check** the box and **enter** any other report, disclosure, certification or clearance the seller is to furnish.

12.2 *Property conditions(s)*: **Check** the appropriate box within the following subsections to indicate the status of delivery of the Transfer Disclosure Statement (TDS).

a. *Attached TDS*: **Check** the box to indicate the seller's TDS has been prepared and handed to the buyer, and if so, **attach** it to this agreement. Thus, the property's condition as disclosed is accepted by the buyer upon entering into the purchase agreement offer.

*Editor's note — Use of the TDS form is mandated on one-to-four unit residential property. [See **first tuesday** Form 304]*

b. *Delayed TDS delivery*: **Check** the box to indicate the TDS is to be **later delivered** to the buyer to confirm the condition of the property is as disclosed prior to entry into the purchase agreement. On receipt of the TDS, the buyer may either cancel the transaction for failure of the seller or listing agent to disclose known property defects prior to the acceptance of the purchase agreement (or counteroffer), or give notice to the seller of the defects known and not disclose prior to acceptance and make a demand on the seller to correct them prior to closing.

c. *Repair of defects*: **Authorizes** the buyer to either cancel the transaction or adjust the price should the seller fail to correct the defects noticed under sections 12.2b or 12.3a.

12.3 *Buyer's inspection*: **Authorizes** the buyer to inspect the property twice during the escrow period to verify its condition is as disclosed by the seller prior to the time of acceptance.

a. *Initial property inspection*: **Requires** the buyer to inspect the property immediately after acceptance to put the seller on notice of material defects to be corrected by the seller prior to closing. [See **first tuesday** Form 269]

b. *Final walk-through inspection*: **Requires** the buyer to inspect the property again within five days before closing to confirm repairs and maintenance of the property have occurred. [See **first tuesday** Form 270]

12.4 *Seller's Natural Hazard Disclosure (NHD) Statement*: **Check** the appropriate box to indicate whether the mandatory NHD statement disclosing the seller's knowledge about the hazards listed on the form has been prepared and handed to the buyer. If it has been received by the buyer, **attach** a copy of the purchase agreement. If the NHD signed by the seller will be handed to the buyer after acceptance, the buyer has ten days after the buyer's receipt of the seller's NHD statement in which to approve it or cancel.

Editor's note — Disclosure by the seller is mandated on one-to-four unit residential property. [CC §1103]

12.5 *Hazard disclosure booklets*: **Check** the appropriate box(es) to indicate which hazard booklets have been received by the buyer, together with the seller's prepared and signed disclosures accompanying each booklet.

12.6 *Other property disclosures*: **Check** the appropriate box(es) to indicate other disclosures made by the seller regarding the location of the property. **Enter** a reference to any

local (option) ordinance disclosure statement attached as an addendum to the purchase agreement and **attach** it. [See **first tuesday** Form 307]

12.7 *Operating costs and rents*: **Check** the appropriate box(es) to indicate the information the seller is to disclose regarding the operating expenses of ownership and any rents. Should the property be subject to rental or lease agreements with tenants, **prepare** a leasing and operating addendum and attach it to the purchase agreement as a referenced addendum. [See **first tuesday** Form 275]

a. *Disclosure approval*: **Authorizes** the buyer to cancel the purchase agreement and escrow if the operating expenses and income disclosures are unacceptable.

12.8 *Homeowner's association (HOA)*: **Check** the appropriate box to indicate whether the HOA documents have been or are to be delivered to the buyer.

a. *Monthly payments*: **Enter** the dollar amount of the monthly payments assessed by the HOA.

b. *CC&Rs*: **Enter** the nature of any violation of the CC&Rs by the seller.

c. *HOA charges*: **Provides** for the seller to pay all HOA charges on the transaction.

d. *Condition of the assessments*: **Provides** for the buyer to approve the HOA's condition of assessments statement prior to closing.

e. *Disapproval of HOA documents*: **Authorizes** the buyer to terminate this purchase agreement within ten days after his receipt of HOA documents when the disclosures are made after entering into the purchase agreement. Disclosure of HOA conditions in escrow trigger a statutory contingency allowing the buyer to cancel the purchase agreement.

12.9 *Safety compliance*: **Requires** smoke detectors and water heater bracing to exist or be installed by the seller.

12.10 *Buyer's possession*: **Check** the appropriate box to indicate when possession of the property will be delivered to the buyer, whether at closing or under an **attached** buyer's interim occupancy or seller's holdover agreement. [See **first tuesday** Forms 271 and 272]

12.11 *Property maintenance*: **Requires** the seller to maintain the present condition of the property until the close of escrow.

Editor's note — See section 12.3b for the buyer's final inspection to confirm maintenance at closing.

12.12 *Fixtures and fittings*: **Confirms** this agreement includes real estate fixtures and fittings as part of the property purchased.

Editor's note — Trade fixtures are personal property to be listed as items on an attached inventory at section 1.

12.13 *Sex offender disclosure*: **Complies** with requirements that the seller disclose the existence of a sex offender database on the sale (or lease) of one-to-four residential units.

Editor's note — By the existence of the disclosure in the form, the seller and brokers are re-
lieved of any duty to make further disclosures regarding registered sex offenders.

13. Closing conditions:

13.1 *Escrow closing agent:* **Enter** the name of the escrow company handling the closing.

a. *Escrow instructions*: **Check** the box to indicate the purchase agreement is to act as the mutual escrow instructions of the EP investor and the seller. The escrow company will typically prepare entirely new instructions to close the transaction. [See **first tuesday** Form 401]

b. *Escrow instructions*: **Check** the box to indicate escrow instructions have been prepared and attached to this purchase agreement. **Prepare** and **attach** the prepared escrow instructions to the purchase agreement and **obtain** the signatures of the parties. [See **first tuesday** Form 401]

13.2 *Closing date*: To indicate the method to be used to set the date on which escrow is to close, **enter** either the specific date for closing in the first blank, or the number of days anticipated as necessary for the parties to perform and close escrow in the alternative blank. Also, prior to seven days before closing, the parties are to deliver all documents needed by third parties to perform their services by the date scheduled for closing.

a. *Escrow charges*: **Requires** each party to pay their customary escrow closing charges, amounts any competent escrow officer can provide on inquiry.

13.3 *Undisclosed lien adjustments*: At the EP investor's option, adjustments for liens not disclosed in the agreement may be made first into the down payment and then into any carryback note.

13.4 *Title conditions*: **Enter** wording for any further-approval contingency provision the buyer may need in order to confirm that title conditions set forth in the preliminary title report will not interfere with the buyer's intended use of the property, such as "closing contingent on buyer's approval of preliminary title report."

13.5 *Title insurance*: **Provides** for title to be vested in the name of the buyer or his assignee. **Enter** the name of the title insurance company that is to provide a preliminary title report in anticipation of issuing title insurance. **Check** the appropriate box to indicate the type of title insurance policy to be issued on closing.

   a. *Policy endorsements*: **Enter** any endorsements to be issued with the policy.

   b. *Payment of premium*: **Check** the appropriate box to indicate whether the buyer or seller is to pay the title insurance premium.

13.6 *Fire insurance*: **Requires** the buyer to provide a new policy of hazard insurance.

13.7 *Prorates and adjustments*: **Authorizes** prorations and adjustments on the close of escrow for taxes, insurance premiums, rents, interest, loan balances, service contracts and other property operating expenses, prepaid or accrued.

13.8 *Personal property*: **Requires** the seller to execute a bill of sale for any personal property being transferred in this transaction as called for in section 1.

13.9 *Property destruction*: **Provides** for the seller to bear the *risk of loss* for any casualty losses suffered by the property prior to close of escrow. Thus, the buyer may terminate the agreement if the seller is unable to provide a marketable title or should the property improvements suffer major damages.

14. Brokerage fee:

14.1 *Fee amount*: **Enter** the total amount of the fee due all brokers to be paid by the seller. The amount may be stated as a fixed dollar amount or a percentage of the price.

Editor's note — The defaulting party pays all brokerage fees and the brokerage fee can only be altered or cancelled by mutual instructions from the buyer and seller.

14.2 *Fee sharing*: **Enter** the percentage share of the fee each broker is to receive.

Editor's note — The percentage share may be set based on an oral agreement between the brokers, by acceptance of the listing broker's MLS offer to a selling office to share a fee or unilaterally by an agent when preparing the buyer's offer.

14.3 *Agency law disclosures*: **Attach** a copy of the Agency Law Disclosure addendum for all parties to sign.

*Editor's note — The disclosure is mandated to be acknowledged by the buyer and accompany the offer so the seller acknowledges it on acceptance of the offer, a prerequisite to the buyer's broker enforcing collection of his fee from the seller when the property sold contains one-to-four residential units. [See **first tuesday** Form 305]*

14.4 *Disclosure of sales data*: **Authorizes** the brokers to report the transaction to trade associations or listing services.

15. *Buyer's broker's bond*: **Check** the box to indicate the broker representing the buyer in this equity purchase transaction has complied with the bonding requirement of the equity purchase laws.

16. *Statutory cancellation period*: The seller has the **right to cancel** the EP agreement until midnight of the fifth business day (Monday through Saturday, excluding specified holidays) following the day the EP agreement is accepted or until 8 a.m. on the day scheduled for a trustee's foreclosure sale of the property, whichever occurs first. [CC §1695.4(a)]

Cancellation Notice:

Enter the EP investor's name as the buyer (twice) and **enter** the appropriate time and date for the expiration of the seller's cancellation period of five business days after acceptance.

17. *Supplemental tax notice*: This is a notice to the buyer, mandated to be included in purchase agreements for one-to-four residential units located in California, disclosing that he will owe property taxes that are not provided for in loan impound accounts and must be separately paid by the buyer.

Agency confirmation:

Buyer's broker identification: **Enter** the name of the buyer's broker. **Obtain** the signature of the buyer's broker or the selling agent acting on behalf of the broker. **Check** the appropriate box to indicate the agency created by the broker's (and his agent's) conduct with the parties.

Seller's broker identification: **Enter** the name of the seller's broker. **Obtain** the signature of the seller's broker or the listing agent acting on behalf of the broker. **Check** the appropriate box to indicate the agency created by the broker's (and his agent's) conduct with the parties.

Signatures:

Buyer's signature: **Enter** the date the EP investor signs the purchase agreement. **Obtain** the EP investor's signature on the purchase agreement. **Enter** his name, address, telephone and fax numbers, and email address.

Seller's signature: **Enter** the date the seller signs the purchase agreement. **Obtain** the signature of each seller on the purchase agreement. **Enter** his name, address, telephone and fax numbers, and email address.

Notice of Cancellation:

*Editor's note — This section is not part of the purchase agreement. It is the separate notice which the seller-in-foreclosure uses if he intends to cancel the transaction. However, it must be **filled out and handed** to the seller with the buyer's offer.*

Enter the date the seller signs his acceptance of the EP agreement. **Enter** the time and date on or before which the seller may cancel the agreement. **Enter** the EP investor's name and the address where the Notice of Cancellation is to be delivered. **Enter** the time (midnight or 8:00 a.m. on the date of foreclosure) and date by which the seller may cancel the agreement (five business days after acceptance).

Editor's note — The Notice of Cancellation presented in duplicate at the end of this agreement is not dated or signed by the seller on acceptance. The seller will later sign and deliver the cancellation section only if he decides to cancel the transaction within the five-business-day cancellation period.

Chapter 3

The EP investor operates without an agent

This chapter examines how equity purchase (EP) legislation has affected the traditional relationship between real estate brokers, investors and sellers of owner-occupied, one-to-four residential properties in foreclosure.

Changing legislation, brokers representing investors

Equity purchase (EP) legislation houses a scheme that regulates real estate brokers and their agents when they act as **agents for investors** in negotiations to acquire one-to-four unit residential properties that are in foreclosure and occupied in whole or in part by the owner as his principal residence, called an *equity purchase transaction.*

The EP scheme has recently been altered. The broker **representing an investor** in an EP transaction used to be required to deliver to the seller-in-foreclosure a written **EP disclosure** statement confirming he was:

- a **licensed** real estate broker; and

- **bonded** by a surety insurer for any losses incurred by the seller due to the broker's conduct. [Calif. Civil Code §1695.17(a)(1)]

The failure of the investor's selling agent to make EP bonding disclosures to the seller-in-foreclosure had two repercussions, both falling on the investor. The first was a seller's contingency. Until the bonding disclosure was received by the seller, the EP agreement could be cancelled at the discretion of the seller any time before escrow closed. After closing, the transaction could be rescinded due to a failure to obtain and disclose compliance with bonding requirements.

The second was the EP investor's liability for any of the seller's **money losses arising** out of the broker's nondisclosure of licensing and failure to meet bonding requirements. [CC §1695.17(b)]

However, the EP investor was entitled to *indemnity* from his broker for any money losses suffered by the investor due to the broker's nondisclosure of bonding and licensing to the seller. Indemnity was available to the EP investor who, without active fault on his part, was legally forced to pay for losses created by the broker's nondisclosure and lack of bonding requirements. [**San Francisco Examiner Div., Hearst Pub. Co.** v. **Sweat** (1967) 248 CA2d 493]

However, these draconian requirements placed on brokers representing EP investors were abolished in December of 2007 when the statutory bonding requirements were rendered unenforceable for vagueness. [**Schweitzer** v. **Westminster Investments** (2007) __CA4th__]

Harsh EP legislation; everyone loses

For the typical broker, obtaining a surety bond is economically prohibitive. Thus, the recently voided EP bonding requirements long ago essentially removed licensed real estate brokers from representing investors who want to locate and purchase a one-to-four unit residential property in foreclosure that serves as the seller's principal residence.

Thus, newly converted EP investors have been learning how to "go it alone," without brokerage assistance. Professional EP investors typically do not use agents to locate and negotiate the acquisition of properties. With aspiring EP investors unable to enter the foreclosure market with the assistance of an agent, fewer investors compete to buy foreclosures than if the EP scheme had not existed.

Further, sellers-in-foreclosure have been denied the full assistance of their listing broker. The EP statutes, while restricting brokers who would otherwise represent EP investors, also effectively wiped out the ability of an unbonded listing broker to bring one of his investor clients to the table as a buyer and negotiate an EP transaction as a **dual agent**. [CC §2079.13(d)]

Broker as principal

The unenforceable bonding requirement, for all its unintended negative consequences, did not restrict the ability of an individual, who may coincidentally be licensed as a broker or sales agent, to act solely as a **principal** purchasing property in an EP transaction for his own account.

Thus, a licensed real estate broker or sales agent may himself be the EP investor, eliminating agency law addenda, licensee disclosures and any future bonding compliance from the purchase agreement since no licensee is acting as an agent for the buyer in the transaction. The licensed real estate broker or sales agent acting solely as an EP investor is a buyer who merely happens to hold a real estate license — a fact that need not be disclosed to the seller-in-foreclosure.

Here, the licensee is not acting as an agent for anyone. One cannot act as their own agent as an agent would act on behalf of another. Thus, no conflict of interest exists to the disclosed.

Conversely, a real estate licensee, while **employed** as the listing broker by a seller-in-foreclosure to locate a buyer, may decide to directly or indirectly buy his client's property. He may do so, but the broker must disclose to his seller-client that the broker or an affiliate is **also acting as a principal** in the transaction, in addition to being, or having been, the seller's agent. [Calif. Business and Professions Code §§10176(d), 10176(g), 10176(h)]

Representing the seller

As a result of the EP scheme, prudent brokers are less inclined to solicit and accept a listing from a seller-in-foreclosure than from an owner of comparable property not in foreclosure. A couple of reasons for this predisposition exist. One used to be the excessive bonding requirements placed on the broker for acting as an investor's selling agent.

Another is the unacceptable exigency arising from the fact the property must be sold and escrow closed before the date of the trustee's foreclosure sale. For anything less, the broker has failed to **fully perform** the employment and meet the seller's expectations under the listing. The difficulty for the agent is that foreclosure periods are roughly four months in length and houses during recessionary periods take ten to twelve months on average to sell.

Lastly, the seller has a solvency problem. Unless the delinquent loan is brought current (or a forebearance agreement entered into) prior to five business days before the trustee's sale, called *reinstatement*, or paid in full before the trustee's sales, called *redemption*, the home will be sold at the trustee's sale. The typical seller-in-foreclosure can do neither, unless a buyer comes to the rescue. [CC §§2924c(e), 2903]

The listing broker for a seller-in-foreclosure needs time to find a buyer and close escrow. The time constraints of marketing a property in foreclosure place the broker under extra pressure to locate a buyer if he is to earn a fee for his efforts.

As always, the listing broker must diligently perform his agency duty owed the seller to care for and protect him while marketing the property. The seller-in-foreclosure **initially expects** the broker he listed with to convert his equity to cash by negotiating a sale of the property that will close before the property is lost to the foreclosing lender. This expectation exists in spite of huge monthly inventories of unsold homes of ten or more per buyer.

If the insolvent seller loses his property by foreclosure, he may well make a demand on the broker for the amount of his lost equity, claiming a lack of due diligence or unprofessional conduct on the part of the broker — a risk brokers do not lightly undertake when listing any property.

Other EP agents

The listing of a property must be placed in a Multiple Listing Service (MLS) publication to initially broadcast to the brokerage community that a property is available for sale. But when a property in foreclosure is placed in a MLS, additional information must be released on the foreclosure aspect to be fair to other members.

A broker placing a listing in MLS of an owner-occupied residence in foreclosure needs to inform brokers representing buyers that the property is owner-occupied and in foreclosure, and advise these selling agents to:

- represent a buyer-occupant; or

- submit an offer as a principal.

Only a **buyer-occupant** who purchases the property avoids complying with EP law. However, buyer-occupants are frequently unwilling to purchase property in foreclosure since the property is often:

- *improperly encumbered* — a buyer-occupant may not want to assume the existing loan, or the property cannot be financed for an amount sufficient to pay off the existing loan requiring short sale negotiations to avoid foreclosure's; and

- *physically unattractive* — due to deferred maintenance by a financially impaired owner.

Thus, a property in foreclosure is attractive primarily to an investor-type. Investors are willing to buy property and take risks presented by delinquencies and maintenance requirements during what is usually a recessionary sales market. The property must be rehabilitated, and financing and operating costs carried until the property is resold or rented — at a profit or a loss. When someone is losing their home they are hostile and do not tend to put money into it, an attitude reflected in the maintenance of the property.

To further complicate the seller's plight, the legislature placed further marketplace restrictions on the sale of a residence-in-foreclosure by reducing the ability of the listing broker to locate a buyer through **advanced fee** restrictions and foreclosure consultant rules controlling the conduct of brokers and agents.

Owner-in-foreclosure consultants

Often, an owner-in-foreclosure will do anything in his power to prevent his residence from being sold at a foreclosure sale.

Owners-in-foreclosure often prudently seek the services of a financial advisor or investment counselor, called a *foreclosure consultant* in this situation.

A **foreclosure consultant** is any person who, for a fee from the owner-in-foreclosure, agrees to:

- stop or postpone the foreclosure sale;

- prevent lienholders from enforcing or accelerating their note;

- help the owner reinstate the loan or negotiate an extension of the reinstatement period;

- advance funds to the owner; or

- arrange a loan for the owner. [CC §2945.1(a)]

However, a licensed real estate broker or his licensed agent acting on behalf of a seller in foreclosure, is not acting as a *foreclosure consultant* when the broker:

- receives only a **contingency fee** (paid on closing) from the owner for selling the residence in foreclosure;

- receives **no advance fees or costs** from the owner;

- **makes a loan** as a principal for an amount sufficient to cure defaults, or **arranges a loan** as a mortgage loan broker employed by the owner; and

- receives **no ownership interest** in the property directly from the owner, except as a principal making a loan as a lender (beneficiary) secured by a trust deed. [CC §2945.1(b)(3)]

Regarding the direct receipt of an ownership interest in the property from the owner, consider a real estate broker who *arranges* a loan for an owner-in-foreclosure. The loan is funded by a trust deed investor and secured by a trust deed lien on the owner's residence. The loan's closing statement notes the broker is acting as a real estate licensee arranging the loan transaction.

Later, the trust deed investor forecloses on the trust deed by a trustee's sale. The trustee's deed **conveys title** to both the broker and the trust deed investor as the highest bidders.

The owner now claims the broker has breached his duties while acting as a *foreclosure consultant* since the broker later obtained an interest in the owner's residence, directly from the owner, by purchasing the residence at the trustee's foreclosure sale under the trust deed loan previously arranged by the broker.

The broker claims he is exempt from being classified as a foreclosure consultant since he was acting in the capacity of a licensed real estate broker when the loan was arranged for the owner and the trustee's sale was a public auction.

Here, the broker breached his duties owed to the seller both as a foreclosure consultant and as a real estate licensee when he acquired an ownership interest at the trustee's sale and was not the lender. To have properly acquired ownership of the property at a trustee's sale (a voluntary sale under trust deed provisions), he would have had to first lend his own funds and have been named as the beneficiary in the trust deed when the loan was made.

The broker arranged a loan for which a real estate license was required by real estate law. However, he also came under the foreclosure consultant law and violated it at the same time when he later acquired an ownership interest at the foreclosure sale. [**Onofrio** v. **Rice** (1997) 55 CA4th 413]

Again, owners who are in foreclosure are the losers. A broker normally can bid and acquire property at a foreclosure sale, unless he arranged the loan for the homeowner-in-foreclosure.

Such cases make doing EP business risky and reduce the available buyers at the trustee's sale — a *voluntary sale* agreed to by the owner in the trust deed that is exercised by the owner by defaulting, called a *put option*.

Advance fees

When a broker collects a fee or any marketing costs **in advance** from a seller-in-foreclosure, the broker is considered a foreclosure consultant subject to statutory restrictions in addition to licensing laws.

However, a foreclosure consultant may not collect an advance fee, another legal "catch-22" for the loan broker attempting to be paid a fee or collect loan costs up front that is typical of a loan broker's arrangement with borrowers. If as a broker he does accept an advance of costs (appraisal fees, credit report charges or property inspection report fee), he is at once classified as a consultant and violator of that law. Also, a foreclosure consultant cannot secure his contingent fee by a lien on the property. [CC §§2945.4(a), 2945.4(c)]

A broker taking a listing from a seller-in-foreclosure without an advance fee arrangement assumes the risk that the uncreditworthy seller will be unable to pay the fee should he refuse a full listing offer or be unable or unwilling to close should he enter into a purchase agreement.

Living "rent-free" can quickly become habit-forming for a seller-in-foreclosure. A seller-in-foreclosure who is no longer making monthly payments may retain possession without any obligation to pay rent except for those days he remains in possession after the trustee's sale — when he no longer owns the property.

The foreclosure consultant law is another example of how EP legislation works to the detriment of the seller-in-foreclosure — and the brokerage community.

However, EP legislation overlooks the fact the broker who takes an advance fee is already **heavily regulated** by the Department of Real Estate (DRE). The broker must place any advance fees in a trust account, provide accounting to the client before withdrawing funds and use a fee agreement cleared by the DRE. [See **first tuesday** Form 106]

But to do so as authorized by the DRE violates a different law — as a foreclosure consultant.

Broker for a foreclosure consultant

When a broker arranges for a seller-in-foreclosure to employ a foreclosure consultant, or pay a fee or transfer title to a foreclosure consultant, the broker is considered the agent of the foreclosure consultant, a sort of *subagent* of the seller. [CC §2945.9(b)]

Further, a foreclosure consultant retained by a seller-in-foreclosure is barred from acquiring any interest in a residence in foreclosure — even if he hires a broker to represent him to buy the property. [CC §2945.4(e)]

Unbelievably, a foreclosure consultant's agent or employee can only be a licensed real estate broker who:

- provides the seller-in-foreclosure with a written statement under penalty of perjury that he is a licensed real estate broker; and

- is bonded by a surety insurer for an amount equal to twice the value of the residence in foreclosure. [CC §2945.11(a)(1)]

Failure of the foreclosure consultant's broker to provide the broker's statement to the seller-in-foreclosure will, at the seller's option, void the advisory agreement with the foreclosure consultant. [CC §2945.11(b)]

Further, an agreement between the foreclosure consultant and the seller-in-foreclosure cannot contain provisions attempting to limit the liability of the foreclosure consultant for money damages caused by the foreclosure consultant's broker. [CC §2945.10]

Editor's note — Assembly Bill (AB) 2154 in 1991 attempted, but failed, to repeal the statutory bond requirements previously created by foreclosure consultant legislation to exclude licensed real estate brokers, if the broker:

- *is performing an activity for which he is licensed;*

- *is acting as an agent in regard to "listed" property (whether the listing is taken by the broker or another broker);*

- *has complied with the agency disclosure statutes;*

- *discloses to the seller-in-foreclosure the recovery available through the Real Estate Recovery Fund, or private bonding or E and O insurance (which the seller may verify through inquiry) for the negligent acts of the broker; and*

- *discloses to the seller-in-foreclosure the recovery may be insufficient to cover the seller's potential losses in the transaction.*

The sponsors reported the bill was pulled after hostile amendments were added at the urging of legal aid groups who felt AB 2154 inadequately protected sellers-in-foreclosure. The bond legislation is not likely to be repealed until sufficient members of the legislature realize the deleterious consequences to sellers-in-foreclosure and brokers created by the bonding requirements, let alone the entire scheme of the equity purchase law.

The subagent characterization end run

In an attempt to avoid the bonding requirement of the selling agent employed by an investor to negotiate the purchase of an owner's residence in foreclosure, the selling agent's role is being recharacterized by some brokers as a finder employed by the listing broker or by the listing broker's listing agent. The subterfuge will not escape the reality and economic function of the EP investor's relationship to the selling agent, who is locating suitable property for the investor to purchase or negotiating between the investor and the listing agent.

Also, a finder by definition is an unlicensed individual who is not and cannot be in anyway involved in the search for a match (the property) or purchase negotiations. Negotiations on behalf of an EP investor begin with an analysis of the property sought, locating a qualifying property and relaying information on it to the investor.

Lastly, does recharacterizing the investor's agent as a subagent of the seller or finder employed by the listing agent make him a dual agent? This fee splitting arrangement harks back to some commission provisions in so-called deposit receipts prior to the mid-1980s when the seller employed all agents in the transaction as his agents — even though one was exclusively the buyer's agent, until also employed by the seller.

Chapter 4

The unconscionable advantage some investors create

This chapter analyzes a seller-in-foreclosure's after-closing right to rescind the sale and recover his home when a buyer-investor takes unconscionable advantage of the seller, and where an intervening purchaser or lender acquires an interest.

The suppression of further marketing

As the strength of real estate sales deteriorate and the previous virtuous cycle of a real estate boom turns vicious, it is the best of times for buyers with cash to invest. With the rapid increase in stocks of inventory for sale and prices dropping, they can find opportunities to either build up their holdings with good real estate on the cheap, or acquire and flip property for a handsome profit.

The match investors then seek out is an owner in foreclosure who does not have the good luck of the investor or the time to maneuver. Both find themselves in their present financial position because of decisions they made in the recent past.

The opportunity allowing investors to bottom fish and acquire real estate with low-ball offers submitted to the financially down-and-out homeowners will also cause a few investors to otherwise over reach. In doing so, they might suppress the owner's ability to further market the property and locate a better match for himself than the one offered by the investor.

The mix of their financial positions is a picture of strong versus the weak, of greed compounded by another's growing fear of loss, of all the time in the world to act and of time running out.

In this emotional environment, the investor is buoyed by the success of the moment's negotiations. Conversely, the seller-in-foreclosure is humiliated by his financial failure to provide homeownership for his family. These forces occasionally drive some investors to suppress any further marketing of the property by the seller-in-foreclosure as a condition of entering into a purchase agreement with the investor.

The use of a *confidentiality agreement*, while prudent in contracting between a buyer and seller of somewhat equal bargaining positions, serves only to interfere with the seller's chances to use the investor's offer to shop around and locate another buyer at a better price. Even the foreclosure sale the owner will soon face is a very public auction with every bid made known to each prospective bidder — until the highest bidder takes home the property.

On the other hand, the investor has no duty to be charitable about the terms of his offer or to bail out a homeowner who did not see his plight coming. Most first-time homeowners lack proper education to give them a clue that a recession will affect them adversely, much less an appreciation for the economic forces that control all ownership and trust deed interests in real estate.

Yet, the investor's proper view of an equity purchase (EP) transaction is an exchange of cash for property. It is his opportunity, by taking the risk of investing now, to get more cash out of an immediate resale of the real estate than he invested or, as a long-term investor building his net worth and cash flow, by ownership of the real estate as a rental.

An EP investor has greater burden placed on his duty to care for and protect his interests when purchasing a home of a seller-in-foreclosure than had the seller not been in foreclosure. Being able to justify that he paid a reasonably fair price for the property will be of great help later should the seller decide to exercise his right to rescind the sale within two years after closing based on a claim of unconscionable advantage taken by the investor. The claim has two aspects, one of which is the price paid.

A fair price calls for an analysis of the property's condition, the price trend in the resale market, the costs of carrying the ownership and a discounted amount to cover a reasonable profit for the risk taken to buy, fix up and resell the property.

A prudent step when preparing to set a price to pay for a property, regardless of whether it is in foreclosure, is an investor's (or any buyer's) location of comparable properties that have been sold within six months. With the use of a valuations spread sheet, called a *comparable market analysis* (CMA), the investor checks out the amenities of the comparable properties and calculates by comparison the value of the property he is interested in buying.

From the value set by the use of the CMA, the investor calculates the price he must pay to provide room to accomplish his resale objective — a profit from his investment on resale. [See Form 318 accompanying this chapter]

The un-American low-price combination

The procedures used or conduct employed by the EP investor may deprive the seller-in-foreclosure of *a reasonable choice* between different buyers and their offers. Without allowing the seller to seek out an alternative to the investor's offer, an unconscionable advantage may have been given to the investor by depriving the seller of a meaningful choice. The unconscionable advantage that deprives the seller of a reasonable choice of action occurs when the EP investor *exploits* the additional element of **oppression or surprise** while at the same time exacting an unreasonably low and highly favorable purchase price.

Oppression by the EP investor arises out of the inequality in bargaining power resulting in no real negotiations between the seller-in-foreclosure and the EP investor — a "take-it-or-leave-it" environment devoid of **competing buyers**. The economics of a foreclosure environment produces a one-sided bargaining advantage for the investor. This power cre-

ated can be improperly used by the investor to insist that his offer is not "shopped around" in a marketing effort by the seller or his listing agent to solicit a better deal during the five-business-day cancellation period.

Surprise occurs due to the post-closing discovery of terms that are hidden in lengthy provisions of the agreement. The price and how it will be paid is not a surprise as it is well known to the seller-in-foreclosure. However, on a later rescission, it is the price that will likely be the only provision in the agreement contested by the seller.

The greater the marketplace oppression or post-closing surprise in the transaction, the less an unreasonably favorable price paid by an EP investor will be tolerated. [**A & M Produce Co.** v. **FMC Corporation** (1982) 135 CA3d 473; **Carboni** v. **Arrospide** (1991) 2 CA4th 76]

Prudent investor conduct

Thus, to lessen the ability of the seller to later show an unconscionable advantage existed in he investor's conduct, the investor begins negotiations by entering into an EP agreement on a form that meets all statutory requirements. [See **first tuesday** Form 156]

Also, an EP transaction involving the seller's **listing broker** or a **counteroffer** lessens and certainly weakens any future attempt by the seller to show an unconscionable advantage was exercised by the investor. They actually negotiated, and a middle man (agent) was involved as a gatekeeper.

The investor might be called upon to further defend his actions by demonstrating the EP agreement was not entered into through:

- misrepresentation of facts or law in *deceitful conduct* by the investor;

- *undue influence* arising out of a prior or special relationship with the seller; or

- *duress* applied in the negotiations by the investor to obtain the seller's acceptance and close the transaction.

Two-year right of rescission

Consider the consequence of recording a Notice of Default (NOD) on a homeowner's personal residence after several months of unpaid installments.

The homeowner, now in foreclosure, is willing to sell on almost any terms to salvage whatever remains of his credit and investment in the property.

The property is listed for sale with a broker. The broker promptly markets the property to locate a buyer, both indirectly through MLS and directly to buyers who will occupy the property as their personal residence.

After nearly a month in foreclosure, an offer is submitted directly to the seller by an equity purchase (EP) investor, acting on his own account without broker representation. Under the offer, the seller-in-foreclosure will receive cash for his equity. Additionally, the investor agrees to cure the seller's loan delinquencies on close of escrow.

The seller contacts his listing broker for advice. After reviewing the offer, the broker recommends the seller accept the investor's offer. The broker has no leads or potential buyers who have shown an interest in the property. However, the listing broker will use the existence of the cancelable purchase agreement to entice potential buyers to make an offer — at a better price. If an acceptable backup offer is received within the cancellation period, the seller will accept the backup offer and cancel the EP agreement.

The broker advises his client he has five business days after his acceptance of the EP offer to cancel the sale, and may do so for any reason, since the sale involves the seller's home, which is in foreclosure.

The seller-in-foreclosure accepts the EP investor's offer. The five-business-day **cancellation period** expires without receiving a backup offer, and escrow is opened on the EP agreement. The EP transaction is later closed and the property conveyed to the investor.

Does the EP investor receive good title when he accepts the grant deed?

No! The EP investor's title remains subject to the seller-in-foreclosure's *right of rescission* for two years after closing. If at any time during the two years following the close of escrow the seller believes the **investor's conduct** and the **price paid** gave the investor an unconscionable advantage, the seller may attempt to rescind the transaction and recover the home he sold. [Calif. Civil Code §1695.14]

However, a seller is not likely motivated to repurchase his home simply because he came by funds sufficient to do so within two years of closing the sale. Market conditions must be such that the property is now worth more than the price the seller received. The closer the timing of the investor's purchase to the lowest point for the pace of sales in the real estate cycle the more likely the pace of sales will soon pick up and then be followed with price increases within the two-year rescission period.

In 2007, the **volume of sales** (and prices) appears likely to diminish and not stabilize until well into 2010. The demographics of the buying-age portions of the population do not indicate a surge in household formations and home demand until the year 2014-2019 as the "Y generation" children of post World War II boomers come of age.

Seller's right to rescind a closed sale

To protect owners who are selling their homes while in foreclosure from buyer-investors who are "rip-off artists," the California legislature gave sellers of their personal residences when in foreclosure a two-year **right of rescission** after closing a sale with an investor.

During the two-year period following closing, a seller-in-foreclosure rescinds the completed EP transaction by:

- notifying the EP investor of his decision to rescind the transaction, called a *notice of rescission*; and

COMPARABLE MARKET ANALYSIS FOR SETTING VALUES

This Comparable Market Analysis (CMA) worksheet is prepared by the seller of a property, or his agent, to provide an estimate of the value of the seller's property based on the sales price of other similar properties sold within the past few months, each adjusted in price to reflect the dollar valuation of their distinctions from the seller's property. On locating recent sales through the County Records and completing a visual inspection of the comparable sales, note in the column for each comparable property any distinguishable itemized features from the seller's property, and note the dollar amount of the adjustment to the comparable property's price by deducting the dollar value of the feature the comparable property has which the seller's property does not, or adding the dollar value of the feature the comparable property does not have which the seller's property has.

Date Prepared:_____   By:_____

Features:	Subject property	Comparable No.1		Comparable No. 2		Comparable No. 3	
Address:							
Proximity to Subject							
Sale Price	$		$		$		$
Sale Price/Gross Liv. Area	$ per sq. ft.	$ per sq. ft.		$ per sq. ft.		$ per sq. ft.	
Data Source							
Verification Source							
1 Sales Information:							
1.1 Date of sale							
1.2 Concessions (sales/financing)							
1.3 Fee simple/leasehold							
1.4 Age of improvements							
1.5 Special HOA assessments							
1.6 Bonded assessments							

VALUE ADJUSTMENT	DESCRIPTION	DESCRIPTION	+(-) $	DESCRIPTION	+(-) $	DESCRIPTION	+(-) $
2 Zoning Compliance (nonconforming/ illegal):							
2.1 Easement/ encroachment							
2.2 Use restrictions (CC & Rs)							
2.3 Retrofitting/water conservation							
3 Location-Neighborhood Trend:							
3.1 Street amenities							
3.2 Lot size/shape							
3.3 Vehicles access							
3.4 Schools/churches/ institutions							
3.5 Transportation/ shopping							
3.6 Inside/corner lot							
3.7 Utilities available							
3.8 Environmental hazards/nuisances							

4	Landscaping:							
4.1	Quality							
4.2	Maintance							
4.3	Soil condition/ drainage							
4.4	Topography							
5	Improvements:							
5.1	Age of improvement							
5.2	Constructions type							
5.3	Highest and best use							
5.4	Design/style							
5.5	Energy efficiency							
5.6	Maintance/ obsolencence							
5.7	Exterior conditions							
5.8	Interior conditions							
5.9	Garage/carpet							
5.10	Central AC/heating							
5.11	Gutters and downspouts							
5.12	Windows/screens							
6	Livable Space:							
6.1	No. of bedrooms							
6.2	No. of baths							
6.3	Kitchen/appliances							
6.4	Living room							
6.5	Dining room							
6.6	Family room							
6.7	Basement/storage							
6.8	Attic/access							
7	Amenities:							
7.1	Fire place/woodstove							
7.2	Pool							
7.3	Fences							
7.4	Patio/Porch/deck							
8	Price of Comparable:		☐ + ☐ -	$	☐ + ☐ -	$	☐ + ☐ -	$
9	Adjusted Price of each Comparable:			% $		% $		% $
10	Value of Subject Property:							

FORM 318 7-06 ©2007 **first tuesday**, P.O. Box 20069, RIVERSIDE, CA 92516 800-794-0494

- returning all funds and items of value received from the investor/buyer under the EP agreement, called *restoration*. [CC §§1691, 1695.14(b)]

To *perfect* his claim for restoration of the property to his ownership, the seller-in-foreclosure also records the **notice of rescission** in the county in which the real estate is located.

The notice of rescission describes the real estate and contains the names of the rescinding seller, the EP investor and any *successor-in-interest* of the investor who is not a *bona fide purchaser* (BFP).

Once served with a notice of rescission, the EP investor (or his non-bona fide successor) has 20 days to reconvey title to the rescinding seller, free of any encumbrances he or his non-bona fide successor placed on title after acquiring the property. [CC §1695.14(b)]

If an investor, after acquiring ownership, **further invests** any amount of money or effort into rehabilitating or carrying the expenses of property ownership, the rescinding seller has no obligation under EP law to reimburse the investor for any expenditures.

The investor's improvements during the two-year rescission period are not considered *good faith improvements*. The expenditures are made while the investor holds a **voidable ownership** interest in the property. The investor's conduct, which created the *unconscionable advantage* over the seller-in-foreclosure, charges him with the knowledge of his defective title. Equity purchase law then acts to sanction him, if the seller rescinds and establishes the investor's offending conduct.

If the EP investor fails to timely reconvey title to the seller on notice of rescission, the seller can sue the investor to enforce the rescission and recover the residence. The prevailing party in the rescission action is entitled to his attorney fees. Remember, the seller-in-foreclosure is basically insolvent, but he has reason to believe the return of the property will be financially rewarding. [CC §§1695.14(b), 1695.14(d)]

Unconscionable advantage and restoration

A seller's notice of rescission during the two-year rescission period after closing is effective to recover the property only if the seller can demonstrate the EP investor took *unconscionable advantage* of him when negotiating the purchase of the property.

Showing the existence of and defending against an unconscionable advantage demonstrated by the **investor's conduct** is problematic for both the seller-in-foreclosure and the EP investor. The legislature has not defined what exactly constitutes an act of unconscionable advantage.

What was a reasonable sales price under the circumstances surrounding the transaction when the EP purchase agreement was entered into might appear to be unconscionable to the seller in the future — due only to fast fluctuating market factors and rapid asset inflation following the sale, **not the conduct** of the EP investor. Thus, an investor assumes the risk a fast rising economy or a quick downward shift in interest rates, or both, may provoke the seller to attempt to rescind (without a valid legal reason).

If real estate values rise rapidly and measurably after closing, the "greed factor" may set in, turning a formerly desperate, thankful seller-in-foreclosure into an astute rescinding seller.

However, any **increase in the value** of the property after acceptance of the EP investor's offer may not be considered in the restoration of the parties to their original position. The test of **unconscionable advantage** is not determined based on events taking place after the seller enters into the EP purchase agreement.

Market circumstances existing at the time of negotiations, or when the parties entered into the agreement, are the economic considerations that form one of the two elements used to test for unconscionable advantage. [**Colton** v. **Stanford** (1890) 82 C 351]

Unconscionability has two linked aspects:

- the lack of a **meaningful choice of action** for the seller-in-foreclosure when negotiating to set the price and sell the home to the EP investor, legally called *procedural unconscionability*; and

- a purchase price or method of payment that is **unreasonably favorable** to the EP investor, legally called *substantive unconscionability*.

Price, like any other provision in a purchase agreement, can be considered unconscionable. When determining the unconscionability of the purchase price, the justification for the price at the time of the sale will be examined. [**Perdue** v. **Crocker National Bank** (1985) 38 C3d 913]

While a low sales price may be justified, the investor may have employed terms that constitute an unconscionable **method of payment** for that price, including:

- a carryback note held by the seller with an unreasonably low interest rate, long amortization or no due date, bearing no relationship to current market rates and payment schedules and lacking any understanding of imputed interest at applicable federal rates for the seller's income tax reporting;

- an exchange of worthless land, stock, gems or zero coupon bonds, at face value with a 20-year maturity date; or

- any form of payment that is uncollectible, unredeemable and lacking any present value.

However, the existence of **unreasonable pricing** and payment alone is not enough to show an unconscionable advantage sufficient for rescission of the closed transaction. Both the lack of a meaningful choice and reasonable terms must exist to show an unconscionable advantage existed.

Title insurance

Title insurance companies have few qualms about insuring property purchased during the foreclosure period. The reason: title insurance does not defend or cover the insured investor against the seller's rescission claims. The seller's claim by definition is based on the conduct of the buyer, an exclusion from coverage.

Some title companies insist the seller-in-foreclosure sign an **estoppel affidavit** declaring the seller:

- fully understands the nature of the equity purchase transaction;

- appreciates the finality of the consequences of the sale;

- agrees the purchase price is reasonable and fair under the circumstances; and

- the transaction is not merely financing that allows the seller to reacquire title to the property.

The signed affidavit makes it a little more difficult for the seller-in-foreclosure to later decide to rescind the transaction and recover his home, since it would increase the seller's burden of proving unconscionable advantage.

However, the affidavit does not and cannot waive the seller-in-foreclosure's two-year right of rescission if unconscionable pricing and an oppressive marketplace environment due to the conduct of the buyer actually existed. Any waiver of the seller's rescission rights is void as a violation of the home equity sales law. [CC §1695.10]

The BFP on a flip of the property

Consider an investor who acquires ownership in an EP transaction with a seller-in-foreclosure. The investor then resells (flips) the property for a fair market price to a **bona fide purchaser (BFP)** before the seller's two-year right of rescission expires and before the seller records a *notice of rescission*.

The seller then seeks to recover title to the residence and follows the necessary steps to rescind the transaction.

However, rescission is not available to the seller-in-foreclosure against the BFP or an encumbrancer for value (money lender) if the property is purchased or encumbered prior to the seller recording a notice of rescission. [CC §1695.14(c)]

A BFP is a person who, in good faith, purchases property and pays a fair price without knowledge of a claim against title. The BFP's **knowledge** of the fact the property was previously purchased by the investor during the foreclosure period does not affect the resale buyer's status as a BFP since no claim has been made by recording a notice of rescission. [CC §1695.14(c)]

Despite the BFP status preventing the seller from recovering the property, the seller can **recover money** from the EP investor. The dollar amount of the recovery is based on the value of the lost equity at the time of the sale to EP investors, not the resale value. The money recovery claim must be filed within four years of the investor's violation of the EP statutes.

Further, and more menacing for the EP investor, is the automatic entitlement of the seller to additionally recover three times his actual loss as punitive damages mandated by statute. [CC §1695.7]

The BFP's title insurance

Obtaining title insurance poses no problem for the BFP. A title insurance company will insure over the seller-in-foreclosure's two-year right of rescission, unless a notice of rescission has been recorded (or the title company has other knowledge of the seller's claim).

Title insurance only insures against what is not known by the buyer at the time the insurance is obtained or not listed as an exclusion from coverage.

Yet, the title insurance company has a duty to defend the BFP against any later rescission claim made by the seller-in-foreclosure against the BFP.

Also, a BFP must deal at **arms length** with the EP investor.

If the title insurance company can show the insured buyer is not a BFP, but a successor-in-interest involved in a title flipping scheme with the EP investor for the purpose of avoiding the seller-in-foreclosure's right of rescission, the title insurance company can refuse to defend the insured buyer against the seller's enforcement of his right of rescission. [Calif. Insurance Code §330 et seq.]

Sale-leaseback to the insolvent seller

A resale buyer from an EP investor (or any seller) has a duty owed to himself to inquire as to the property rights of any **person in possession** of the property before the resale buyer can qualify as a BFP. [CC §1695.14(c)]

The seller-in-foreclosure may still occupy the property under a sale-leaseback arrangement. The BFP must inquire as to the occupant's rights (as must the title company under an ALTA policy).

If the seller-in-foreclosure holds an option to purchase under the sale-leaseback, then the sale-leaseback is in law a mortgage, not a sale, and the investor is a lender, not a buyer. Thus, the lender vested as the title holder has nothing to sell beyond his right to receive money as holder of a lien on the property for repayment of a debt under the grant deed as a mortgage-in-fact. [CC §1695.12; see Chapter 21]

Possession of property by any person other than the current vested owner of record imparts *constructive notice* to a potential buyer to inquire as to the right, title and interest of the person in possession. [**Gates Rubber Company** v. **Ulman** (1989) 214 CA3d 356]

SECTION B

Equity Purchase
Time Frame

Chapter 5

Reinstatement and redemption periods during foreclosure

This chapter reviews the time periods for curing delinquencies on a real estate loan and when the loan must be paid in full.

Recession-induced defaults

A government declared recession (two quarters of declining gross domestic product) is a period commencing roughly 24 to 30 months into a regime of a continuous incremental rise in short-term rates orchestrated by the Federal Reserve (Fed). August of 2005 (and of 1988 and 1999) saw the planting of the first seeds of one such recession when the Fed started the continuous periodic bidding up of short-term rates. Thus, the Fed deliberately engineered a pace of slower growth for the economy; a deceleration of economic activity — the sales of real estate.

The rise in short-term rates until they exceed the long-term rates is designed to reduce the long-term growth of price inflation in, among other things, real estate assets. In a word, the real estate boom was over as of August 2005, commencing a recognition of the plight of those who acquired real estate during the boom and were now unable to unload it for the price they paid.

Flipping property within six months of purchase and seeking a profit based solely on an inflating market had run its course, a sort of nation-wide *Ponzi scheme* fed primarily by home builders and Wall Street bankers. The process will occur again following the next real estate boom — most likely in the period of 2015 to 2020. The boom will be a repeat of the boomer acquisitions in the late 1980's, but this time fueled by the X generation's household formations and the retirement of the boomers in condos they purchase.

*Editor's note — The **first tuesday** online journal contains a section that reviews the economic trends of real estate. The journal can be viewed at www.firsttuesdayjournal.com.*

As a recession takes its toll on real estate prices, the attitudes of sellers, brokers and their agents, lenders and the media (for merely reporting the adverse economic and financial condition of the market) turn decidedly gloomy. Further, the general public (for lack of a high school education on economic principals) has a generally pessimistic view of the market place, an *anti-market bias*.

This **anti-market bias** only hastens and deepens the recession's effect on real estate prices. During real estate recessions, sellers nearly panic as their efforts to find a buyer consume ever more months, lenders seize up in an aversion to all risk (nothing short of paranoia) and brokers and agents (especially those new to the business) look for work in other fields of endeavor in droves — 40% or more of sales agents will annually let their licenses expire.

Popular thought, expressed in a variety of ways, is that real estate will never be as good again, that it cannot recover to match the action of the boom-time days, and that the market has gone permanently south, allowing no right-minded person to be fool enough to venture into the quagmire.

Well, permanence is never the case, and investors, by their tolerance for risk, as well as well-educated individuals who are informed on economic principles, do not view real estate as does the herd.

A stretch by the seller too far

It is also the time when sellers experimentally talk of lease-option sales and land sale contracts in an occasionally self-destructive effort to do everything possible to eliminate the long-standing entry barriers for buyers that cripple an owner's sales efforts. Specifically, owners openly collaborate with buyers to avoid brokers, escrow, title insurance, lender involvement and disclosures, such as inspections, city occupancy compliance, pest control, property conditions and natural hazards. The list of gatekeeper obstructions goes on. All this to attract buyers.

It is not that the equity purchase (EP) investor wants any part of these short-sighted but well-intended sales devices to encourage him to buy; he is paying cash. But it is into this environment he will step to make offers, at or near the bottom of the recession when volume and prices neutralize, just before or as the sales volume starts to consistently increase.

Another set of conditions serving to fine tune the time for submission of a purchase offer are the specific circumstances surrounding the foreclosure to which the seller is subjected. Timing of the foreclosure process is mechanical; foreclosure for the seller is a ticking clock counting down for a detonation event: the foreclosure sale. [See Figure 1 accompanying this chapter]

Meanwhile, the EP investor, in a bit more talented approach and certainly with a less gloomy outlook, is tracking those owners who are victims of the public's overreaction to the real estate bust. At the same time, investors see that property prices have been dragged down below the historical trend line of market values, a condition aggravated by ever more property being placed on the market than sellers should sell or brokers should list to maintain a stable real estate market. Also adding to adverse sales conditions is the fact buyers will not return in sufficient numbers to increase prices until it is socially acceptable.

With monthly inventories of homes for sale stacked up at 10 to 13 per buyer per month, brokers seem totally unaware that excessive listing

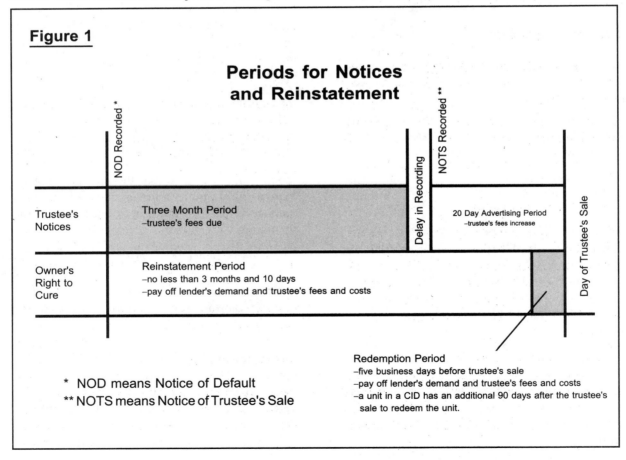

Figure 1

Periods for Notices and Reinstatement

NOD Recorded *

NOTS Recorded **

Delay in Recording

Day of Trustee's Sale

Trustee's Notices

Three Month Period
–trustee's fees due

20 Day Advertising Period
–trustee's fees increase

Owner's Right to Cure

Reinstatement Period
–no less than 3 months and 10 days
–pay off lender's demand and trustee's fees and costs

Redemption Period
–five business days before trustee's sale
–pay off lender's demand and trustee's fees and costs
–a unit in a CID has an additional 90 days after the trustee's sale to redeem the unit.

  * NOD means Notice of Default
** NOTS means Notice of Trustee's Sale

only exacerbates already depressed prices and declining sales volume, a supply and demand issue not overlooked by EP investors and other scavengers of real estate.

The culmination of these events creates a profitable environment for risk tolerant buyers; some acting for the short term, all benefitting in the long term. At some point during the decline in sales volume and sales prices, roughly 24 to 30 months after the start of a methodical decline in short-term rates, the pace of the decline begins to slow. Soon, prices and sales volume neutralize, dropping no further and becoming stable.

Gradually, more buyers gain confidence and begin to buy real estate in greater numbers. As the volume of sales picks up, sellers realize the prices they have been receiving are too low. Twelve to 15 months into a clear trend of increasing sales volume, the prices of comparable properties start to increase. Thus, the germination of yet another real estate boom takes root.

The time for offers

In this matrix of recessionary market activity, the EP investor will locate profitable acquisitions and make offers.

The timing for the submission of offers is set by two conditions:

- current sales volume in the real estate market; and

- foreclosure circumstances of the seller.

As fewer buyers compete to pocket real estate during a recession, the EP investor's timing for making offers requires he wait until the vacuum created by the dearth of buyers creates a window for his easy entry as a cash buyer. At that moment, cash is recognized as king of the transaction.

It is time to submit an offer when the investor locates a property in foreclosure during the period of price stabilization at the bottom of the recessionary period and the property has an equity sizable enough to justify an offer for a few thousand dollars.

The foreclosure circumstances unique to each property in foreclosure during this window period control the proper time to submit an offer on that property.

Timing for submitting an offer to purchase property in foreclosure conveniently breaks down into three phases:

- the period of foreclosure ending before the trustee's auction sale is held;

- the trustee's auction sale itself; and

- the real estate owned (REO) status of the property immediately after the trustee's sale when it is acquired by the lender.

The period following the recording of an NOD before the trustee's sale provides little opportunity for an investor when the loan amount exceeds the property's value. Thus, the property has no equity for the investor to buy. The opportunity that does then exist is a generally troublesome *short sale* effort. Lenders are not emotionally capable of taking a loss while they still hold a note and trust deed.

By waiting until the trustee's sale to bid and acquire a property, an investor might be able to acquire the property at the right price. Of course, he will need to pay cash to buy the position in title held by the lender.

Especially juicy are foreclosures on first trust deed loans that have a loan-to-value ratio of 60% to 70% of value and are in foreclosure because the property is over encumbered with second trust deeds, abstracts of judgment and tax liens.

The foreclosure sale of the first trust deed works to wipe out the junior lienholders who over encumber the property. Thus, to acquire the property for a cash bid in the amount of the first, the trustee's sale eliminates all junior lienholders and leases. The trustee's deed clears from title all liens, except for property taxes, any Mello-Roos-type improvement district bonds and trust deed loans senior to the foreclosed trust deed.

For those properties in foreclosure with a principal loan amount exceeding the value of the property and where the owner lacks the ability or time to negotiate a short pay, the trustee's sale provides little opportunity for the investor to bid in the property at the right price. Lenders typically bid in the property for all amounts due, called a *full credit bid*, including principal, accrued interest, prepayment penalties, late charges and foreclosure costs.

The lender who takes title to the real estate at the trustee's sale puts the investor tracking the property at the third stage — the time to submit a purchase agreement offer to the lender.

Hopefully, the investor has conducted some due diligence investigation into the condition and merits of the property and is ready to submit an offer to the lender immediately following the trustee's sale. A delay in submitting an offer will likely find the property's management already assigned to the lender's REO department. Money will then be spent clearing out occupants, cleaning up the property and eliminating deferred maintenance. Without offers to consider, they soon list the property with MLS-type brokers at full retail prices.

Unlike acquiring property at a trustee's sale, a purchase from the seller-in-foreclosure or the lender as an REO will be escrowed, disclosures will be made and, most importantly, a policy of title insurance will cover defects in title (like strange liens with priority) that would not be covered on a trustee's sale.

Editor's note — Information about recorded NODs and scheduled trustees' sales in California can be purchased at the following websites: www.countyrecordsresearch.com; www.foreclosures.com; www.redloc.com; and www.retran.net.

Nullifying the call during foreclosure

The lender holding a trust deed and note, called the *beneficiary*, may call the entire principal balance of the note due and immediately payable on any default in the terms of either the note or trust deed. Trust deeds contain a boilerplate provision called an *acceleration clause* that authorizes the lender to call the loan on a default.

Another provision in the trust deed, called the *power-of-sale provision*, authorizes the beneficiary to instruct the trustee appointed under the trust deed to initiate a non-judicial trustee's foreclosure to sell the property described in the trust deed.

As a result of the tandem effect of the power-of-sale provision and the acceleration clause, the trustee's *recording* of a Notice of Default (NOD) both initiates the trustee's foreclosure procedures and causes all sums due on the note and trust deed to become due and payable without further notice.

Consider a homeowner who has defaulted on the payment of principal and interest due on the note and property taxes due under the trust deed. An NOD has been recorded, commencing foreclosure to enforce payment of all sums owed under the note and trust deed.

An investor submits a purchase agreement offer, which the homeowner accepts. The terms include the transfer of ownership to the investor subject to the existing note and trust deed that is in foreclosure. The owner will pay all delinquencies and foreclosure charges at the close of escrow from equity purchase funds received from the investor.

Escrow is opened and a request for a beneficiary statement is sent to the beneficiary holding the note and trust deed by escrow. The beneficiary is a private party who has commenced foreclosures before on this trust deed and cancelled the NOD when the homeowner paid all the foreclosure costs and brought the delinquent payments and late charges current.

The beneficiary responds to the request for a beneficiary statement by sending a payoff demand, not a beneficiary statement. The beneficiary claims he is enforcing the acceleration clause in the trust deed and will only accept payment in full now that the NOD has been recorded, triggering the call.

The NOD states the amount of the delinquencies, past, present and future. Thus, escrow is able to determine the amount due to cure the defaults stated in the NOD. The trustee is contacted and the total of the foreclosure fees and charges incurred by the date scheduled for close of escrow are determined.

Between the information in the NOD and the stage of the foreclosure proceeding, escrow can determine the amount due to cure the defaults and pay foreclosure costs. The investor deposits closing funds with escrow on escrow's call for funds. Escrow is closed and the delinquencies and foreclosure costs are forwarded to the trustee, payable to the beneficiary, a tender of the homeowner's proceeds of the sale to cure the defaults.

The beneficiary rejects the tender, claiming the entire amount of his note is due as agreed in the trust deed. Further, the beneficiary claims the due-on clause in the trust deed has been triggered by the buyer's failure to obtain the beneficiary's consent and now requires a full payoff of the note.

Can the escrow, by tendering only the amount of the delinquencies and foreclosure costs necessary to cure the defaults, cause the note and trust deed to be brought current and reinstate the trust deed as though a default had not occurred?

Yes! After the NOD has been recorded and prior to five business days before the trustee's sale, the owner (or any junior lienholder or buyer) of the real estate encumbered by the trust deed lien that is in foreclosure can terminate the foreclosure proceedings by either:

- paying the **delinquent amounts** due on the note and trust deed as described in the NOD and foreclosure charges, called *reinstatement* [Calif. Civil Code §2924c]; or

- paying the **entire amount** due on the note and trust deed, plus foreclosure charges, called *redemption*. [CC §2903]

Since the call triggered by a violation of the due-on clause based on the unconsented-to transfer to the investor is not stated in the NOD, the due-on call cannot be enforced under this NOD.

Note defaults and reinstatement

A trust deed on which a foreclosure has been initiated is considered **reinstated** when the beneficiary receives:

- all amounts referenced as delinquent in the notice of default (NOD), including principal, interest, taxes, insurance, assessments and advances;

- installments that become due and remain unpaid after the recording of the NOD, and any future advances made by the beneficiary after the recording of the NOD to pay taxes, senior liens, assessments, insurance premiums and to eliminate any other impairment of the security; and

- costs and expenses incurred by the lender to enforce the trust deed, including trustees fee's or attorney fees. [CC §2924c(a)(1)]

After an NOD is recorded, an owner or any junior lienholder of real estate can bring current any monetary or curable default stated in the NOD at any time **prior to five business days** before the trustee's sale, called the *reinstatement period*. If the sale is postponed, the **reinstatement period** is extended, ending the day before the five business days prior to the postponed sale date. [CC §2924c(e)]

Up until the time the NOD is recorded by a trustee, the tender of all delinquencies must be accepted by the beneficiary.

After recording the NOD, the lender's trustee must allow **three months** (not 90 days) to pass before advertising and posting notice of the date of the trustee's sale. [CC §2924; see Figure 1]

The lender's trustee must begin advertising and post a *Notice of Trustees Sale* (NOTS) at least 20 days before the date of the sale. The property can be sold by the trustee no sooner than the twenty-first day after advertising begins and the posting of notice occurs. [CC §2924f(b); see Figure 1]

The owner in foreclosure is not allowed to delay the trustee's sale by requesting a postponement. [CC §2924g]

Thus, the owner, or junior lienholder, has a minimum of approximately 105 days to cure the default and reinstate the note and trust deed before foreclosure.

To determine the last day for reinstatement of the note and trust deed, consider a trustee's sale that is scheduled for a Friday. Count back **five business days** beginning with the first business day prior to the scheduled Friday sale. Since weekends are not business days, the fifth day counting backward from the scheduled trustee's sale is the previous Friday (if no holidays exist). Thus, the very last day to reinstate the loan is on the Thursday eight calendar days before the trustee's sale.

The lender's failure to identify or include the dollar amount of all known defaults in the NOD does not invalidate the NOTS for the defaults stated in the NOD. Further, the lender can enforce payment of any omitted defaults by recording another, separate NOD. [CC §2924]

On reinstatement of the note and trust deed, the NOD is rescinded by the trustee, removing the recorded default from the title of the property. [CC §2924c(a)(2)]

Additionally, any **call is eliminated** and the loan is returned to installment status when the note and trust deed have been reinstated. Upon reinstatement, the owner continues his ownership of the property as though the loan had never been in default.

Redemption

Failure to cure a default before the reinstatement period expires allows a trust deed holder to require the owner to **redeem the property** by:

- paying all sums due under the note and trust deed; and

- reimbursing the costs of foreclosure prior to completion of the trustee's sale.

The owner's *right of redemption* exists until the moment the trustee completes the bidding and announces the property has been sold. Any owner, junior lienholder or other person with an interest in the property may satisfy the debt and redeem the property prior to the completion of the trustee's sale. [CC §2903]

To redeem the property, the owner or junior lienholder are required to pay the principal and all interest charges accrued on the principal, permissible penalties, foreclosure costs and any future advances made by the foreclosing lender to protect his security interest in the property.

Unless all amounts due on the note and trust deed resulting from the owner's default are paid in full during the redemption period, the owner will lose the property at the trustee's foreclosure sale.

Lender remedies on a default

An owner's default on a trust deed loan encumbering his property can arise under a provision in either the note or the trust deed. However, a default on the note triggers a default on the trust deed. It is the default on a trust deed that permits a foreclosure.

When the owner fails to pay installments of principal and interest as they become due under the terms of the note, he is then in default on the note. Thus, a default also exists on the trust deed.

The owner's default prompts the trust deed noteholder to immediately call the loan due under the acceleration clause in the note and trust deed by commencing foreclosure proceedings and recording a notice of default (NOD).

Additionally, when the owner fails to meet his obligations regarding the **care, use and maintenance** of the secured real estate, he is in default under the *waste provision* in the trust deed. The default on the trust deed exists even though the owner may be current on all payments and the note is not in default.

The owner's failure to maintain the property or pay property taxes, hazard insurance premiums, assessments and amounts due on senior trust deed liens is considered a default on the current trust deed.

When the owner defaults on the trust deed, the lender may simply call the note due by recording an NOD that initiates a trustee's foreclosure sale.

A trust deed noteholder may advance funds to cure a default on the trust deed, such as the owner's failure to pay hazard insurance premiums, and then add the advance to the debt owed by authority of the trust deed's *future advances provision*. The trust deed noteholder may then demand the immediate repayment of the advance from the owner.

Let the grace period run before NOD

Consider a trust deed note held by a carryback seller that calls for installments to be paid by the first day of each month. A provision in the note imposes a charge when the monthly installments are not received within 10 days after the installment's due date. No mention of a *grace period* for a late payment exists in the note.

The seller consistently receives installments within the 10-day period after the installments become due, but never by the **due date** itself. Eventually, the carryback seller gives the buyer reasonable advance notice (30 days) that the installment for the following month **must be paid** by the first day of the month, the payment's actual due date. If it is not paid by the first, the seller advises the buyer he will begin foreclosure proceedings by recording a notice of default (NOD).

The following month, the buyer fails to deliver the installment by the first. The carryback seller records an NOD beginning foreclosure proceedings within the 10-day no-charge period.

The payment is received by the seller within 10 days after the due date.

The seller claims the monthly installment was delinquent since it was not paid by the first day of the month, thus placing the buyer in default on the second day of the month.

The buyer claims a default did not exist when the NOD was recorded since the NOD was recorded prior to incurring the agreed-to late charge.

Can the carryback seller begin foreclosure proceedings for the past-due monthly installment before the late charge is incurred?

No! The payment, while due, is not yet considered *delinquent* due to the existence of a late charge provision. Foreclosure proceedings may not be initiated for a past due payment during the period before a late charge is incurred. When a note provision imposes a late charge on the expiration of a specified time period without receipt of the amount due, this extended time for payment without penalty qualifies as a *grace period*.

Since a **grace period** exists, a foreclosure may not be initiated to enforce payment of the installment until after the grace period runs, when the payment becomes *delinquent* if unpaid. [**Baypoint Mortgage Corporation** v. **Crest Premium Real Estate Investments Retirement Trust** (1985) 168 CA3d 818]

Trust deed defaults and reinstatement

A property owner's *ability to reinstate* a loan by curing a default under a trust deed provision relating to the property and its title, not the note, depends on the trust deed provision in default.

For example, an owner of real estate encumbered by a trust deed fails to pay property taxes. The trust deed lender records a notice of default (NOD), describing the delinquent property taxes as the owner's default under the trust deed.

Can the property owner reinstate the loan and retain the property by eliminating the default?

Yes! The default is *monetary*, entitling the owner to reinstate the loan by simply paying the delinquent property taxes and the trustee's fees and charges incurred in the foreclosure proceeding.

Also, **monetary defaults** on trust deed provisions, such as the owner's failure to pay assessments, ground lease rent and hazard insurance premiums, may be cured and the loan reinstated on the owner's tender of the full dollar amount of the default. [CC §2924c]

Defaults cured only by redemption

Some trust deed defaults do not allow an installment debt to continue since reinstatement of the note on those defaults is only available if voluntarily agreed to by a lender. Defaults triggering a call and requiring *redemption* of the property by a payoff of the entire debt include a breach of a due-on clause, a waste provision or a violation of law provision.

For example, consider real estate that is encumbered by a trust deed that requires the owner to maintain his property in good condition and repair.

The owner fails to repair the aging improvements on his property and allows the trees and lawn to die.

The trust deed lender becomes concerned since the owner's activities causing waste on the property has decreased the value of his security, called *impairment*. Due to the owner's failure to maintain the property in good condition (and thus the loan-to-value ratio due to a reduced property value), the lender records a notice of default (NOD) against the property.

Unlike a failure to maintain hazard insurance, here the owner cannot cure the default in the trust deed (waste) by tendering less than the entire remaining balance of the debt. Thus, the owner is unable to reinstate the loan.

In order to retain ownership of the property after the loan had been called due to waste, the owner must **redeem the property** by tendering full payment of **all sums due**, including foreclosure costs.

Alternatively, the trust deed gives the lender the authority to cure the waste and add that cost to the principal balance of the note, under the **future advances clause**.

However, when waste by the owner is committed in **bad faith**, the lender foreclosing by a trustee's sale must consider an *underbid* in a dollar amount equal to the property's reduced fair market value should the lender acquire the property at the trustee's sale. With an **underbid** for an amount equal to the property's fair market value, the lender can sue the owner to recover the reduction in the property value below the amount due, which was caused by the bad faith waste, even if the note is a nonrecourse debt. [**Cornelison** v. **Kornbluth** (1975) 15 C3d 590]

Foreclosure of CID assessment lien

When a condo owner fails to pay his assessment fees to a common interest development (CID), the association of the CID can initiate foreclosure procedures. However, the CID must first notify the owner that his condo will be sold at a trustee's sale if the fees are not brought current or the late charges remain unpaid. [CC §1367.1(a)]

If the assessment fees and related charges are not paid within 30 days of the initial notification, the association can then record a notice of delinquent assessment as a trust deed lien on the owner's condo. The association must send the owner a copy of the notice of delinquent assessment within ten calendar days of the recordation. [CC §1367.1(d)]

After the notice of delinquent assessment is recorded, the owner has 30 days before the association can initiate foreclosure proceedings by recording an NOD. [CC §1367.1(g)]

The owner's right to redeem the condo lasts until 90 days after the trustee's sale. Further, the notice of trustee's sale must include a statement advertizing that the condo is being sold subject to the owner's 90-day right of redemption. [CC §1367.4(c)(4)]

SECTION C

Property
Analysis

Chapter 6

Condition of Property: disclosure by seller-in-foreclosure

This chapter explains the affirmative duty imposed on a seller-in-foreclosure and his listing agent to disclose their knowledge about the property's condition to prospective buyers.

Mandated on sales of one-to-four units

Any seller of a one-to-four unit residential property, whether or not it is their principal residence or in foreclosure, must **complete and deliver** to prospective buyers a statutory form called a *Transfer Disclosure Statement* (TDS), sometimes generically called a Condition of Property Disclosure Statement. [Calif. Civil Code §§1102(a), 1102.3; see **first tuesday** Form 304]

The seller must prepare the mandatory TDS with **honesty and in good faith**, regardless of whether he retains a broker and listing agent to assist in its preparation. [CC §1102.7]

When the seller prepares the TDS, he must set forth any material property defects **known or suspected** by him to exist.

Any adverse conditions known to the seller that **negatively affect** the value and desirability of the property are *material defects* that must be disclosed, even though they may not be referenced in the preprinted TDS. Disclosures to an investor or any other buyer are not limited to the items listed on the form. [CC §1102.8]

Provisions used by the seller to have a buyer **waive delivery** of the statutorily-mandated TDS, such as the use of an "as-is" provision in the purchase agreement, are *void* as against public policy.

A buyer has the legal ability to obtain a judgment against a seller for losses caused by non disclosures. However, when the seller is in foreclosure and without sufficient funds to shelter himself and his family, a judgment is of little financial help to the EP investor since the likelihood of collecting money from an insolvent seller is remote.

Thus, the investor must take all steps readily available to complete a due diligence investigation into the property's physical improvements so the purchase price will be based on the actual condition of the property. [See **first tuesday** Form 156 §12.2]

Delivery of the TDS

While it is the seller who must prepare the TDS, it is the agent who obtains the EP offer from the investor who must hand the investor the seller's TDS. When the sales transaction is directly between the seller-in-foreclosure and EP investor, without the participation of an agent in negotiations, the seller has the obligation to deliver the TDS to the investor. Under the circumstance of foreclosure, the investor may need to provide the form and insist it be prepared and returned to him before he submits an offer. [CC §1102.12]

The failure of the seller or any of the agents to **deliver** the seller's TDS to the investor will not invalidate a sale of property after it has closed. However, the seller and the listing broker will be liable to the investor for the amount of actual monetary losses (cost to cure or reduced value) caused by undisclosed defects known to them at the time of acceptance, a point of law that has always existed in California. [CC §1102.13]

For the seller's disclosure statement to be an effective pronouncement to the investor, **material defects** in the integrity of the property must, as a practical matter, be disclosed to the investor before the price of the property is set by acceptance of an offer or counteroffer. [Calif. Attorney General Opinion 01-406 (August 24, 2001)]

Thus, when the seller's TDS on a one-to-four unit residential property is delivered to the investor after the seller enters into a purchase agreement, the investor has the right to:

- **cancel** the purchase agreement on discovery of undisclosed defects known to the seller and unobserved by the investor or the investor's agent prior to acceptance [CC §1102.3];

- **make a demand** on the seller to correct the defects or reduce the price accordingly before escrow closes [See **first tuesday** Form 156 §12.2]; or

- **close escrow** and make a demand on the seller for the costs to cure the defects known to the seller and not disclosed prior to acceptance. [**Jue** v. **Smiser** (1994) 23 CA4th 312]

Closing escrow without resolving the issue of previously undisclosed property conditions is not a viable method for settling a claim for corrections of defects or a price adjustment since the seller-in-foreclosure is basically insolvent.

EP investor's right to cancel

The Condition of Property Disclosure Statement (TDS) is to be delivered to a prospective buyer *as soon as practicable*, and in any event, before closing. **Delivery** of the seller's TDS to the investor is fully satisfied and no right to cancel exists for the investor (due to the disclosures) if the TDS is previously delivered or attached to the purchase agreement offer made by the investor or the counteroffer entered into by the seller. [CC §1102.3]

If the TDS is belatedly delivered to the investor — after the EP agreement has been entered into — the investor may, among other remedies, **elect to cancel** the purchase agreement under a statutory three-day right to cancel. The investor's statutory cancellation right runs for three days following the day of the in-escrow delivery of the TDS. [CC §1102.3]

However, an investor is not left merely to cancel the purchase agreement and "go away" on his in-escrow receipt of an unacceptable TDS.

As an alternative to canceling the purchase agreement due to a delayed receipt and review of the seller's TDS (or a home inspection report), the investor may **make a demand** on the seller to cure any material defect (affecting value) that was known to the seller and not disclosed or known to the investor prior to entering into the purchase agreement.

The same rule holds for the listing agent who has knowledge of defects and does not disclose the facts to the investor before the investor and seller enter into the purchase agreement. Here, the agent's broker provides a "deep pocket" for the investor's recovery of his money losses, since the seller is insolvent. [See **first tuesday** Form 269]

If the seller will not cure the defects, the investor may tender a **price reduced** by the cost to repair or replace the defects known to the seller and undisclosed on the date the purchase agreement was entered into. [See **first tuesday** Form 156 §12.2]

Reliance limited to seller's awareness

On listing his principal residence for sale, the seller of a one-to-four unit residential property in foreclosure signs and hands his listing agent a completed Condition of Property Disclosure Statement (TDS).

A preprinted limitation-of-liability provision contained in the statutory TDS states the disclosures made by the seller on the form:

- **may not be relied on** by an investor as a *warranty* of the actual condition of the property; and

- are **not part of the terms** of the purchase agreement (even though the disclosure statement may be attached to it).

On the disclosure statement, the seller indicates by not checking the box that he is **unaware** of any building code violations on the property. The listing agent adds nothing as he has no knowledge to the contrary and his visual inspection brought nothing to his attention as a violation.

An EP investor is located and an equity purchase agreement entered into. During the seller-in-foreclosure's five-business-day right to cancel, the investor is handed the TDS, which he approves. After the seller's right to cancel expires and prior to closing escrow, a county building inspector contacted by the investor during his due diligence investigation advises the investor that building code violations exist on the property.

Here, the seller **disclosed his lack of actual knowledge** of any code violations in the TDS. The disclosure in the statement enables the seller to avoid liability for building code violations that actually existed, were adverse to the value of the property and were unknown to the seller.

A seller completes the mandatory Condition of Property Disclosure Statement only as a disclosure of his **state of awareness** (actual knowledge) regarding the condition of the property. Thus, the statement does not itself disclose the **actual conditions** that may exist on the property. In a word, it is not a *warranty* of the actual state of the property's condition. Instead, it is a statement of the state of the seller's **awareness** of the property's condition.

Since the TDS is not a warranty, the TDS itself is not a basis for a price adjustment to cure the actual defects if the TDS was honestly prepared.

Again, the EP investor must look beyond the TDS to his alternative remedies, which include:

- canceling the transaction on discovery of a material adverse property condition not previously disclosed;

- requiring the violations be cured before closing escrow; or

- reducing the price by the cost to cure the violations. [See **first tuesday** Form 156 §12.2]

Excuse my state of mind

Serving as a **lack-of-awareness** disclosure, the statutory Transfer Disclosure Statement (TDS) has become discredited as the primary source of information for buyers about the integrity of the physical condition of the property being purchased. At the very least, however, it does contain those defects the seller is willing to disclose.

In practice, a listing agent hands the seller's TDS to a prospective investor (or the investor's agent) to **induce reliance** on its content as establishing the integrity of the property's condition. With the TDS in hand, the investor then sets the price, terms and conditions in his offer to purchase the property, or, if delivered after he is under contract, waive contingencies and proceed to close escrow.

The listing agent does not present the disclosure to the investor as a "red flag warning," accompanied by a contingency provision in the EP agreement stating the investor is to hire a home inspector since the TDS is only the seller's state of awareness. A home inspector's report states the actual condition of the property and warrants that condition.

However, the EP investor, mindful of the lack-of-awareness limitation on the effectiveness of the TDS, cannot give any weight to the seller's disclosure statement, except for the defects actually disclosed.

Thus, the "not-a-warranty" limitation-of-liability provision in the TDS puts every buyer on notice that the TDS is not a part of any purchase agreement. The fact the TDS is an addendum to the purchase agreement or counteroffer assures its delivery to the investor before they enter into the purchase agreement.

Attaching the TDS to the purchase agreement does not make the TDS a representation of the actual condition of the property. Thus, the question remains: just what role ought the TDS play, other than to get the seller on record as to the defects he will disclose in his effort to salvage something from his equity?

Investors must learn not to use the seller's Condition of Property Disclosure Statement (TDS), handed them by the listing agent, as a basis for setting a definitive price and terms of purchase. To everyone's benefit, the well-informed investor will require a home inspection report as the subject of a further approval contingency provision in the EP agreement, whether the report is obtained by the seller or the investor.

With the report, the investor is fully informed and guaranteed about the actual physical condition of the property. The need for price adjustments or corrections based on the "in escrow" discoveries is then remedied under purchase agreement provisions for defects discovered after entering into the purchase agreement. [See **first tuesday** Form 156 §12.2]

Include a home inspector

A competent listing agent will aggressively recommend to his seller that a **home inspector** be retained at the earliest opportunity, before the property is marketed. The inspector will conduct a physical examination to determine the actual condition of the property and issue a report on his findings. [See chapter 7]

A home inspector typically detects and reports property defects overlooked by the seller and not observed during a visual inspection by the listing agent or the investor. Significant defects that remain undisclosed tend to surface after closing as claims made by the investor against the listing broker for deceit. A home inspector troubleshoots for defects discovered by a physical inspection of the property's grounds and improvements that may not generally be observable on a visual inspection by the untrained eye of a broker and his listing agent.

Listing broker's mandatory inspection

A **seller's broker** (or the broker's listing agent) is obligated to personally carry out a visual in-

spection of the property. The seller's disclosures on the TDS prepared by the seller are then reviewed by the broker or the listing agent for discrepancies. The broker or his agent then add any information about material defects that have gone undisclosed by the seller (or the home inspector) and were known to the listing agent or observed during the agent's visual inspection of the property.

An EP investor has **two years** to pursue the seller's broker and listing agent to recover losses caused by the broker's or his agent's **negligent failure** to disclose observable and known defects adversely affecting the physical condition and value of the property. Undisclosed defects permitting recovery are those that would have been observed by a *reasonably competent* broker during a visual on-site inspection. A listing agent is expected to be as competent in his visual inspection and reporting as a reasonably competent broker would be. [CC §2079.4]

However, the investor will be unable to recover money from the seller's broker if the broker or listing agent did not actually know a defect existed, and did conduct a competent visual inspection of the property. [CC §1102.4(a)]

Following their mandatory visual inspection, the seller's broker or his listing agent may include on the TDS **specific items** entered based on disclosures in a home inspector's report. Should the items relied on later be contested by the investor as incorrect or inadequate, the broker and his agent are entitled to *indemnification* from the home inspection company issuing the erroneous report for his share in the responsibility for the omission. [**Leko** v. **Cornerstone Building Inspection Service** (2001) 86 CA4th 1109]

Nondisclosure by the seller

Now consider a residence that has a defect in its foundation adversely affecting the value of the property. The defect is known to the seller, but it is not readily observable by a buyer or broker.

The seller's Condition of Property Disclosure Statement (TDS) does not reflect the seller's knowledge of the defective foundation.

An EP agreement is entered into between the seller-in-foreclosure and EP investor. The TDS is attached to the EP agreement to acknowledge the investor's receipt and avoid a right-to-cancel contingency triggered by a delayed disclosure. Escrow is opened, the cancellation period expires and the property is conveyed to the investor on closing.

Within four years after escrow closes, the defective foundation worsens and becomes obvious to the investor. The investor makes a demand on the seller for his costs incurred to cure the defect. The seller's two-year period for rescission due to an unconscionable advantage has expired. Further, all aspects of the EP procedure and documentation were complied with at the time of purchase. Thus, the EP investor does not feel threatened by a cross claim for violating EP laws.

Is the seller-in-foreclosure liable to the EP investor for the cost incurred to repair the defective foundation?

Yes! Any seller, whether or not he is represented by a listing broker, has a duty to the buyer to disclose on the statutory Transfer Disclosure Statement all facts **known to the seller** about the condition of the property that:

- are **not readily observable** by a buyer on the buyer's inspection of the property; and

- **affect the value and desirability**, and thus the integrity, of the property in the hands of the buyer. [**Prichard** v. **Reitz** (1986) 178 CA3d 465]

The illegal "as-is" sale

Consider a listing agent who, on conducting his visual inspection of a property, has reason to believe the property fails to conform to building and zoning regulations due to the conversion of the garage to living space and the addition of a carport.

The listing agent knows a prospective EP investor who is interested in purchasing the property, but is unaware of the possible violations. If he learns of the violations, he might view the property's value differently.

The investor submits an EP offer. The listing agent prepares a counteroffer and includes an "as-is" disclaimer provision that the seller-in-foreclosure signs. The provision states the agent "makes no representations regarding the property and incurs no liability for any defects, the EP investor agreeing to purchase the property "as is." The counteroffer is submitted to the EP investor and accepted.

After closing, the city refuses to provide utility services to the property on the change of ownership due to building code and zoning violations.

The investor makes a demand on the seller's broker and listing agent for the investor's money losses due to overpricing and the cost of corrective repairs. The investor claims the seller's broker and listing agent breached their *general agency duties* owed the investor since they failed to disclose material defects that adversely affected the value of the property, facts **known** to the listing agent but not the investor.

The broker claims the investor waived his right to collect any money losses when he signed the counteroffer with the "as-is" disclaimer.

Does use of an "as-is" disclaimer provision shield a listing broker from liability for the investor's loss of money and property value caused by the building and zoning violations that were **suspected to exist** by the broker's listing agent and not known or suspected by the EP investor?

No! The seller's broker and listing agent have a **general duty**, owed to all parties in the transaction, not just their seller, to personally conduct a competent visual inspection of the property sold. Based on their duty to conduct a reasonably competent inspection, they are to disclose **all known and observable** property conditions that adversely affect the value and desirability of the property and are not already known to the buyer.

A breach of the seller's listing broker's general duty owed to a buyer occurs when the broker or his listing agent fail to disclose his knowledge or observations about **potential adverse conditions** existing on a property. The breach of the duty is not excused by writing an "as-is" disclaimer into the purchase agreement in lieu of factual disclosures about his suspicions concerning the property's condition. [**Katz** v. **Department of Real Estate** (1979) 96 CA3d 895]

The words "as is" should never be used. "As is" implies a failure to disclose something known to the seller or the listing agent. A buyer purchases property in its condition "as disclosed" and agreed at the time his offer is accepted, in spite of the seller's urgency to negotiate a sale and his need for an early closing due to the pressure of foreclosure. Any failure to timely disclose material defects subjects the seller to liability for the decreased value of the property or the cost to eliminate the undisclosed defect. [CC §1102.1(a)]

"As is" provisions become unnecessary to explain the condition of the property when information regarding defects is included in the seller's TDS and handed to the investor. The seller simply discloses the defects, whether he does or does not eventually agree to make repairs when considering the acceptance of an offer to buy.

Further, public policy prohibits the sale of one-to-four unit residential property "as is," whether or not the property is occupied by the owner as his principal residence or is in foreclosure. All buyers purchase property "as disclosed" by the seller, the seller's broker and the broker's agents, and as actually observed by the investor, **prior to entering** into the purchase agreement, unless negotiations on entering into a purchase agreement call for the seller to correct some or all of the previously disclosed defects. [CC §1102.1(a)]

Chapter 7

Verify the seller's disclosures: Retain a home inspector

This chapter reviews the equity purchase (EP) investor's use of a home inspector to confirm the physical condition of the property is as represented by the seller-in-foreclosure and listing agent prior to entering into an equity purchase (EP) agreement.

Protection for the prospective investor

An equity purchase (EP) investor locates an owner-occupied, one-to-four unit residential property that is in foreclosure and appears to qualify for the investor's purposes. A walk through of the property with the listing agent confirms the property suits the investor's needs.

The EP investor then requests information on the property from the listing agent, including a title profile, a transfer disclosure statement (TDS) and a home inspection report (HIR). The listing agent responds by suggesting the investor should submit an offer. He explains the "necessary disclosures for closing" will be delivered after an acceptable offer has been submitted to the seller.

The indication the investor gets is that the listing agent is dilatory, failing to have prepared a **listing package**. Worse, no information on the property will likely be made available until it is nearly time to close escrow. As for the listing agent, he felt it was a waste of his time to do any of the paperwork until a sale had been agreed to. Negotiations by use of a letter of intent would have been more to the liking of the listing agent. [See **first tuesday** Form 185]

The investor decides he should make an offer at a price and on terms he believes are justified. The investor has checked out comparable sales from information provided to him by the title company. Also, he has some knowledge about properties in the immediate area. As a result of the walk-through and no adverse disclosures by the seller or the listing agent, the investor knows of no problems presented by the physical condition of the property.

The offer anticipates nondisclosures

In any event, an EP agreement is prepared with *contingency and remedy provisions* regarding disclosures and investigation into the condition of the property.

Contingency and remedy provisions included in the EP agreement, among others, call for:

- the seller to furnish an HIR prepared by an insured home inspector showing the land and improvements to be free of material defects [See **first tuesday** Form 156 §12.1(b)];

- the seller and the listing agent to prepare, sign and deliver a condition of property disclosure (TDS) [See **first tuesday** Form 156 §12.2(b)]; and

- the investor to inspect the property twice — once to initially confirm the condition of the property and once again before closing escrow to confirm maintenance has not been deferred and material defects discovered after entering into the EP agreement have been corrected or eliminated. [See **first tuesday** Form 156 §12.3]

The offer is submitted and promptly rejected by the seller. Eventually, a purchase agreement is entered into that eliminates the provision calling for the seller to furnish an HIR. No previous offer has been submitted to the seller by other prospective buyers who obtained an HIR on the property that the EP investor could review.

The investor contacts a home inspection company and orders an inspection and report. The inspection takes place and the HIR is received and reviewed by the investor. The seller and the listing agent have not delivered a TDS or any of the other disclosures or inspection reports that both the seller and the listing agent are duty bound to deliver to prospective buyers. [Calif. Civil Code §§2079, 1102; see Form 269 accompanying this chapter]

The home inspector's written report lists significant defects he has observed during his physical inspection of the property's condition, all of which the seller should have known about. Repair/replacement costs are estimated by a building contractor at $4,500 to eliminate the defects not disclosed by the seller or observed by the investor on his cursory review of the living and storage space within the structure.

Remedies keep the deal alive

The investor makes a **written demand** on the seller to cure (repair) the defects discovered by the home inspector based on the terms agreed to in the EP agreement. [See **first tuesday** Form 156 §12.3(a); and Form 269]

A copy of the HIR and a contractor's estimate of the cost to cure the itemized defects are attached to the investor's request for repairs. Thus, the investor substantiates his demand on the seller to cover previously undisclosed defects.

The seller and his listing agent now prepare a TDS. On it, they note all the defects listed in the HIR and on the investor's notice demanding repairs. The TDS is delivered to the investor. The seller then refuses to make any of the corrections demanded by the investor, claiming he has disclosed the defects in the TDS as he agreed he would do in the EP agreement.

Eventually, the investor is told by the listing agent to either close escrow or cancel. Meanwhile, the seller's five-business-day right to cancel has expired without his having cancelled the EP agreement.

Can the EP investor require the seller to cure the *material defects* found by the home inspector and close escrow?

Yes! The seller must deliver the property to the investor in the condition as disclosed by the seller and his listing agent and observed by the investor at the time the investor's purchase agreement offer was accepted, not in the condition stated in an **untimely disclosure** made in the TDS handed to the investor during escrow.

The seller's and listing agent's **failure to disclose** the adverse conditions existing on the property that affect its value prior to acceptance is an omission of material facts, called *negative fraud*.

For the investor, the most significant issue arising out of the discovery of defects concerns the price he agreed to pay in the EP agreement. The seller and investor agreed on a price for the property based on the conditions **disclosed and known to the investor** at the time the offer was accepted.

Thus, the price represents the agreed value of a used but defect-free property, except for any defects observed by the investor or disclosed to the investor and therefore known prior to entering into the EP agreement. The price, as it turns out, exceeds the property's fair market value by the amount of the costs that will be incurred to cure the defects and deliver the property in the condition "as disclosed" prior to acceptance.

Confirm the seller's disclosures

A seller and his listing broker must disclose to a prospective buyer by use of a TDS all known and observable property conditions that adversely affect the value of the property. The TDS must be handed to the prospective buyer **as soon as possible**, that is, at the earliest convenience.

A Transfer Disclosure Statement completed by the seller and listing agent without the benefit of a HIR too often inaccurately or entirely fails to reveal significant property defects or code violations that actually exist and are not known to the seller or listing agent.

DATE:_____, 20_____, at_____, California.

TO SELLER: _____

FACTS:

1. Buyer entered into a purchase agreement with you dated _____, 20_____ agreeing to buy real estate referred to as _____
    _____.

2. The purchase agreement calls for an **initial inspection** of the real estate by Buyer, or a representative of Buyer.

    2.1 The inspection is to confirm that the condition of the real estate is substantially the condition reasonably expected by Buyer based on observations by Buyer and representations made by Seller or Seller's Agent to Buyer or Buyer's Agent prior to acceptance of the purchase agreement.

3. The purchase agreement calls for Buyer to notify Seller, on completion of Buyer's initial inspection, of any material defects discovered by Buyer which were undisclosed and unknown to Buyer prior to acceptance of the purchase agreement.

4. The purchase agreement further calls for Seller to repair, replace or correct the noticed defects prior to closing the transaction and delivering possession to Buyer.

5. By this notice of material defects in need of repair, replacement or correction, Buyer does not intend to cancel the purchase agreement or avoid Buyer's obligation to perform on the purchase agreement.

    5.1 Buyer will close as scheduled or as soon thereafter as any noticed defects have been eliminated by repair, replacement or correction and completion has been verified by Buyer.

THUS:

6. Buyer hereby confirms the condition of the property on the initial inspection satisfies Buyer's expectations of its physical condition regarding both the land and its improvements, **except** for the following itemized material defects in the condition of the property.

    6.1 Buyer hereby notifies Seller of the material defects in the condition of the property which were undisclosed and unknown to Buyer prior to acceptance of the purchase agreement and makes a demand on Seller to repair, replace or correct the following itemized defects prior to closing:

    _____
    _____
    _____
    _____
    _____
    _____
    _____
    _____
    _____
    _____
    _____
    _____
    _____
    _____
    _____.

I agree to the terms stated above.	Seller hereby acknowledges receipt of a copy.
Date:_____, 20_____	Date:_____, 20_____
Buyer: _____	Seller: _____
Buyer: _____	Seller: _____

FORM 269　　　　08-01　　　©2008 **first tuesday**, P.O. BOX 20069, RIVERSIDE, CA 92516 (800) 794-0494

When the seller has not obtained an HIR prior to entering into a purchase agreement, the EP investor should always order one on either opening escrow or the expiration of the seller-in-foreclosure's five-business-day right of cancellation. In any event, the EP investor should get an HIR before the expiration of any contingency regarding his confirmation that the property is in the condition he was led to expect during the negotiations leading up to entry into a purchase agreement.

An investor needs a home inspection report in the interest of avoiding:

- after-closing discoveries of defects that require correction; and

- after-closing claims he may have against the seller, who borders on insolvency, or the broker who is insured, to recover the value lost or the costs incurred to correct the defects.

Armed with an HIR containing findings of material defects not disclosed, observed or known to the investor at the time the EP agreement was accepted, the investor can then make the necessary demands on the seller to cure or correct defects. Thus, the investor ensures the property will be delivered in the condition **as disclosed** by the seller on entering into the EP agreement, including defects known to the seller or the agent and disclosed in the TDS received prior to acceptance of the investor's offer.

A **home inspection report** is undoubtedly the single most welcomed bit of information a buyer can get on a property that appears suitable to acquire. With it, the buyer has assurance no defects or shortcomings in the improvement exist outside those identified in the report — if not already corrected and eliminated by the seller.

As a cover for the physical condition of the improvement, which represents roughly 75% of the price paid for the property, the home inspection report is equivalent to title insurance covering the deed to the property. If conditions are not as stated in a property inspection report or title policy, they are cured or paid for by the companies issuing the report or the policy. Home inspectors should be used who carry errors and omissions (E&O) insurance to cover their failure to locate and report defects.

The inspection and report

A home inspection is a **physical examination** conducted on site by a home inspector. Unlike the listing agent's mandatory *visual inspection* and report on his observations in the TDS, the physical inspection of a one-to-four unit residential property by a home inspector is performed in exchange for payment of a **noncontingent fee**.

The purpose of the physical examination of the premises is to identify *material defects* in the condition of the land and the structure, systems and components of the improvements on the property. **Material defects** are conditions that affect the property's:

- market value;

- desirability as a dwelling;

- habitability from the elements; and

- safety from injury in its use as a dwelling.

The **home inspection** is a *non-invasive examination* of the mechanical, electrical and plumbing systems of the dwelling. Also covered are the components of the structure, such as the roof, ceiling, walls, floors and foundations. **Non-invasive** indicates there will be no intrusion into the roof, walls, foundation or soil by dismantling or taking apart the structure that would disturb components or cause repairs to be made to remove the effects of the intrusion. [Calif. Business and Professions Code §7195(a)(1)]

The **home inspection report** is the written report prepared by the home inspector to set forth his findings during his physical examination of the property. The report identifies each system and component of the structure inspected, describes any material defects the home inspector found or suspects and makes recommendations

FINAL WALK-THROUGH INSPECTION
Final Condition-of-Property Confirmation

DATE:_____, 20_____ at _____, California.

TO SELLER: _____

FACTS:

1. Buyer entered into a purchase agreement with you dated _____, 20_____, agreeing to buy real estate referred to as _____
_____.

2. The purchase agreement calls for a **final walk-through inspection** of the real estate by Buyer, or a representative of Buyer.

   2.1 The purpose of the final walk-through is to verify that the condition of the real estate at the time of closing is substantially the condition reasonably expected by Buyer based on observations by Buyer and representations made by Seller or Seller's Agent to Buyer or Buyer's Agent prior to acceptance of the purchase agreement.

3. The purchase agreement calls for Buyer to notify Seller on completion of Buyer's final walk-through inspection of the following:

   3.1 any lack of maintenance during the escrow period; or

   3.2 failure of Seller to make repairs and correct defects, defects which Seller was given notice after Buyer's receipt of the Condition of Property — Transfer Disclosure Statement (TDS) and initial property inspection. [See **ft** Forms 269 and 304]

4. By this notice of the need for repair or maintenance, Buyer does not intend to cancel the purchase agreement or avoid Buyer's obligation to perform on the purchase agreement.

   4.1 Buyer will close as scheduled or as soon thereafter as completion of any repairs and maintenance can be verified by Buyer.

ACCORDINGLY:

5. Buyer hereby confirms the condition of the property on the final walk-through inspection satisfies Buyer's expectations of its physical condition regarding both the land and its improvements, **except** for the following list of items regarding the condition of the property.

   5.1 Buyer hereby notifies Seller of the condition of the property which is not in working order or has not been corrected as previously requested and makes a demand on Seller to repair, replace or correct the following itemized condition(s) prior to closing: _____
_____
_____
_____
_____
_____
_____
_____
_____
_____
_____
_____
_____
_____.

I agree to the terms stated above.	**Seller hereby acknowledges receipt of a copy.**
Date:_____, 20_____	Date:_____, 20_____
Buyer: _____	Seller: _____
Buyer: _____	Seller: _____

FORM 270   08-01   ©2008 **first tuesday**, P.O. BOX 20069, RIVERSIDE, CA 92516 (800) 794-0494

about the conditions he observed. The report will suggest any further evaluation needed to be undertaken by other experts for conditions observed by the inspector that are beyond his expertise or the scope of his inspection. [Bus & P C §7195(c)]

When ordering the report, the investor should also request that the home inspector conduct an inspection on the energy efficiencies of the property and include his findings in the report. On a request for an **energy efficiency inspection**, the home inspector will report on items including:

- the R-value of the insulation in the attic, roof, walls, floors and ducts;

- the quantity of glass panes and the types of frames;

- the heating and cooling equipment and fans;

- water heating systems;

- the age of major appliances and the fuel used;

Existing home inspection reports and liability limitations

Prospective buyers of a property are **entitled to rely** on an existing home inspection report (HIR) when they decide to buy the property, waive their right to cancel escrow or require corrections before closing.

The investor's reliance on an existing HIR, obtained by the owner or a prior prospective buyer imposes liability on the home inspector for his failure to exercise the level of care expected of a home inspector when examining the property and reporting its defects. Liability for the unreported defects is imposed even though the home inspection contract or report contain provisions restricting use of the report solely to the person who requested it. [**Leko** v. **Cornerstone Building Inspection Service** (2001) 86 CA4th 1109]

Further, any provision in the home inspection contract or condition in the home inspection report that purports to waive or limit the home inspector's liability for the negligent investigation or preparation of the HIR is unenforceable. The home inspector is liable for the full amount of losses caused by his failure to locate defects and report them. [Bus & P C §7198]

Occasionally, a boilerplate provision in the home inspector's contract or the home inspection report will state the buyer's period for recovery is limited to one year after the inspection occurred. However, any limitation the home inspector may place on the **time period** for the buyer to discover the defect and make a claim is also unenforceable. The statutory four-year period is needed to provide time for buyers to realize the home inspector produced a faulty report. [**Moreno** v. **Sanchez** (2003) 106 CA4th 1415]

An investor ordering out or relying on an existing home inspection report needs to verify the home inspection company has **professional liability insurance coverage**. Do not rely on their that word one exists; get a copy of the declaration page from the insurance policy. The existence of the home inspector's E&O coverage reduces the risk of loss when acquiring one-to-four unit residential property.

- thermostats;

- energy leakage areas throughout the structure; and

- the solar control efficiency of the windows. [Bus & P C §7195(a)(2)]

The EP investor's remedies for deceit

If a home inspection report reveals property defects previously undisclosed and unknown to the investor, the investor may:

- make a demand on the seller to correct or eliminate the defects, and refuse to close escrow until the seller has either complied or agreed to an adjusted price [See Form 269]; or

- refuse to close escrow for lack of the seller's compliance with the demand for corrections.

An option available to an EP investor, though not financially viable due to the seller's insolvency, is to close escrow and then make a money demand on the seller for his losses. The losses will be either the difference between the purchase price set in the EP agreement and the price adjusted for the undisclosed defects as called for in the EP agreement or the cost incurred to cure the defects. [**Jue** v. **Smiser** (1994) 23 CA4th 312]

If the EP agreement entered into by the seller and investor contains a **price adjustment provision**, the investor can, before closing, enforce a reduction of the purchase price. The price adjustment will be for the amount of the costs necessary to bring the property into the condition as it was disclosed by the seller or the listing agent or

known to the investor at the time of acceptance. [See **first tuesday** Form 156 §12.2]

Also, when the seller fails to convey the property in the condition as disclosed by his conduct prior to acceptance, he has failed to deliver the property as agreed. Thus, the investor is justified in refusing to close escrow until the seller compensates the investor for or corrects the defects discovered during escrow.

However, if the investor is made aware of basic facts indicating adverse conditions existed on the property at the time the investor enters into the EP agreement, facts that would cause an ordinary buyer to be put on notice to investigate into their consequences, the investor has no grounds for claiming a loss for the condition he knew existed on entering into the EP agreement.

Final pre-closing inspection

An EP investor must personally **reinspect the property** just before close of escrow to confirm:

- the quality of any repairs made by the seller; and

- the maintenance of the general condition of the property after entering into the EP agreement.

The investor's right to a final pre-closing inspection of the property is agreed to in the EP agreement. [See **first tuesday** Form 156 §12.3(b)]

On final inspection of the property, the investor lists any property defects not already addressed, such as equipment and fixture malfunctions or deferred maintenance, on the final walk-through inspection statement. [See Form 270 accompanying this chapter]

Chapter 8

Hazard disclosures by the broker

This chapter discusses the use of the Natural Hazard Disclosure (NHD) Statement by a seller-in-foreclosure and listing agent to fulfill their obligations to inform prospective equity purchase (EP) investors about the nature of a property's location.

A unified disclosure for all sales

The listing broker in transactions involving the sale of any type of real estate has a duty owed to a prospective buyer **to disclose**, along with other facts that have a significant adverse impact on a property's *value and desirability*:

- the broker's **actual knowledge** of any *natural hazards* affecting the value of the property; and

- information contained in **public records** concerning *natural hazards*. [Calif. Civil Code §1103(c)]

If a seller has not listed the property with a broker, then the seller must disclose any natural hazards known to him or contained in public records. The seller in a for-sale-by-owner (FSBO) transaction must disclose his knowledge of the natural hazards of his property's location and use a statutorily mandated form to do so. [See **first tuesday** Form 314]

Natural hazards come with the **location** of a parcel of real estate, not with the man-made aspects or conditions of the property, as are environmental hazards. Locations where a property might be subject to natural hazards include:

- special flood hazard areas, a federal designation;

- potential flooding and inundation areas;

- very high fire hazard severity zones;

- wildland fire areas;

- earthquake fault zones; and

- seismic hazard zones. [CC §1103(c)]

The existence of a hazard presented by the geographic location of a property affects its value and desirability to prospective EP investors. Hazards, by their nature, limit an investor's ability to develop the property, obtain insurance or receive disaster relief.

Whether a seller markets his property himself or lists the property with a broker, the seller must disclose to prospective investors any natural hazards **known to the seller**, as well as those **contained in public records**.

To unify and streamline the disclosure by a seller (and his listing agent) about those natural hazards that affect a property, the California legislature created a statutory form entitled the *Natural Hazard Disclosure (NHD) Statement*.

The NHD form is used by a seller and his listing agent for their preparation (or acknowledgement of their review of a report prepared by an NHD expert) and disclosure of natural hazard information. The information is either known to the seller and listing agent (and the NHD expert) or available to them as shown on maps in the public records of the local planning department. [CC §1103.2; see **first tuesday** Form 314]

Actual use of the NHD Statement by sellers and their agents is **mandated** on the sale of **one-to-four unit residential properties**, called *targeted properties*. While some sellers of targeted properties are excluded from mandatory use of the form, their listing agents are not. Thus, the form, filled out and signed by the seller and the listing agent, must be included in listing packages handed to prospective EP investors on every one-to-four unit residential property.

Editor's note — Any attempt by a seller or listing agent to use an "as-is" provision or otherwise provide for a buyer to agree to waive his right to receive an NHD statement signed by the seller is void as against public policy. [CC §1103(d)]

Regarding sales of property other than one-to-four unit residential property, use of the statutory NHD Statement is **optional**. However, delivery of the information by use of one form or another is not optional. A natural hazard disclosure is mandated on all types of property. [CC §1103.1(b)]

All sellers, and any listing or selling agent involved, have an initial common law duty owed to prospective buyers to disclose conditions on or about a property that are **known to them** and might adversely affect the EP investor's willingness to buy or influence the price and terms of payment he is willing to offer.

Natural hazards, or the lack thereof, irrefutably affect a property's value and desirability. If a hazard is known to the seller or his agent, or noted in public records, the hazard must be disclosed to prospective buyers before they agree to purchase the property. If not disclosed, the EP investor can cancel the transaction, called *termination*. If the transaction has closed escrow, the buyer may *rescind* the sale and be **refunded** his investment, called *restoration*. [**Karoutas** v. **HomeFed Bank** (1991) 232 CA3d 767]

The NHD is to be prepared, signed and available for delivery to prospective buyers before the seller accepts an offer or makes a counteroffer, requisites to the requirement that the NHD be delivered to the prospective buyer *as soon as practicable*. [Calif. Attorney General Opinion 01-406 (August 24, 2001); CC §1103.3(a)(2)]

Investigating the existence of a hazard

Natural hazard information must be obtained from the public records. If not obtained, the seller and listing agent cannot make their required disclosures.

To obtain the natural hazard information for delivery to the EP investors, the seller-in-foreclosure and his listing agent are required to exercise *ordinary care* in gathering the information. They may gather the information themselves or the seller may employ an NHD expert to gather the information. The expert then prepares the NHD form for the seller and the listing agent to review, add any comments, sign and deliver to the EP investor. [CC §1103.4(a)]

Thus, the seller-in-foreclosure and listing agent may obtain natural hazard information:

- directly from the public records themselves; or

- by employing a natural hazard expert, such as a geologist.

For the seller-in-foreclosure and the listing agent to rely on an NHD report prepared by others, the listing agent need only:

- **request** an NHD report from a reliable expert in natural hazards, such as an engineer or a geologist who has studied the public records (as some natural hazards clearly do not pertain to engineering or geology);

- **review** the NHD form prepared by the expert and **enter** any actual knowledge the seller or listing agent may possess, whether contrary or supplemental to the expert's report, on the form prepared by the expert or in an addendum attached to the form; and

- **sign** the NHD Statement provided by his NHD expert and **deliver** it with the NHD report to the EP investor. [CC §1103.2(f)(2)]

When prepared by an NHD expert, the NHD report must also note whether the listed property is located within 2 miles of an existing or proposed airport, an environmental hazard zone called an *airport influence area* or *airport referral area*. The EP investor's occupancy of property within the influence of an airport facility may be affected by noise and use restrictions, now or later, which may be imposed on the EP investor's uses as set by the airport's land-use commission. [CC §1103.4(c)]

Also, the expert's report must note whether the property is located within the jurisdiction of the San Francisco Bay conservation and development commission.

Broker's use of expert limits liability

The Natural Hazard Disclosure scheme, while not making the practice mandatory, encourages brokers and their agents to use natural hazard experts rather than gather the information from the local planning department themselves. The use of an expert who himself relies on the contents of the public record to prepare his report relieves the listing agent of any liability for errors not known to the agent to exist.

Neither the seller-in-foreclosure nor any agent in the transaction is liable for the erroneous preparation of an NHD Statement they have delivered to the EP investor, if:

- the NHD report and form is prepared by an **expert in natural hazards**, consistent with his professional licensing and expertise; and

- the seller and listing agent used **ordinary care** in selecting the expert and in their review of the expert's report for any errors, inaccuracies and omissions of which they have **actual knowledge**. [CC §§1103.4(a), 1103.4(b)]

The seller and the listing agent need not enter into an *indemnification agreement* with the natural hazard expert to avoid liability for errors. By statute, the expert who prepared the NHD is liable for his errors, not the seller or listing agent who relied on the report of a properly selected expert to fulfill their duty to check the public records.

However, if brokers are sued based on the inaccuracy of the expert's report, an indemnity agreement entered into by the expert, given in exchange for the request to prepare a natural hazard report, will cover the cost of any litigation that might unnecessarily haul the uninsured broker into court.

The listing agent's dilatory delivery of an expert's NHD to the EP investor after the offer has been accepted, will not protect the broker from liability for the EP investor's lost property value due to the nondisclosure before acceptance. If the agent **knew or should have known** of a natural hazard based on the readily available local planning department's parcel list, he is exposed to liability. Liability exposure includes costs the EP investor may incur to correct or remedy the undisclosed hazardous condition and the dollar amount of the price that exceeds the property's fair market value when taking the undisclosed hazard into consideration. [CC §1103.13]

Further, the seller's agents and the expert who originally prepared the NHD are not exposed to liability from others affiliated with the transaction, such as lenders or insurers, who might receive the erroneous NHD Statement and rely on it to analyze the risk they undertake by their involvement. [CC §1103.2(g)]

Documenting compliance with NHD law

Compliance by the seller-in-foreclosure and listing agent to deliver the NHD Statement to the EP investor is required to be documented by a provision in the purchase agreement. [CC §1103.3(b); see **first tuesday** Form 156 §12.4]

However, should the seller or the listing agent fail to provide the investor with an NHD before entering into the EP agreement, the seller is statutorily penalized for the untimely disclosure in escrow. The EP investor, on an **in-escrow disclosure**, is allowed either a three-day right of cancellation should he be handed the NHD Statement, or a five-day right of cancellation should the NHD Statement be mailed to the investor. [CC §1103.3(c)]

Further, delivery of the NHD after acceptance of an offer, when it could have been previously obtained or prepared by the seller or listing agent and timely delivered, imposes liability on the seller and listing agent. Liability is based on any money losses (including a reduced property value) inflicted on the EP investor by the disclosure should the EP investor choose not to exercise his right to cancel and instead perform on the agreement and close escrow. [CC§1103.13; **Jue v. Smiser** (1994) 23 CA4th 312]

Delivery of the NHD to the EP investor

If the EP investor has a selling agent, the selling agent has the duty to hand the EP investor the NHD Statement received from the seller or the listing agent, called *delivery*. [CC §1103.12(a)]

The **EP investor's agent**, on receiving the NHD form from the listing agent, owes the EP investor a special agency duty to care for and protect his EP investor's best interest by reviewing the NHD Statement himself for any disclosure that might affect the property's value or its desirability for his EP investor. The EP investor's agent is then required to deliver the NHD to the EP investor and make any recommendations or explanations the EP investor's agent may have regarding its content. [CC §§1103.2, 1103.12]

If the EP investor does not have a broker, the seller-in-foreclosure's agent is responsible for delivering the NHD Statement to the investor.

However, the listing agent is not required to understand the effect hazards have on the property or the EP investor. Also, the listing agent has absolutely no duty to voluntarily explain to a prospective EP investor the effect a known natural hazard (which is itself disclosed) might have on the property or the EP investor. The task of voluntarily explaining the consequence of living with a natural hazard is the duty of a EP investor's agent.

Delivery may be in person or by mail. Also, delivery is considered to have been made if the NHD is received by the spouse of the EP investor. [CC §1103.10]

Sellers-in-foreclosure occasionally act as "For Sale By Owners" (FSBOs) and directly negotiate a sale of their property with EP investors in transactions that exclude brokers and agents. Here, the seller-in-foreclosure is responsible for preparing or obtaining and signing an NHD statement and delivering the NHD Statement to the prospective EP investor.

No warranty, just awareness

A seller-in-foreclosure's NHD Statement is **not a warranty or guarantee** by the seller-in-foreclosure or listing agent of the natural hazards affecting the property. The NHD Statement is a report of the seller-in-foreclosure's and listing agent's (or the NHD expert's) knowledge (actual and constructive) of any natural hazards affecting the property.

However, the NHD Statement may be relied on by the EP investor. The NHD is designed to assist in the decision to buy the property, and at what price and on what terms. These conditions all need to exist before entering into a purchase agreement to avoid misleading the EP investor, called *deceit*. [AG Opin. 01-406]

Disclosures concerning the value and desirability of a property, such as an NHD Statement, contain **price-sensitive information**. Thus, the statement must be delivered to the investor before he enters into a purchase agreement in order to accomplish the intended result of the disclosure. If not timely disclosed, the seller and listing agent subject themselves to claims for price adjustments (offsets) that may be made by the investor either before or after closing. Alternatively, the investor may cancel the purchase agreement and have his deposit refunded.

Good brokerage practice is to deliver the NHD to a prospective buyer before he makes an offer or accepts a counteroffer, while he is still considering pricing and the terms of purchase. Disclosures should not be made later when the investor is under contract to buy and entitled to ownership of the property at the price and on the terms agreed.

Properly, the investor's offer in an EP agreement will include a copy of the seller's NHD Statement as an addendum (along with all other disclosures), noting the transaction is in compliance with NHD law.

As for an **escrow officer** handling a sale in which the listing agent fails to provide the investor with the NHD prior to opening escrow, the escrow officer has no duty to the seller or investor to prepare, order out or deliver the NHD to the investor. The obligation remains that of the seller and listing agent. However, escrow may accept instruction to perform any of these activities, in which case escrow becomes obligated to follow the NHD instructions agreed to by the escrow officer. [CC §1103.11]

Other disclosure statements distinguished

The NHD Statement handed to a prospective EP investor of one-to-four unit residential property is an additional disclosure unrelated to the environmental hazards and physical deficiencies in the soil or improvements located on or about a property that are presented in the Transfer Disclosure Statement (TDS) or the purchase agreement. [See **first tuesday** Form 304 §C(1)]

The TDS discloses health risks resulting from **man-made** physical and environmental conditions affecting the use of the property. They are limited to facts known to the seller and listing agent without concern for a review of public records on the property at the planning department or elsewhere. The NHD Statement discloses risks to life and property that exist **in nature** due to the property's location and are known and readily available from the public records (planning department).

Editor's note — The following discussion details the different hazards that must be disclosed on the NHD Statement.

Flood zones

Investigating flood problems was facilitated by the passage of the National Flood Insurance Act of 1968 (NFIA).

The NFIA established a means for property owners to obtain flood insurance with the National Flood Insurance Program (NFIP).

The Federal Emergency Management Agency (FEMA) is the administrative entity created to police the NFIP by investigating and mapping regions susceptible to flooding.

Any flood zone designated with the letter "A" or "V" is a *special flood hazard area* and must be disclosed as a natural hazard on the NHD Statement. [See **first tuesday** Form 314 §1]

Zones "A" and "V" both correspond with areas with a 1% chance of flooding in any given year, called 100-year floodplains, e.g., a structure located within a special flood hazard area shown on an NFIP map has a 26% chance of suffering flood damage during the term of a 30-year mortgage.

However, Zone "V" is subject to additional storm wave hazards.

Both zones are subject to mandatory flood insurance purchase requirements.

Information about flood hazard areas and zones can come from:

- city/county planners and engineers;
- county flood control offices;
- local or regional FEMA offices; and
- the U.S. Corps of Engineers.

Additional information concerning flood hazard areas can be obtained in the Community Status Book. The book lists communities and counties participating in the NFIP and the effective dates of the current flood hazard maps available from FEMA.

The Community Status Book can be obtained via the web at:
http://www.fema.gov/fema/csb.shtm.

Flood Insurance Rate Maps and Flood Hazard Boundary Maps are all available at the FEMA Flood Map store by calling (800) 358-9616 or via the web at: http://msc.fema.gov/.

Another flooding disclosure that must be made on the NHD Statement arises when the property is located in an area of **potential flooding**. [See **first tuesday** Form 314 §2]

An area of potential flooding is a location subject to partial flooding if sudden or total **dam failure** occurs. The inundation maps showing the areas of potential flooding due to dam failure are prepared by the California Office of Emergency Services. [Calif. Government Code §8589.5(a)]

Once alerted by the listing agent to the existence of a flooding condition, the EP investor or his agent must inquire further to learn the significance of the disclosure.

Very high fire hazard severity zone

Areas in the state that are subject to significant fire hazards have been identified as *very high fire hazard severity zones*. If a property is located in a very high fire hazard severity zone, a disclosure must be made to the prospective EP investor. [See **first tuesday** Form 314 §3]

The city, county or district responsible for providing fire protection have designated, by ordinance, very high fire hazard severity zones within their jurisdiction. [Gov C §51179]

The fire hazard disclosure on the NHD form mentions the need to maintain the property. Neither the seller-in-foreclosure nor the listing agent need to explain the nature of the maintenance required or its burden on ownership. Advice to the EP investor on the type of maintenance and the consequences of owning property subject to the maintenance are the duties of the EP investor or his agent.

For example, an EP investor acquiring a residence located in a very high fire hazard severity zone must:

- maintain a firebreak around the structure of a distance of no less than 30 feet or to the property line, whichever is nearer, unless the local agency requires up to 100 feet or more;

- remove tree branches extending within 10 feet of any chimney or stovepipe;

- clear dead or dying wood from trees adjacent to or overhanging the structure;

- remove leaves, needles or other dead vegetative growth from the roof; and

- maintain a screen over the chimney or stovepipe. [Gov C §51182]

State Fire Responsibility Areas

If a property is in an area where the financial responsibility for preventing or suppressing fires is primarily on the state, the real estate is located within a *State Fire Responsibility Area*. [Calif. Public Resources Code §4125(a)]

Notices identifying the location of the map designating State Fire Responsibility Areas are posted at the offices of the county recorder, county assessor and the county planning agency. Also, any information received by the county after receipt of a map changing the State Fire Responsibility Areas in the county must be posted. [Pub Res C §4125(c)]

If the property is located within a **wildland area** exposed to substantial forest fire risks, the seller-in-foreclosure or his listing agent must disclose this fact. If the property is located in a wildland area, it requires maintenance by the owner to prevent fires. [Pub Res C §4136(a); see **first tueday** Form 314 §4]

In addition, the NHD Statement advises the investor the property is located in a **wildland area** and that the **state has no responsibility** for providing fire protection services to the property, unless the Department of Forestry and Fire Protection has entered into a cooperative agreement with the local agency. No further disclosure about whether a cooperating agreement exists need be made by the seller or listing agent. [See **first tueday** Form 314 §4]

However, if property disclosures place the property in a wildland area, the EP investor or his agent needs to inquire and investigate into what agency provides fire protection to the property.

Earthquake fault zones

To assist the seller's agent or the expert preparing the NHD in identifying whether the listed property is located in an earthquake fault area, maps have been prepared by the State Geologist.

The State Mining and Geology Board and the city or county planning department have maps available that identify special studies zones, called *Alquist-Priolo Maps*. [Pub Res C §2622]

The maps are used to identify whether the listed property is located within one-eighth of a mile on either side of a fault.

Also, the NHD Statement requires both the seller and the listing agent to disclose to the investor whether they have knowledge the property is in a fault zone. [See **first tuesday** Form 314 §5]

Seismic hazards

A *Seismic Hazard Zone* map identifies areas that are exposed to earthquake hazards, such as:

- strong ground shaking;

- ground failure, such as liquefaction or landslides [Pub Res C §2692(a)];

- tsunamis [Pub Res C §2692.1]; and

- dam failures. [Pub Res C §2692(c)]

If the property for sale is susceptible to any of the earthquake (seismic) hazards, the seismic hazard zone disclosure on the NHD Statement must be marked "Yes." [See **first tuesday** Form 314 §6]

Seismic hazard maps are not available for all areas of California. Also, seismic hazard maps do not show Alquist-Priolo Earthquake Fault Zones. The California Department of Conservation creates the seismic hazards maps.

The seismic hazard maps that exist are on the web at http://www.consrv.ca.gov/shmp/.

If the NHD indicates a seismic hazard, the EP investor or his agent must then determine which type of seismic hazard exists, the level of that hazard and the distinctions. The listing agent has no obligation to voluntarily explain his disclosure to the EP investor, but must respond honestly to an inquiry.

For example, property located in Seismic Zone 4 is more susceptible to **strong ground shaking** than areas in Zone 3. But which zone the property is located in is a question the EP investor or his agent must answer. Most of California is in Zone 4, except for the southwest areas of San Diego County, eastern Riverside and San Bernardino Counties, and most of the Northern California Sierra Counties.

Homes in Zone 4 can be damaged even from earthquakes that occur a great distance away.

Ground failure is a seismic hazard that refers to landslides and liquefaction. Liquefaction occurs when loose, wet, sandy soil loses its strength during ground shaking. Liquefaction causes the foundation of the house to sink or become displaced. The condition is prevalent in tidal basins that are fills.

A **tsunami** is a large wave caused by an earthquake, volcanic eruption or underwater landslide. Coastal areas are the ones at risk for loss of property and life.

Tsunami inundation maps are available from the National Oceanic and Atmospheric Administration (NOAA) led National Tsunami Hazard Mitigation Program (NTHMP) at: http://www.pmel.noaa.gov/tsunami-hazard.

Also, FEMA's Flood Insurance maps consider tsunami wave heights for Pacific coast areas.

Dam failure results in flooding when an earthquake causes a dam that serves as a reservoir to rupture. The city or county planning department has maps showing areas that will be flooded if a local dam fails.

Areas susceptible to inundation due to dam failure caused by an earthquake are also noted on the NHD Statement as a potential flooding area.

Chapter 9

Property operating data investigation

This chapter advises equity purchase (EP) investors to evaluate an owner-occupied residential property in foreclosure based on expenses and rent generated by ownership of the property.

Profiling a property by its expenses

On acquiring a single-family residential property, the buyer will either:

- **retain ownership** and occupy the property or rent it to a tenant; or

- **flip ownership on a resale** to another buyer who will occupy the property or rent it to a tenant.

When acquiring a property, the buyer will pay or cause tenants to pay the monthly expenses incurred to maintain and occupy the property. The buyer who occupies the property as his residence will pay all of these expenses. The tenant who leases the property from the buyer will directly or indirectly pay all these operating costs; those paid directly will be in addition to rent owed, those paid indirectly will be paid by the landlord from the rent.

All expenditure for the costs of maintaining a property and expenses of occupying and using it are known to the seller of every property sold. These maintenance costs and occupancy expenses affect a property's value, be the costs low and advantageous, high and adverse, or neutral in effect when weighed against the costs and expenses of owning and occupying comparable properties. Thus, costs and expenses have an impact and must be gathered and analyzed as guidance to establishing a property's:

- present value;

- rental rate; and

- resale value.

Logically, a prudent investor acquiring a residence in foreclosure should request that the seller provide him with the information before he makes an offer to buy the property, as should well-advised buyers of any property. When making the request for the seller-in-foreclosure to disclose the monthly costs and expenses of ownership and occupancy (exclusive of loan information), the EP investor should hand the seller an occupant's property expense profile (OPEP) sheet to fill out and return to the investor. [See Form 562 accompanying this chapter]

Duties owed the EP investor

A listing agent owes a *general duty* to a prospective buyer of any property to gather and present readily available data on the costs and expenses the buyer will experience on acquiring the listed property. These data are components of ownership obligations and may adversely affect the property's value. Thus, they might influence a buyer's decision about his purchase of the property.

The property operating data submitted to the buyer by a listing agent can be relied on and need not be investigated for their accuracy by the investor unless it is noted to be a forecast, although estimates involve reasonableness and require a high degree of accuracy as they cannot be the product of conjecture.

In turn, the duty of care a buyer owes to himself when he does not have an agent to advise him require the buyer to review the skeletal property operating data received from the seller and listing agent. From the data he must determine what inquiry or investigation is needed to understand and appreciate the ramifications of the data disclosed.

OCCUPANT'S PROPERTY EXPENSE PROFILE
(OPEP)

DATE:_____, 20_____, at _____, California.

Prospective Occupant _____

1. **PROPERTY TYPE:** _____
    1.1 Location: _____
    1.2 OPEP figures are estimates reflecting:
         a. ☐ current expenses of occupancy.
         b. ☐ forecast of anticipated expenses of occupancy.
2. **MONTHLY OPERATING EXPENSES:**
    2.1 Electricity . . . . $_____
    2.2 Gas. . . . . $_____
    2.3 Water . . . . $_____
    2.4 CATV . . . . $_____
    2.5 Phone. . . . . $_____
    2.6 Rubbish . . . . $_____
    2.7 Sewage. . . . . $_____
    2.8 Insurance _____. . . . . $_____
    2.9 Taxes _____. . . . . $_____
    2.10 General obligation bonds . . . . $_____
    2.11 Lawn/Gardening . . . . $_____
    2.12 Pool/Spa . . . . $_____
    2.13 Janitorial/Maids . . . . $_____
    2.14 Maintenance and repair . . . . $_____
    2.15 Other _____ . . . . $_____
    2.16 **Total Operating Expenses**. . . . . $_____
    2.17 **Monthly Loan/Lease Payment**. . . . . $_____
    2.18 **Total Monthly Expenses** . . . . $_____
3. **DEPOSITS:**
    3.1 Rental Security Deposit . . . . $_____
    3.2 Electricity Deposit . . . . $_____
    3.3 Water Deposit . . . . $_____
    3.4 Sewage and Rubbish Deposit. . . . . $_____
    3.5 Gas Service Deposit . . . . $_____
    3.6 Phone Service Deposit. . . . . $_____
    3.7 Other _____ . . . . $_____
    3.8 **Total Deposits** . . . . $_____

OWNER: I have read and approve this information.

Date_____, 20_____

Owner's Name _____

Signature _____

Date Prepared: _____, 20_____	**PROSPECTIVE BUYER/TENANT: I have received and read a copy of this estimate.**
Broker:_____	Date: _____, 20_____
Agent: _____	Name: _____
Phone: _____, Cell: _____	Signature: _____
Fax: _____	Name: _____
Email: _____	Signature: _____

FORM 562   01-08   ©2008 **first tuesday**, P.O. BOX 20069, RIVERSIDE, CA 92516 (800) 794-0494

In essence, the seller's listing agent literally hands off to the EP investor the decision as to which points raised by the OPEP figures need to be checked out to get a better picture of the property's ongoing costs and expense he will incur on his acquisition of ownership.

The monthly operating expense data are one basis for comparing different available properties and their respective values with the seller's property. Comparison allows the EP investor to select the best overall value.

Participation by a broker to negotiate on behalf of the EP investor has been (prior to Decmber, 2007) and will most likely be effectively eliminated in the future by EP statutes due to broker bonding requirements.

But a broker could be hired by the EP investor to independently advise him on a particular property. Bonding requirements, past and future, for investment brokers will dissuade these brokers from also acting on behalf of the EP investor directly negotiating with the seller-in-foreclosure or the seller's broker. [See Chapter 3]

Thus, an investor who wants an operating analysis of a property he is considering for purchase has the burden of investigating and completing or confirming the numbers on an Occupant's Property Expense Profile (OPEP) sheet himself. Alternatively, he could hire a broker to investigate and analyze the operating costs without interfacing with the seller or listing agent. [**Kendall** v. **Ernest Pestana, Inc.** (1985) 40 C3d 488]

However, while the seller-in-foreclosure will know the costs and expenses incurred to own and occupy the property, he may not know about the property's possible rental income rate, data needed by an EP investor to analyze the property as a long-term investment. A seller who provides *good faith estimates* about the property's operating potential as a rental cannot be held liable for inaccuracies as long as the estimated figures are labeled as "estimates." [Calif. Civil Code §1102.5]

Seller's good-faith assistance

To assist a listing agent to marshall information about a property's operations for the preparation of an OPEP to be handed to prospective buyers, the seller must, *in good faith*, provide the listing agent with the costs and expenses he is incurring as the owner.

A seller, having employed a listing agent to market his property and locate a buyer willing to pay the listed price, owes a duty to the listing agent to make a good-faith effort to cooperate and assist the agent to meet the objectives of the employment. Otherwise, the seller *wrongfully interferes* with the agent's ability to successfully market the property (and earn a fee). Without accurate ownership expense data, property cannot be honestly marketed to prospective buyers.

In turn, the listing agent's duty owed to the seller is to deliver to his seller the best business advantage **legally achievable**. This duty is tempered by the listing agent's *general duty* owed to prospective buyers to provide them with accurate factual information about the integrity of the property, including reasonable OPEP estimates, that may adversely affect the value of the property, and do so before the buyer enters into a purchase agreement.

To meet this affirmative disclosure duty owed prospective buyers, the listing agent must provide prospective buyers or their agents with information **known or readily available** to the seller or listing agent about the operations of the property that **might affect** the decisions of a reasonably prudent buyer regarding acquisition of the property. As a result, the listing agent must present known facts to a prospective buyer in a manner that will not mislead or deceive the buyer by omitting known factors that adversely affect the property's value.

If the seller is the source of the property's operating cost and expense data entered on the OPEP sheet and no reason exists for the listing agent to believe the data is false, the listing agent has no duty to prospective buyers to investigate the truthfulness (accuracy) of the information. However, for the agent to avoid liability for erroneous data obtained from others, the **source of the data** must be disclosed since the data is presented as current conditions — facts.

Estimating rental income

Residential properties controlled by EP statutes include properties containing one-to-four residential units, **one of which is occupied** as the seller-in-foreclosure's principal residence.

With a multi-family income property, the income producing capacity of the property is established by:

- the **scheduled rental income** for each rented unit, and the market rental rate for the unit occupied by the seller-in-foreclosure; and

- the uncollectible portion of the scheduled rents based on prospective vacancies and nonpayment of rent, called a **vacancy factor**.

For the seller-occupied unit, its scheduled rental income must be estimated based on the rental rates charged for comparable properties in the area. As always, the EP investor or his broker must do some investigation into the rental rates charged by landlords of comparable units.

The EP investor should be warned: *estimated, anticipated, forecasted or projected rental income* and expense figures provided by most listing brokers are highly suspect due to generally negligent guesswork in their preparation. However, the EP investor cannot hold the seller-in-foreclosure or the seller's broker liable for estimates made in good faith and based upon the best possible information when they later prove to be erroneous. [CC §1102.5]

The seller-occupied unit in a triplex or fourplex structure is typically of grander proportions and containing upgraded amenities than the other units. The upgraded seller-occupied unit typically will not command a rent that is pro rata to the size/square footage of the other units, a con-

dition called *over-built*. Thus, the estimates of rental income scheduled for the upgraded seller-occupied unit must be viewed with some suspicion. Comparable units for setting the rent should be of same size and occupancy design.

Completing the APOD

After the EP investor receives the property's income and expense information and confirms or prepares the annual property operating data (APOD) sheet, he can calculate expenses as a percentage of rental income to reveal the property's cost-effectiveness as compared to other like-type properties. [See **first tuesday** Form 352]

Expenses, as a percentage of scheduled income, are calculated on the APOD in the column to the right of the dollar amount. Percentages are obtained by dividing each expense item by the 100% scheduled income.

Percentages calculated for each operating expense alert the EP investor to costs that vary from a standard cost range used for income property analysis.

For example, if the percentage allocated to utility expenses is abnormally large compared to other units, this cost should be evaluated to determine:

- what can be done, if anything, to bring the utility expenses within the normal percentage range; and

- what effect the expense has on the value of the property.

Subtracting the operating expenses from income calculates the **net operating income** (NOI). Net operating income represents the income used to determine the **property's value** — before payments on the financing secured by the property or depreciation.

Net operating income, when divided by the EP investor's desired annual yield — called the *capitalization rate* or "cap rate" — constitutes another basis for establishing the value of the property to the EP investor besides comparison.

Loan payments

Loan payments entered on the APOD should only be the principal and interest payment, separated from any impounded (escrowed) funds collected by the lender with the principal and interest payment. Impounds are merely a **reserve** for some of the owner's operating expenses that will be paid through the lender from the impounded funds. Impounds paid are not a loan charge, they are the owner's operating expenses.

Impounds typically change on transfer of the property, primarily due to an increase in property taxes triggered by reassessment on a change of ownership. Calculate the increase in the impounds and note the estimated future impound payment, not the seller-in-foreclosure's present impound payment.

The exact balances and terms of existing financing are forwarded to escrow in the *beneficiary statement* provided by the lender on request. Information from the beneficiary statement confirms the seller-in-foreclosure's representations of the loan amount, payments, interest impounds and delinquencies. [See Chapter 20]

An *assumption* of the loan by the EP investor will likely include some modification of the loan payment schedule, particularly in a high or rising long-term interest rate market. [See Chapter 15]

Other valuation considerations

In addition to the ongoing monthly ownership costs and occupancy expense information collected, the EP investor should consider other facts affecting the marketability of the property, including:

- the *physical condition* of the property's improvements and soil;

- *title conditions* and *zoning* use restrictions;

- the *area surrounding* the property location and the hazards of the location; and

- the *capital investment* required to own the property.

The EP investor should **physically inspect** the property for any deferred maintenance and rehabilitation costs. Additionally, a home inspector's investigation and report of the property condition helps avoid surprise discoveries after escrow closes. [See Chapters 6 and 7]

A **preliminary title report** will expose any recorded title problems, such as judgment liens, assessment bonds or easements.

Further, the EP investor should confirm with local agencies the uses allowed by the current zoning, as zoning affects the future income and expenses of the property. [See Chapter 10]

In addition to all the various property analyses, an EP investor who intends to flip the property for a profit should prepare a **capital cost analysis** of the residence he is considering acquiring to ensure the property's economic feasibility as a profitable investment. [See **first tuesday** Form 365]

SECTION D

Title
Condition

Chapter 10

Preliminary title reports

This chapter examines the use of a preliminary title report by an equity purchase (EP) investor to review the condition of title and eliminate contingency provisions, and by escrow to prepare closing documents.

An offer to issue title insurance

An investor enters into an equity purchase (EP) agreement to acquire a one-to-four unit residential property that is the seller's principal residence. The property is encumbered by a trust deed and a notice of default has been recorded.

Closing of the transaction is contingent on the investor's receipt and review of a preliminary title report, commonly called a *prelim*. He wants to confirm the property is subject only to the liens disclosed by the seller before he proceeds further with his due diligence investigation.

Any taxes or monetary liens of record not disclosed in the EP agreement are to remain of record. However, the amount of any undisclosed lien will be deducted from the cash down payment. [See **first tuesday** Form 156 §13.3]

Escrow is instructed to order a prelim from a title insurance company for approval of the condition of title by the investor. To keep acquisition costs at a minimum, escrow is also instructed to close without obtaining a policy of title insurance. As a result, the escrow office attaches an advisory notice to the instructions as mandated to warn that title insurance is necessary to ensure the buyer's interest. [Civil Code §1057.6; see **first tuesday** Form 401-1]

The prelim received by escrow indicates the title is clear of all encumbrances, except those disclosed by the seller. Believing the title condition is as represented by the seller, the investor waives the further-approval contingency regarding approval of the prelim. Escrow closes on receiving a "date-down" on the prelim from the title company — without the issuance of an abstract or policy of title insurance.

However, the preliminary title report failed to disclose a recorded abstract of judgment that had attached to title as a judgment lien. Later, the judgment creditor enforces his judgment lien by commencing a foreclosure on the property. The investor makes a demand on the seller to pay the judgment and obtain a release of the lien, but the seller rejects.

The investor then clears title of the lien and makes a demand on the title company for the amount of the payoff since he relied on their erroneously prepared prelim. The investor claims the title company is liable for his losses since it failed to disclose the judgment lien on the preliminary title report, a negligent misrepresentation of title.

Can an investor, escrow officer or agent rely on the preliminary title report as assurance the title condition is "as represented" in the report?

No! A preliminary title report is not a representation of the condition of title. Unlike an *abstract of title* issued by a title company, a prelim cannot be relied on by anyone. A title insurer has no duty to accurately report title defects and encumbrances on the preliminary title report (as exceptions in the proposed policy). [**Siegel** v. **Fidelity National Title Insurance Company** (1996) 46 CA4th 1181]

A preliminary title report prepared by a title insurance company is no more than a conditional **offer to issue** a title insurance policy based on the terms and conditions stated in the prelim. The offer is subject to any modifications later made by the title company before the policy is issued, a very conditional offer. [Calif. Insurance Code §12340.11]

Use of the prelim

A preliminary title report discloses the current vesting, including general and special taxes, assessments and bonds, covenants, conditions and restrictions (CC&Rs), easements, rights of way, liens, and any interests of others that may be reflected on the public record as affecting title, collectively called *encumbrances*.

The closing of the purchase escrow should be conditioned on the investor's approval of the prelim. The investor, real estate agent and escrow officer review the report on its receipt for encumbrances on title inconsistent with the terms for the seller's delivery of title as stated in the EP agreement and escrow instructions.

Also, agents are looking for title conditions that might interfere with any **intended use or change in the use** of the property known to be contemplated by the investor. Interferences could be in the form of unusual easements or use restrictions obstructing the investor's announced plans to add improvements.

Finally, escrow relies on the preliminary report to carry out its instructions to record grant deeds, trust deeds, leaseholds or options that will be insured.

Escrow instructions typically call for closing when the deed can be **recorded and insured**, subject only to taxes, CC&Rs and other encumbrances specified in the instructions.

Ultimately, it is the escrow officer who, on review of the prelim, must advise the seller of any need to eliminate encumbrances on title that will interfere with closing as instructed.

The prelim and a last-minute *date-down* of title conditions are used by escrow to reveal any additional title problems to be eliminated before closing and, as instructed, obtain title insurance for the documents being recorded.

Should the date-down of the prelim reveal encumbrances not previously reported in the prelim, either due to error or a later recording, the title company can **withdraw its offer** and issue a new prelim — a different offer to issue a policy that will include the recently discovered encumbrances, unless removed.

Prelim vs. abstract of title

Title companies have long been aware of the public's reliance on the prelim. This reliance was consistently reinforced by the California courts holding title insurers liable for their erroneous reports. However, legislation drafted by the title insurance industry was enacted in 1981 to eliminate liability for their faulty preparation of preliminary title reports.

Prelims were once compared to abstracts of title. An *abstract of title* is a written statement that may be relied on by those who order them as an accurate, factual representation of title to the property being acquired, encumbered or leased. [Ins C §12340.10]

An abstract of title is a **statement of facts** collected from the public records. An abstract is not an insurance policy and does not have a dollar limit on the title company's liability for indemnity. Since the content of an abstract is intended by the insurance company to be relied upon **as fact**, the insurer is liable for all money losses of the policy holder flowing from its failure to properly prepare the abstract. Not so under a policy of title insurance, which limits the dollar recovery to policy limits. [**1119 Delaware** v. **Continental Land Title Company** (1993) 16 CA4th 992]

To shield title companies from an *abstractor's liability* on the issuance of a defectively prepared prelim, the prelim is now defined as being neither an abstract of title nor a representation of the condition of title. The prelim is a report furnished in connection with a buyer's **application** for title insurance. [Ins C §12340.11]

Chapter 11

Title insurance coverage

This chapter discusses the risks covered by title insurance under the different types of policies available to the EP investor.

Identifying an actual loss

A policy of title insurance is the means by which a title insurance company *indemnifies* — reimburses or holds harmless — a person who acquires an interest in real estate against a monetary loss caused by an **encumbrance on title** that:

- is not listed in the policy as an *exception*; and

- the insured was unaware of when the policy was issued. [Calif. Insurance Code §12340.1]

A policy of title insurance is issued on one of several forms, which are the prototypes used by the entire title insurance industry in California. The policies are typically issued to **buyers** of the fee simple interest in real estate, **tenants** acquiring long-term leases on real estate and **lenders** whose loans are secured by real estate.

As an **indemnity agreement**, a title policy is a contract. The terms of coverage in the policy set forth the extent of the title insurance company's obligation, if any, to indemnify the named insured for a *money loss* caused by an **encumbrance on title** that is not listed in the policy's exceptions. [Ins C §12340.2]

An insured lender or buyer cannot recover a **reduction in profits** caused by an unlisted defect in title as lost profits are not covered by title insurance. The title policy only indemnifies the insured against a **reduction in the value** of the property below the policy limits, not a reduction in future profits on either a foreclosure or resale of the property. [**Karl** v. **Commonwealth Land Title Insurance Company** (1993) 20 CA4th 972]

Encumbrances unknown, undisclosed

Almost all losses due to the reduction in value of real estate below the policy limits arise out of an encumbrance. An encumbrance is any condition that affects the ownership interest of the insured, whether the interest insured is a fee, leasehold, life estate or the security interest of a lender.

The word encumbrance is all encompassing. Any right or interest in real estate held by someone other than the owner that diminishes the value of the real estate is an encumbrance.

Encumbrances on title include:

- covenants restricting use;

- restrictions on use;

- reservations of a right of way;

- easements;

- encroachments;

- trust deeds or other security devices;

- pendency of condemnation; and

- leases. [**Evans** v. **Faught** (1965) 231 CA2d 698]

Use of property not covered

Physical conditions on the property itself are not encumbrances affecting title, they are existing uses affecting ownership. Uses that exist and are visible (open and notorious) as physical features on the property include:

- canals;

- highways;

- irrigation ditches; and

- levees.

Accordingly, title policies do not insure against observable physical conditions existing on the property. Observable physical conditions are not encumbrances, although they may be authorized by an encumbrance on title, such as an easement. A buyer is always presumed to have contracted to acquire property subject to physical conditions on the property that impede its use or impair its value. In the case of encumbrances, recorded or not, no such presumption exists.

Consider an EP investor who under an EP agreement contracts to acquire title free of all encumbrances except those agreed to in the purchase agreement. Even if the investor is on notice of an encumbrance affecting title and he has not agreed in the purchase agreement to take title subject to the encumbrance, the seller is responsible for its removal, extinguishment or compensation.

However, for title insurance purposes only, the buyer/investor's knowledge of an encumbrance affecting title at the time of closing **removes the known encumbrance** from coverage even if it is not listed as an exception. Thus, the insured buyer assumes the risk of loss due to the known encumbrance, but only as to the title insurer, not the seller.

Underwriting conditions

A title insurance policy is not an *abstract of title*. Thus, a policy of title insurance does not *warrant* or *guarantee* the nonexistence of title encumbrances, as does an abstract. Instead, the insured is *indemnified*, up to the policy's dollar limits, against a money loss caused by a title condition not listed as an exception or known to the insured prior to issuance of the policy.

Under a title insurance policy, the title company only assumes (covers) the risks of a **monetary loss** caused by an encumbrance not listed as an

exception to coverage, and unknown to the insured buyer or lender at the time of closing. The title company has no obligation to clear title of the encumbrance.

Consider an owner who discovers the size of an easement was understated in the title policy.

Due to the actual dimensions of the easement, the owner cannot develop the property as anticipated.

The owner makes a claim on the title company for the **lost value** of the property based on its potential for development as allowed by the understated easement, not for his loss of value on the price he paid for the property (which is the dollar amount of the title policy limits).

Instead, the title company only pays the owner an *inflation adjusted price* based on the price the owner paid for the property — an amount set by the policy limits and the inflation endorsement.

The owner claims the title company's *negligence* in the disclosure of the easement caused a loss in property value equal to the difference between the purchase price paid and the potential value of the property for development.

However, the title company is not liable under a policy for lost profits in the unrealized potential value of the property. It was the existence of the easement that caused the loss of profits, not the issuance of a title insurance policy. [**Barthels** v. **Santa Barbara Title Company** (1994) 28 CA4th 674]

Introduction to title policy forms

Title insurance is bought to assure real estate buyers, tenants and lenders the **interest in title** they acquire is what they bargained for from the seller, landlord or borrower. While title insurance is not a guarantee of the condition of title acquired, it does provide a **monetary recovery** up to the policy's dollar limits for the conveyance of any lesser interest than the interest insured.

On closing a real estate transaction, a policy of title insurance is issued on one of several forms used throughout the entire title insurance industry in California. The policies are typically issued to **buyers** of real estate, **tenants** acquiring long-term leases and **lenders** whose loans are secured by real estate.

Two basic forms exist and are the industry prototypes for:

- insuring the condition of record title only, accomplished by the issuance of a *California Land Title Association (CLTA) policy*; and

- insuring both the record title conditions and observable on-site activities that affect title, accomplished by the issuance of an *American Land Title Association (ALTA) policy.*

In analysis, a **policy of title insurance** is broken down into six operative sections, including:

- the risks of **loss covered**, called *insuring clauses*, which are based on an unencumbered title at the time of the insured transfer;

- the risks of **loss not covered**, comprising encumbrances arising after the transfer or known to or brought about by the insured, called *exclusions*, which are a boilerplate set of title conditions;

- **identification** of the insured, the property, the vesting, the estate in the property, the dollar amount of the coverage, the premium paid and the policy (recording) date for the conveyance insured, called *Schedule A*;

- the **recorded interests**, i.e., any encumbrances affecting title (and for an ALTA policy any observable on-site activities) that are **listed as risks** agreed to and assumed by the insured and not covered by the policy, called *exceptions*, which are pre-printed for CLTA coverage and itemized for all types of coverage in *Schedule B*;

- the **procedures**, called *conditions*, for **claims made** by the named insured and for *settlement* by the insurance company on the occurrence of a loss due to any encumbrance on title that is not an exclusion or exception to the coverage granted by the insuring clauses; and

- any **endorsements** for additional coverage or removal of exclusions or pre-printed exceptions from the policy.

Insuring clauses

The coverage under the broadly worded **insuring clauses** of a policy of title insurance indemnifies the named insured for risks of loss **related to the title** due to:

- anyone making a claim against title to the real estate interest;

- the title being unmarketable for sale or as security for financing;

- any encumbrance on the title; and

- lack of recorded access to and from the described property.

Exclusions from coverage

All title insurance policies, in their **exclusions section**, exclude from coverage those losses incurred by the insured buyer, tenant or lender due to:

- **use ordinances** or (zoning) laws;

- **unrecorded claims known** to the insured, but not to the title company;

- encumbrances or adverse **claims created** or attaching **after** the date of the policy;

- claims arising out of **bankruptcy** laws or due to a **fraudulent conveyance** to the insured;

- police power and **eminent domain**; and

- **post-closing events** caused by the insured.

Schedule A data

All policies of title insurance in their Schedule A set forth:

- the property interest the insured acquired (fee simple, leasehold, life estate, security, etc.);

- the legal description of the insured property;

- the date and time the insured conveyance or lien recorded and coverage began;

- the premium paid for the policy; and

- the maximum total dollar amount to be paid for all claims settled.

Exceptions to coverage

In addition to the policy exclusions, a policy's coverage under its "no-encumbrance" insuring clause is further limited by Schedule B exceptions in the policy. The **exceptions section** contains an itemized list of recorded and unrecorded encumbrances that are known to the title company and affect the insured title. While the existence of these known encumbrances are insured against in the insuring clauses, they are removed by Schedule B as a basis for recovery under the policy.

In addition to the itemized list of exceptions, a CLTA policy includes a set of **pre-printed exceptions** setting forth risks assumed by the insured buyer, tenant or lender, which include:

- taxes, assessments, liens, covenants, conditions and restrictions (CC&Rs), or any other interests, claims or encumbrances that have not been recorded with the county recorder or tax collector on the date of closing;

- any unrecorded and observable on-site activity, including conflicts regarding boundary lines, encroachments or any other facts that a correct survey would disclose;

- unpatented mining claims; and

- all water rights.

Claims and settlements

Lastly, a policy of title insurance includes a **conditions section** outlining the procedures the named insured must follow when making a claim for recovery under the policy. Also set forth are the settlement negotiations or legal actions available to the title company before they must pay a claim.

Owner's policies for buyers

Several types of title coverage are available for a buyer to choose from when entering into a purchase agreement with the seller, including:

- a CLTA standard policy;

- an ALTA owner's extended coverage policy;

- an ALTA residential (ALTA-R) policy; and

- an ALTA homeowner's policy.

When making an offer, a prospective buyer is informed by his agent about the coverage each type of policy provides. The buyer's need for title coverage must be reviewed when the buyer enters into a purchase agreement since the agreement's title insurance provision calls for the buyer to designate the type of title insurance policy on closing and states who will pay its premium. [See Figure 1 accompanying this chapter]

The CLTA standard policy

The CLTA standard policy is purchased solely by buyers, carryback sellers and private lenders, not institutional lenders or builders who generally need extended coverage offered by an ALTA policy and endorsements.

The CLTA standard policy insures against all encumbrances affecting title to the property that can be discovered by a search of **public records** prior to issuance of the policy. Any encumbrance not recorded, whether or not observable by an **inspection or survey** of the property, is not covered due to the CLTA policy exclusions and standard exceptions.

Public records include those records imparting *constructive notice* of encumbrances affecting title to the property.

For example, a deed conveying a parcel of real estate that is actually **recorded and indexed** by the county recorder's office imparts constructive notice to buyers and lenders who later acquire an interest in the property. [Calif. Civil Code §1213]

Also, the CLTA standard policy (as well as the ALTA policy) protects the buyer against:

- the unmarketability of title or the inability to use it as security for financing;

- lack of ingress and egress rights to the property; and

- losses due to the ownership being vested in someone other than the buyer.

All title insurance policies provide coverage forever after the date and time the policy is issued, limited in recovery to the dollar amount of the policy, which is generally adjusted for inflation.

Coverage is further limited by the **exclusions, exceptions and conditions on claims**.

The CLTA standard policy (as well as the ALTA policy) contains Schedule A *exclusions to coverage* barring recovery by the buyer or joint protection carryback seller for losses due to:

- zoning laws, ordinances or regulations restricting or regulating the **occupancy, use or enjoyment** of the land;

- the character, dimensions or location of any **improvement erected** on the property;

- a **change in ownership** or a parceling or combining of the described property by the insured buyer;

- **police power**, eminent domain or violations of environmental protection laws, unless a notice or encumbrance resulting from the violation was recorded with the county recorder before closing;

- encumbrances **known** to the insured buyer or lender that are not recorded or disclosed to the title company;

- encumbrances not resulting in a **monetary loss**;

- encumbrances that are created or become encumbrances **after issuance** of the policy;

Figure 1   *Excerpt from first tuesday Form 156 — Equity Purchase Agreement*

13.5   Title to be vested in Buyer or Assignee free of encumbrances other than those set forth herein. Buyer's interest in title shall be insured by ___Title Company under a(n) ___ Homeowner(s) policy (one-to-four units), ___ Residential ALTA-R policy (vacant or improved residential parcel), ___ Owner's policy (other than one-to-four units), ___ CLTA Joint Protection policy (also naming Carryback Seller or purchase-assist lender), or ___ Binder (to insure resale or refinance within two years).

a.   Endorsements

b.   ___ Seller, or ___ Buyer, to pay the title insurance premium.

- encumbrances (equitable liens) resulting from the buyer's payment of **insufficient consideration** for the property or delivery of improper security to the carryback seller also insured under the policy; and

- the unenforceability of the insured trust deed lien due to the lender's **failure to comply** with laws regarding usury, consumer credit protection, truth-in-lending, bankruptcy and insolvency.

The CLTA standard policy contains **pre-printed exceptions** listed in the policy as Schedule B, also called *standard exceptions* or *regional exceptions*. It is the inclusion of these pre-printed boilerplate exceptions that makes the CLTA policy a standard policy. An ALTA owner's policy does not contain pre-printed exceptions, only the typewritten exceptions listing the encumbrances that are known to the title company and affect title to the property.

The **pre-printed standard exceptions** in Schedule B of the CLTA standard policy eliminate coverage for losses incurred by the buyer due to:

- taxes or assessments not shown as existing liens in the records of the county recorder, the county tax collector or any other agency that levies taxes on real property;

- unrecorded rights held by others that the buyer could have discovered by an inspection of the property or inquiry of persons in possession;

- easements or encumbrances not recorded and indexed by the county recorder;

- unrecorded encroachments or boundary line disputes that would have been disclosed by a survey; and

- recorded or unrecorded, unpatented mining claims or water rights.

A lower premium is charged to issue a CLTA policy since the title company undertakes a lower level of risk for indemnified losses due to the CLTA pre-printed exceptions as compared to the extended risks covered by the more expensive ALTA owner's policy.

The ALTA owner's policy

Most policies issued today are of the ALTA variety. The CLTA policy format with pre-printed standard exceptions does not provide protection for **unrecorded encumbrances or claims** to title.

The ALTA owner's policy provides greater coverage (and premiums) than the CLTA policy since the exceptions in Schedule B do not include the pre-printed standard exceptions. If the pre-printed exceptions are included in Schedule B and attached to the ALTA policy, the policy becomes an ALTA standard policy, comparable in cost and coverage to the CLTA standard policy since unrecorded encumbrances will not be covered.

The ALTA owner's policy covers **off-record matters** not covered under the CLTA standard policy. As a result, the title company may require the parcel to be surveyed, and those in possession to be interviewed or estopped, before the title company will issue an ALTA policy. Unrecorded interests in title are most often observable by an on-site inspection of the property.

Typewritten exceptions for existing encroachments or boundary conflicts are occasionally added to the ALTA policy (Schedule B) based on the survey.

The exclusions section of an ALTA owner's policy are identical to exclusions in the CLTA policy, except for additional exclusions relating to an insured lender or carryback seller. The ALTA owner's policy is not issued to lenders. Further, a **joint protection ALTA** policy is never issued.

Thus, separate policies and **duplicate premiums** are required for ALTA coverage when a buyer of property records a new loan, a most common event.

The premium for an ALTA owner's policy is larger than the premium for a CLTA standard policy. The ALTA owner's policy provides additional coverage and may, as a requisite to issuance, require costs to be incurred for a survey. Further, the premiums are nearly double to pay for both a lender's policy and the buyer's policy when a new loan is recorded to fund the purchase of real estate acquired by the buyer. This is not the case for a CLTA joint protection policy, one policy insuring both the lender (or carryback seller) and the buyer.

The ALTA residential policy

For buyers of parcels containing one-to-four residential units, an ALTA residential (ALTA-R) policy is available in lieu of the ALTA owner's or homeowner's policies. Parcels insured include lots and units in common interest developments (CIDs), such as condominiums.

The ALTA-R is referred to by the title companies as the "plain language" policy. The ALTA-R is written using wording that avoids legalese. The policy is structured and written to be easily read and understood by the buyer. The ALTA-R form policy contains a **table of contents** and an **owner's information sheet** outlining the policy's features.

The coverage, exclusions and exceptions in the ALTA-R policy are similar to the ALTA owner's policy. In addition, the ALTA-R policy also covers losses due to:

- mechanic's liens incurred by someone other than the buyer; and

- the inability of the buyer to occupy the property should the single family residence violate the CC&Rs listed in the Schedule B exceptions in the policy or existing zoning.

The premium for an ALTA-R form policy is priced lower than the premium for an ALTA owner's policy since the policy is usually issued only on parcels in an existing subdivision or CID that historically has no known problems with easements, encroachments or access.

The ALTA homeowner's policy

A homeowner's policy now exists to provide **more coverage** than the ALTA owner's or the ALTA-R policies. In addition to the risks covered by the ALTA owner's and ALTA-R policies, the homeowner's policy covers several risks to ownership that could arise **after closing**, including:

- the **forging** of the buyer's signature on a deed in an attempt to sell or encumber the buyer's property;

- the construction on an adjoining parcel of a structure **encroaching** onto the buyer's property, excluding a boundary wall or fence;

- the recording of a document preventing the buyer from obtaining a secured loan or selling the property;

- claims of **adverse possession** or **easement by prescription** against the buyer's property; and

- claims by others of a right in the buyer's property arising out of a lease, contract or option **unrecorded and unknown** to the buyer at the time of closing.

The ALTA homeowner's policy also covers losses arising out of a lack of vehicular and pedestrian access to and from the property. Other owner's policies only cover losses resulting from the lack of a legal right to access, not a practical means of access, which is covered by the ALTA homeowner's policy.

Also covered by the ALTA homeowner's policy are losses incurred due to many other risks that may exist at the time of closing, including:

- the correction of any pre-existing violation of a CC&R;

- the inability to obtain a building permit or to sell, lease or use the property as security for a loan due to a pre-existing violation of a subdivision law or regulation;

- the removal or remedy of any existing structure on the property if it was built without obtaining a building permit, excluding a boundary wall or fence;

- damage to existing structures due to the exercise of a right to maintain or use an easement;

- damage to improvements due to mineral or water extraction;

- the enforcement of a discriminatory CC&R;

- the assessment of a supplemental real estate tax due to construction or a change of ownership or use occurring before closing;

- an incorrect property address stated in the policy; and

- the map attached to the policy showing the incorrect location of the property.

Binders

An investor who buys property and plans on reselling the property within two years after his purchase should consider a **binder**, also called a *commitment to issue*.

A binder entitles the investor to title insurance coverage until the investor requests a policy be issued to a new buyer on resale of the property or to a new lender on a refinance, such as occurs when an investor takes title to a residence intending to flip it in a sale to the ultimate user.

Although the binder is 10% to 15% more expensive than a policy, it will cost less than buying two policies — one when the property is purchased, and another on the later resale or refinance.

With a binder, the resale policy will be at no further charge, except for the premiums for any additional liability coverage requested for any increase in the resale price.

Lender's policies

The CLTA and ALTA form title policies available to insure the priority of the lien a lender holds to secure their loan, include:

- a CLTA standard joint protection (JP) policy; and

- an ALTA loan policy.

The CLTA standard JP policy

A lender or a seller who carries back a note and trust deed for part of the sales price has options when calling for title insurance.

The lender or carryback seller can either:

- be named as an additional insured on a CLTA standard JP title insurance policy with the buyer; or

- request a separate ALTA loan policy as a sole named insured.

The JP policy enables one or more individuals or entities to be named as insured.

However, the JP policy is only available under a CLTA standard policy. If either the buyer or the lender in a cash-to-new-loan transaction requests ALTA coverage, a separate ALTA loan policy will be issued to each at approximately double the cost.

The ALTA lender's policy

An institutional lender will usually require its trust deed lien on a parcel of real estate to be insured under an ALTA loan policy as a condition for making a loan secured by real estate.

The ALTA loan policy insures against money losses incurred by lenders and carryback sellers due to the loss of priority of the insured trust deed lien, unless listed in the exceptions, to encumbrances such as:

- a mechanic's lien, if the work was commenced prior to recording the trust deed (which is the same date and time as the date of the policy) and the trust deed did not secure a loan to pay for the construction;

- a mechanic's lien arising out of work financed by proceeds from the construction loan secured by the insured trust deed, if no part of the construction work was commenced before the trust deed was recorded; and

- assessments (Mello-Roos) for street improvements under construction or completed prior to recording the trust deed.

The ALTA loan policy comes at a higher (and separate) premium than the CLTA standard JP policy due to the extended mechanic's lien and assessment coverage. The buyer who borrows to finance his purchase usually pays the premium for the lender's policy.

Endorsements

Endorsements of great variety can be added to the form policies to provide coverage for title conditions and use or economic conditions not covered by the proto-typical policies. Endorsements are usually issued only to lenders, though modified endorsements can be used in owner's policies as well, particularly for developers and builders.

Endorsements cover losses incurred due to violations of CC&Rs, damage from extraction of water or minerals, mechanic's liens, encroachments (conditions covered in an ALTA-R policy) and the effects of inflation. Endorsements are also issued to remove an exclusion or exception that is an unwanted boilerplate provision in a policy.

Chapter 12

Clearing a lien-clouded title

This chapter instructs a prospective equity purchase (EP) investor on how to negotiate the release of judgments or discharge of state/federal tax liens that may encumber a homeowner's residence that is in foreclosure.

Negotiate a release to create equity

An investor enters into an equity purchase (EP) agreement to buy an owner-occupied residence that is in foreclosure, called an *equity purchase* or EP transaction. [See **first tuesday** Form 156]

After expiration of the seller-in-foreclosure's five-business-day cancellation period, escrow is opened and a preliminary title report is ordered. The title report discloses an *abstract* has been recorded referencing a **money judgment** against the seller that has attached to the residence, called a *judgment lien*. The seller did not record a declaration of homestead prior to the recording of the abstract.

The **judgment lien** was not specifically referenced in the purchase agreement. However, the terms of the EP agreement call for the down payment to be reduced by the amount of any unreferenced lien and the responsibility for payment of the lien shifted to the investor. The EP agreement makes it optional for the investor to take title subject to the recorded judgment lien rather than having the debt satisfied and the lien released prior to closing. [See **first tuesday** Form 156 §13.3]

Further, the title insurance company demands either a *partial* or *full release* be recorded clearing title of the lien before they will issue a policy of title insurance eliminating any reference to the judgment lien as excluded from coverage. The investor chooses to have the lien released before closing, rather than opting to offset the down payment and leave the lien on title for later negotiations and its release.

However, the seller is uninformed about **lien avoidance**. Accordingly, the EP investor, with written authority from the seller, takes control by contacting the judgment lienholder, directly or through escrow, to negotiate a partial or full release of the lien so the purchase transaction can be closed. These negotiations are allied to those for a short payoff of a trust deed loan.

The lienholder initially demands full payment of the debt, which is the very reason he recorded his lien.

However, the investor has economic leverage over the creditor in his negotiations for a lien release. When the first trust deed on the property is in foreclosure, the creditor's risk of loss of his abstract lien on the property has been greatly increased. Further, the seller qualifies for an automatic homestead exemption depriving the creditor of any ability in the foreseeable future to collect by his forcing the sale of the property.

Both the trust deed and the homestead claims on title are senior to the creditor's right to recover the amount of his judgment from the property's value.

The trustee's foreclosure sale, should it take place, will wipe out the judgment lien. Unless excess funds flow from the trustee's sale to be distributed to junior lien holders, the judgment creditor will receive nothing.

Also, the homestead exemption available to the head of a household protects up to $75,000 of the homeowner's equity, freeing that amount of equity for the seller from collection on the judgment by a court ordered sale.

The lien about to be wiped out

Generally, a good bargaining tactic for obtaining a **release of a lien** from a seller's residence is a combination of:

- a "gentle reminder" that the lien is on the verge of being *wiped out by foreclosure* of the first trust deed without the likelihood of an overbid to provide funds for the creditor;

- a review of the homeowner's $75,000 *homestead exemption* rights as having a prior claim on equity to the creditor's lien, leaving no ability to collect by forcing a judicial sale; [See Chapter 13]

- an *offer to pay* a lesser amount in full satisfaction of the debt owed to the lienholder; and

- a partial (or full) satisfaction and the execution of a partial (or full) release, allowing the abstract of judgment to remain of record (unless fully released) while *releasing the residence* from its lien so escrow can close.

The objective of the investor's negotiations is to give the lienholder sufficient incentive to cooperate and release the property from the lien without the homeowner filing a bankruptcy petition to approve the sale and remove the lien. The investor (or the seller's agent) is in a better position to deal with the lienholder in an aggressive manner than the seller-in-foreclosure, who has exhausted his goodwill with the judgment creditor.

A financially advantageous situation is created for all parties when:

- the **lienholder** collects a portion of the money owed, which is not available from a sale of the residence if a foreclosure wipes out the judgment lien, or a recorded or automatic homestead exemption exists;

- the **seller** closes the sale of his residence, avoiding the loss of his equity to the lender's foreclosure, and receives any proceeds protected by his homestead exemption; and

- the **equity purchase (EP) investor** keeps his purchase agreement alive by negotiating a release of the lien in exchange for a less-than-full payoff of the lienholder's judgment out of the seller's proceeds from the sale.

Release of recorded instrument

When a judgment lienholder agrees to release a residence from his lien, a signed and notarized **release of recorded instrument** must be obtained from the lienholder and recorded. All aspects of the paperwork can be handled through escrow after negotiations have been completed. [See Form 409 accompanying this chapter]

The release contains all the information necessary to clear the judgment lien from the record title to the property.

When the release is notarized and recorded, the judgment lien attached to the residence is removed from the record and a policy of title insurance can be issued covering title free of the lien.

The abstract of judgment lien

A judgment creditor creates a valid lien on real estate owned by the debtor by recording an *abstract of judgment* issued by a state court. [Calif. Code of Civil Procedure §697.310(a)]

A judgment lien continues in effect for 10 years from the date it is recorded, unless the money judgment is either satisfied or released. [CCP §697.310(b)]

However, the recording of a certified copy of a judgment awarded by a federal court attaches without the need to record an abstract of judgment.

For example, a judgment creditor obtains a federal district court money judgment against an in-

RELEASE OF RECORDED INSTRUMENT

DATE:_____, 20_____, at _____, California.

Items left blank or unchecked are not applicable.

1. From the Document entitled _____,

2. dated _____, and recorded on _____, as Instrument No. _____,
   in the Official Records of _____County, California,

3. pursuant to the judgment entered in the _____ branch of the _____County
   _____ Court, dated _____, renewed _____,
   in a legal action entitled _____,
   docket number _____,

4. held by _____
   and against _____,

5. is hereby released:

   5.1 ☐ all interests in real property situated in the County of record, owned or hereafter
       acquired by _____

   5.2 ☐ the real property situated in the County of record described as
       _____
       _____

THIS FORM IS NOT A RECONVEYANCE OF A TRUST DEED. DO NOT USE THIS FORM TO RECONVEY A TRUST DEED FROM RECORDED TITLE.

Date:_____, 20_____ _____ _____
                                 (Print name)   (Signature)

Date:_____, 20_____ _____ _____
                                 (Print name)   (Signature)

STATE OF CALIFORNIA
COUNTY OF _____)
On _____ before me,
_____
                    (name of notary public)
personally appeared _____
_____,
                    (name of principal)
personally known to me (or proved to me on the basis of satisfactory
evidence) to be the person(s) whose name(s) is/are subscribed to the
within instrument and acknowledged to me that he/she/they executed the
same in his/her/their authorized capacity(ies), and that by his/her/their
signature(s) on the instrument the person(s), or the entity upon behalf of
which the person(s) acted, executed the instrument.

WITNESS my hand and official seal.

Signature: _____
           (Signature of notary public)   *(This area for official notarial seal)*

dividual. A **certified copy** of the judgment is recorded in the county where the individual is the vested owner of real estate.

The owner later obtains a loan secured by recording a trust deed on the property. A dispute between the lender and the judgment creditor arises over who has priority and is entitled to funds remaining after a payoff of the first trust deed.

The second trust deed lender claims the recorded federal judgment is not a valid lien since it is not documented by a recorded abstract of judgment to give the lien priority to the lender's trust deed.

Does the judgment creditor hold a valid lien senior to the lender's trust deed?

Yes! The judgment creditor holds a valid lien senior to the lender's trust deed. A federal judgment creditor creates a lien on real estate owned by the judgment debtor on recording a **certified copy** of the federal judgment. [**In re McDonell** (9th Cir. BAP 1996) 204 BR 976]

A money judgment from a court of the United States becomes a valid lien on real estate on the recording of:

- an abstract of judgment; or

- a certified copy of the money judgment. [CCP §697.060]

The FTB as a judgment creditor

A personal income tax lien on a residence recorded by the Franchise Tax Board (FTB) is enforced under the same procedure as any creditor's judgment lien. The FTB issues and records a *warrant* for the amount claimed due by the state. The **warrant** has the same force and effect as an abstract of judgment issued by a court. [CCP §688.020]

The FTB lien created by recording the **warrant** attaches to real estate owned by the tax payer in the same priority as would a judgment lien. More importantly, the tax payer who is a homeowner and head of the household has a homestead exemption that is senior to the FTB lien and shields

$75,000 of the seller's equity from seizure by the FTB. [CCP §688.030; Government Code §§7170 et seq.]

Unfortunately for the seller and the investor, no statutory or regulatory authority exists for the FTB to negotiate a partial payment of the tax bill in exchange for releasing the residence from the tax lien. At first glance, it appears to be an all or nothing situation.

However, California's **Taxpayer Bill of Rights** provides some relief. Under it, the FTB must release its lien from the residence if the proceeds from the sale would not result in a reasonable reduction of the seller-in-foreclosure's debt to the FTB. Again, negotiations are an all or nothing analysis for a release of the FTB lien on a short sale of the property. [Calif. Revenue and Taxation Code §21016(a)(3)]

Nevertheless, no case law exists testing whether the statute may be used as an offensive weapon by the seller to quiet title to real estate and eliminate the cloud of a state income tax lien when a declaration of Homestead was recorded prior to the FTB warrant.

Releasing an IRS lien

Consider an EP investor whose preliminary title report reveals the existence of a **federal tax lien** junior to a trust deed loan that is in foreclosure.

When property is sold at a trustee's sale and a timely recorded and junior federal tax lien exists, the Internal Revenue Service (IRS) may later *redeem* (purchase) the property from the successful bidder at the trustee's sale by paying him the amount of his bid within 120 days, plus interest and foreclosure costs. Thus, the equity can be acquired by the IRS after the trustee's foreclosure sale to satisfy the delinquent payment of income tax owed by the now wiped-out owner. The IRS will later hold its own auction and resell the residence.

When a second trust deed or judgment lien exists on the residence, the IRS will typically wait until the first trust deed lender completes its foreclosure, wiping out the junior lienholder and **creat-**

ing an equity where none existed before the trustee's sale. The IRS then steps in within 120 days after the trustee's sale and acquires the residence from the buyer at the trustee's sale.

On a regular sale of property, the IRS has the *authority to negotiate* with the seller/taxpayer or his authorized agent (or the EP investor after closing the EP transaction) to accept partial or no payment in exchange for a **certificate of discharge** from the income tax lien. The discharge is authorized when the IRS's recovery under its lien and redemption and resale rights would be economically unfeasible beyond the amount available to the IRS from a sale of the property at current value. [Internal Revenue Code §6325(b)(2)]

Thus, the discharge of the IRS tax lien from title can be negotiated by the investor (or other authorized person) on behalf of the taxpayer by using some of the same persuasive techniques used to negotiate a release of a judgment lien with a creditor or a short payoff with a trust deed lender.

To release the tax lien from title when the property is in foreclosure, the seller submits a written request to the district director of the IRS for a discharge of the residence from the federal tax lien. Instructions and format for application for a Certificate of Discharge are available in IRS Publication 783 at *www.irs.gov*. [Revenue Regulations §301.6325-1(b)]

General information the IRS wants with the Application for a Certificate of Discharge is a preliminary title report, proposed closing statement (HUD-1), two opinions of value (appraisals), and a declaration and signature of the payer under penalty of perjury.

Current IRS policy dictates the IRS, not the seller, must receive all of the proceeds from any equity remaining in the residence up to the amount of the lien.

Additionally, the EP investor should consider whether it is more advantageous to take the residence subject to the IRS tax lien, especially if the property is a "fixer-upper." If little or no equity exists beyond the encumbrances senior to the IRS lien, the EP investor, as the new owner, can negotiate with the IRS for the release of the lien in exchange for a small cash payment — often an amount less than the IRS would have been willing to accept from the seller prior to the EP investor becoming the owner.

However, taking the residence subject to the IRS lien entails a risk of loss for the investor that must be analyzed. The IRS may decide to leave its lien intact on the property since the property is no longer in foreclosure. Thus, they would then be able to participate in the future property value added by inflation, appreciation or the efforts of the investor. [**Han** v. **United States of America** (9th Cir. 1991) 944 F2d 526]

The homestead exemption coup

A homeowner's equity of up to $75,000 for a head of household is protected by California homestead exemption laws. [CCP §704.710 et seq.]

The homestead protection is **automatic** when the judgment lienholder or the Franchise Tax Board (FTB) attempts to enforce its money judgment by a sheriff's sale of the homeowner's residence. The residence cannot be sold by the lienholder when the net proceeds of the sale will be less than the homestead exemption amount.

However, the automatic homestead exemption only applies to execution sales ordered by a court to satisfy money judgments against the homeowner and to any sale of the home in a bankruptcy proceeding.

While merely a defensive tool for the homeowner, the **automatic homestead** exemption becomes a powerful offensive tool in a bankruptcy proceeding. Through bankruptcy proceedings, the homeowner can clear his title of judgment and state tax liens that impair the value of his $75,000 homestead equity in the property. [**In re Herman** (9th Cir. BAP 1990) 120 BR 127; 11 United States Code §522(f)].

However, the automatic homestead exemption is not enforceable against an Internal Revenue Service (IRS) tax lien in bankruptcy. [**U.S.** v. **Heffron** (9th Cir. 1947) 158 F2d 657; 11 USC §545]

Alternatively, the homeowner may have recorded his **declaration of homestead** prior to the date a judgment or FTB lien was recorded. If the recorded homestead is senior to the judgment creditor's or FTB's lien and the net proceeds of a voluntary sale entered into by the owner of the residence will be less than the homestead amount, the owner can quiet title to the property and eliminate the effect of the judgment or FTB tax lien on that property.

However, like the automatic homestead exemption, the recorded homestead has no priority over an IRS tax lien. Thus, the IRS can still force the sale of the residence under its tax lien if a certificate of discharge is not arranged. [**U.S.** v. **Rodgers** (1983) 461 US 677]

In practice, the release of an IRS lien under a Certificate of Discharge from title is always negotiated based on whether it has recorded priority over voluntary encumbrances and judgment liens on the residence. The homestead has no effect on the **lien rights of the IRS**.

Whether it is by an automatic exemption or recorded declaration, the homestead is leverage to be used to induce judgment lienholders and the FTB to voluntarily release their lien from the title to the residence. The effects of foreclosure, a bankruptcy or quiet title action to enforce the homestead exemption and clear title gives lienholders an incentive to negotiate the release.

Preparing the Release of Recorded Instrument

The numbers on the instructions correspond to the numbers given to the provisions in Form 409.

Check and **enter** only the items to be included as provisions in the release.

§1. **Enter** the name of the document that created the lien on the property, e.g., *abstract of money judgment.*

§2. **Enter** the date the document creating the lien was prepared, and the date, instrument number and county of its recording.

§3. If the document is a release of an abstract of money judgment:

- **enter** the identification of the branch (i.e. Pasadena), county name (i.e. Los Angeles) and court (superior) that entered the judgment;

- **enter** the date of the judgment and the date of any renewal;

- **enter** the title of the cause of action in the case, e.g., *breach of contract, negligent misrepresentation, unlawful detainer,* etc.; and

- **enter** the docket number the court assigned to the case. [CCP §697.370]

§4. **Enter** the names of the lienholder and owner named as the judgment debtor. [Gov C §27288.1(b)]

§5. **Check** the box indicating whether the release is:

5.1 a blanket release of all recorded interests in real estate in the county. If all property is released, **check** the box and **enter** the name of the seller again, thus identifying him as the owner whose property interests are being released from the judgment lien; or

5.2 a partial release only for a specific property. If only a specific property is released, **check** the box and **enter** the legal description of the property released.

The lienholder unilaterally executes the release by **signing** it and **dating** his signature.

Notarize the release for recording. **Record** the release to clear the seller's title of the lien. [Gov C §27287]

Chapter 13

Automatic and declared homesteads

This chapter demonstrates the EP investor's application of the various homestead exemptions available to sellers to create net equity where a judgment or tax lien affects title.

Home-equity shield against judgments

A real estate investor tracks *abstracts of judgment* recorded by creditors against owners of real estate as his method for locating financially distressed real estate he might be able to buy.

The investor finds an abstract attached as a lien on the principal residence of an owner who owes the creditor $80,000 on the judgment. The owner recorded a **declaration of homestead** before the abstract was recorded. Also, the property is not presently held out "For Sale."

On completing a *comparable market analysis* (CMA), the investor concludes the property has a value for his investment purposes of approximately $20,000 more than the first trust deed lien. When considering the $80,000 abstract of judgment that attached as a lien, the property appears to be over-encumbered and have no equity.

The owner, initially contacted by the investor's use of a form letter, indicates he needs to sell the home. He has other creditor problems as well as being delinquent on his home loan. He is aware he has a $75,000 homestead to protect him from the judgment creditor selling his home. However, he does not know how his home can be sold when title is clouded by the abstract.

The investor prepares an offer on a regular purchase agreement form since a Notice of Default has not been recorded commencing foreclosure. The price is payable $20,000 cash (down payment) to a new loan. Two contingency provisions are attached to the purchase agreement:

- one calling for a 10% discount on a short payoff of the first trust deed loan from cash funds provided by the investor; and

- the other calling for a release of the property from the **abstract of judgment** held by the creditor.

When submitting the offer to the owner, the investor explains that the approximate $30,000 in down payment and lender discount belongs to the seller (less closing costs), not the judgment creditor, due to the recorded homestead of $75,000.

The investor obtains written authorization to negotiate with the lender and the judgment creditor to arrange for the short pay and the release. The investor and the owner understand the owner's receipt of cash on a short sale may trigger the lender's moral bias that might interfere with their mitigating a loss by avoiding a foreclosure.

The lender will be induced to discount since the title is encumbered with liens of $50,000 in excess of the property's market value. Alternatively, a more compelling reason for a discount is the fact the lender will have to complete a foreclosure due to the existence of the junior lien (abstract). A short pay would be in their best interest to mitigate losses they will otherwise certainly incur due to deteriorating real estate prices in the current phase of the real estate market.

As for the judgment creditor, he will be asked for a release of the owner's home on the close of escrow since he has no claims against the property due to the recorded homestead declaration and the lack of more than $75,000 in equity over the amount of the lender's trust deed lien. It is possible that negotiations for the release of the lien may necessitate the payment of $5,000 to $10,000 to motivate the judgment creditor to release the property from his lien if the threat of a quiet title action to clear title of his cloud does not do so.

Thus, the seller now has the incentive to accept this offer. He will net some cash from a sale in which the buyer (investor) will be handling negotiations to clear up title and perfect an equity in the property.

Homestead by type and amount

A homeowner is sued by a creditor for money owed on an unsecured debt. A **money judgment** is awarded to the creditor who becomes a *judgment creditor*. The homeowner becomes a *judgment debtor*.

An **abstract of judgment** is recorded by the **judgment creditor** in the county where the homeowner's residence is located.

Can the homeowner prevent the recorded abstract from attaching as a lien against the title to his home?

No! However, the type of homestead the homeowner claims — there are two — and the amount of the homestead exemption he qualifies for — there are three — determines the homeowner's ability to:

- **voluntarily sell** the home and buy another home with the homestead amount he has in his equity; or

- bar the judgment creditor from **forcing a sale** of the home to satisfy the judgment.

The owner's homestead interest in title

A *homestead* is the dollar amount of the equity in a homeowner's dwelling that the homeowner qualifies to hold. The amount of the homestead held by the homeowner has priority on title over most judgment liens and some government liens.

Two types of **homestead** procedures are available to California homeowners to establish the priority of the homestead equity they hold in their home:

- the *declaration of homestead*, which is recorded [Calif. Code of Civil Procedure §704.920]; and

- the *automatic homestead*, also called a *statutory homestead exemption*, which is not recorded. [CCP §704.720]

Both homestead arrangements provide the same dollar amount of home-equity protection given to all homeowners in California. However, a homeowner must record a **declaration of homestead** to receive the additional benefits available under the homestead laws allowing the homeowner the right to sell and to reinvest the dollar amount of the homestead in another home.

Neither the declared nor the automatic homestead interfere with:

- *voluntary liens* later placed on the property by the homeowner, such as trust deeds; and

- *involuntary liens* given priority to the homestead exemption under public policy legislation.

Involuntary liens and encumbrances that are given priority by statute and can be enforced as senior to the amount of the homestead exemption include mechanic's (contractor's) and vendor's (seller's) liens, homeowners' association (HOA) assessments, judgments for alimony or child support, real estate taxes and Internal Revenue Service (IRS) liens.

Involuntary liens that are subordinate and junior to the homestead amount include:

- Franchise Tax Board (FTB) personal income tax liens;

- Medi-Cal liens; and

- judgment creditor's liens.

Automatic and declared homesteads

An **automatic homestead** is always available on the principal dwelling occupied by the homeowner or his spouse when:

- a judgment creditor's abstract is recorded against the homeowner and attaches as a lien on the property; and

- the occupancy by the homeowner continues until a court determines the dwelling is a homestead. [CCP §704.710(c)]

The **automatic homestead exemption** applies to the equity in a real estate dwelling (and its outbuildings), a mobilehome, a condominium, a planned development, a stock cooperative or a community apartment project together with the

---

Declaring a homestead as asset preservation

The **recorded homestead declaration** includes:

- the name of the homeowner declaring the homestead;

- a description of the property homesteaded; and

- a statement that the declared homestead is the principal dwelling in which the homeowner resides on the date the homestead is recorded. [CCP §704.930(a); see **first tuesday** Form 448]

The declaration must be signed, notarized and recorded to take effect. [CCP §704.930]

The homestead declaration may be **signed and recorded** by any one of several individuals, including:

- the owner of the homestead;

- the owner's spouse; or

- the guardian, conservator, attorney in fact, or a person otherwise authorized to act for the owner or the owner's spouse. [CCP §704.930(b)]

An individual's personal residence that is vested in a revocable inter vivos (living) trust, or other type of title holding arrangement established for the benefit of the homeowner, can also be declared a homestead by anyone who has an interest in the property and resides there. [**Fisch, Spiegler, Ginsburg & Ladner** v. **Appel** (1992) 10 CA4th 1810]

Additionally, a declaration of homestead in no way restricts the homeowner's ability to voluntarily sell, convey or encumber his homesteaded property. [CCP §704.940]

A recorded homestead declaration does not appear in credit reports or impact the homeowner's credit reputation or ability to borrow funds. Title companies disregard recorded homestead declarations, except in litigation guarantee policies.

land they rest on, as well as a houseboat or other waterborne vessel used as a dwelling. [CCP §704.710(a)]

On the other hand, a **recorded declaration of homestead** applies only to real estate dwellings. Thus, mobilehomes not established as real estate and houseboats are not protected by a recorded homestead, only the automatic homestead. Also, a leasehold interest in real estate with an unexpired term of less than two years is not protected by a recorded homestead declaration. [CCP §704.910(c)]

Real estate to be homesteaded

As long as the homeowner claiming the exemption actually uses the homesteaded property as the principal residence for himself and his family, the type of real estate qualifying for a homestead includes:

- two five-room flats [**Viotti** v. **Giomi** (1964) 230 CA2d 730];

- an 18-unit apartment building where the owner occupies only one unit [**Phelps** v. **Loop** (1944) 64 CA2d 332]; and

- 523 acres of rural land with a house and water rights for the land. [**Payne** v. **Cummings** (1905) 146 C 426]

Amount of equity protected

The dollar amount of whichever home equity protection a homeowner qualifies for is protected whether the homeowner relies on the automatic homestead or records a declaration of homestead.

Homeowners qualify for one of three dollar amounts of **net equity** homestead protection:

- a $50,000 equity for a homeowner with no dependents;

- a $75,000 equity for a head of household; or

- a $150,000 equity for the aged or disabled. [CCP §704.730]

An individual homeowner with **no dependents** other than himself qualifies for the $50,000 homestead exemption. [CCP §704.730(a)(1)]

A homeowner qualifies for the $75,000 homestead exemption as the **head of a household** by providing support for a spouse, dependent children, grandchildren, parents, grandparents or in-laws. [CCP §704.730(a)(2)]

An aged or disabled homeowner qualifies for the $150,000 homestead exemption if the homeowner or his spouse is:

- 65 or older;

- physically or mentally disabled; or

- 55 or older with an annual income of less than $15,000 or, if married, a combined gross annual income of no more than $20,000. [CCP §704.730(a)(3)]

Both a husband and a wife may be the declared homestead owners in the same homestead declaration when both husband and wife own an interest in the property. [CCP §704.930(a)(1)]

However, a couple's combined homestead exemption cannot exceed the exemption limit for a head of household ($75,000), unless one or both qualify as an aged or disabled person ($150,000). [CCP §704.730(b)]

Further, if both spouses are entitled to a homestead exemption, the homestead proceeds will be apportioned to each spouse according to their share of the ownership in the homesteaded real estate. [CCP §704.730(b)]

Abstract avoids homestead increases

The dollar amount of the homestead exemptions is periodically increased to keep up with consumer price inflation (not property price inflation). A homeowner who has recorded a declaration of homestead does not need to record a new declaration to avail himself to the increased amounts. The increased homestead exemption amounts apply to the old declaration.

However, when an involuntary lien is recorded prior to an increase in the amount of the exemption, the amount of equity protected from the attachment is the homestead amount available when the lien was recorded, whether the homeowner is claiming an automatic or declared homestead. Thus, inflation or appreciation in the value of the residence may eventually create a home equity large enough to exceed the homestead amount and provide some recovery for a judgment creditor. [**Berhanu** v. **Metzger** (1992) 12 CA4th 445]

Combating a creditor's sale

A judgment creditor with a recorded abstract of judgment cannot force the sale of an owner's home to collect on a money judgment without first petitioning a court for its sale, whether the homestead is automatic or by recorded declaration. The court must confirm the owner's net equity in his home is a dollar amount greater than the amount of the owner's homestead exemption before the creditor's judgment can be judicially foreclosed by an *execution sale*. [CCP §704.740(a)]

For example, the head of a household owes $325,000 on trust deed loans encumbering his home. An unsecured creditor is awarded a money judgment against the homeowner and an abstract is recorded, attaching as a lien on title to the property.

Before the creditor can begin judicial proceedings against the equity in the home to collect on the judgment from the net proceeds of its sale, the home needs a **net value** in excess of $400,000 — the $325,000 owed on the existing trust deeds plus the $75,000 homestead exemption.

A home with a **net equity** (after transactional costs) of less than the homestead amount leaves nothing for the creditor to sell in order to collect on the judgment.

Forced sale by court order only

The sale of a homesteaded dwelling can be forced by a creditor if a net equity exists beyond the amount of the homestead the home owner holds in the property. To force the sale of a homeowner's dwelling, the creditor must first **file an application** for a judicially ordered sale, called an *execution sale*, stating under oath:

- a description of the property;

- whether a declared homestead has been recorded on the property;

- the names of the person or persons who claim the homestead;

- the amount of the homestead; and

- the dollar amounts of all liens and encumbrances recorded on the property and the names and addresses of the lienholders. [CCP §704.760]

If the homestead is declared and the creditor challenges the **validity of the declaration**, the creditor must prove the property does not qualify for a homestead.

However, if the homeowner has not recorded a declaration of homestead on the property, the homeowner must prove his residency in the dwelling qualifies the property for the automatic homestead exemption. [CCP §704.780(a)(1)]

If the execution sale of the property is ordered by the court and the bids received at the sale are insufficient to satisfy the senior liens and encumbrances, plus the homestead amount and the sales costs, the dwelling will not be ordered sold. [CCP §704.800(a)]

Additionally, a winning bid must exceed **90%** of the fair market value (FMV) of the property as set by the court. [CCP §704.800(b)]

A real estate appraiser is often appointed by the court as a *reference* to assist in determining the FMV of the dwelling. Compensation for the appraiser may not exceed comparable fees for similar services in the community. [CCP §704.780(d)]

If the dwelling is jointly owned by the judgment debtor/homeowner and another person as joint tenants or tenants in common, only the judgment debtor's interest in the property will be sold. [CCP §704.820(a)]

The proceeds from an execution sale of the dwelling are disbursed in the following order:

- pay all senior liens and encumbrances on the property;

- disburse the amount of the homestead equity to the homeowner;

- cover the costs of the sale;

- pay the judgment creditor's court costs; and

- pay the amount due to the creditor from the judgment. [CCP §704.850]

Any remaining proceeds from an execution sale go to the homeowner.

"Drawing down" the homestead amount

Consider a homeowner who records a **declaration of homestead** on his principal residence that is encumbered by a trust deed. A creditor is later awarded a money judgment against the homeowner and records an abstract of judgment.

The homeowner then records a second trust deed on the residence to secure another loan for an amount less than the dollar amount of his homestead exemption.

The homeowner defaults on the first trust deed loan and the first trust deed holder forecloses on the residence. The residence is sold at a trustee's sale on a bid in excess of the amount owed to the first trust deed holder.

The judgment lien creditor claims he is entitled to the excess funds since the judgment lien is prior in time to the later recorded second trust deed.

The second trust deed holder claims he is entitled to the remaining funds since the second trust deed lien is a voluntary encumbrance on the homeowner's equity up to the dollar amount protected by the homeowner's homestead exemption, which entitles him to first recover against funds due the homeowner under the recorded declaration of homestead exemption.

Is the second trust deed holder entitled to the excess funds?

Yes! The second trust deed holder is entitled to payment from the funds remaining after satisfaction of the first trust deed debt since the judgment creditor's **lien is subordinate** to the recorded declaration of homestead exemption amount. Further, the dollar amount of equity subject to the homestead exemption held by the homeowner under the previously recorded declaration was voluntarily encumbered by the second trust deed lien. [**Smith** v. **James A. Merrill, Inc.** (1998) 64 CA4th 94]

Automatic homestead as a shield

An **automatic homestead** exempts some or all of the equity in a homeowner's dwelling up to the dollar amount of the homestead exemption from money judgments obtained by the homeowner's creditors. However, use of the automatic homestead is limited to providing a **shield**, raised by the homeowner, to defend the equity in his house against a forced sale sought by an involuntary creditor.

For example, a homeowner claims his automatic exemption and receives funds in the amount of the homestead equity from a creditor's forced sale of his home. The homestead funds are protected from the creditor's attachment during a six-month reinvestment period. Further, an automatic homestead exemption is provided on the replacement residence to protect the reinvested funds. [CCP §704.720(b)]

Editor's note — Although the proceeds are protected from attachment by the creditor's lien for the six-month reinvestment period, if the property purchased is in the same county where the lien is recorded, it will not prevent the lien from attaching to new property (subject to the homestead exemption) the instant title is transferred into the buyer's name.

Thus, a homeowner/debtor intending to purchase a replacement home in the same county with his protected funds will probably not be able to obtain title insurance for a new loan. Title companies will not make a determination as to whether an exemption on the residence is valid. Also, the abstract lien will attach to the property as a lien senior in time to the new lender's trust deed, unless it is a trust deed carried back by a seller.

The best way to deal with the intervening (judgment) lien in counties where the abstract of judgment is recorded is to purchase property either subject to an existing trust deed or by creating a carryback trust deed. Carryback trust deeds have priority over any lien attaching to the title when the buyer takes title. [Calif. Civil Code §2898]

With the automatic homestead exemption, a homeowner who **voluntarily sells** his residence while title is clouded by a creditor's lien leaves the sales proceeds unprotected by the automatic exemption. This is not the case for a sale subject to a recorded declaration of homestead. The declaration with priority allows the homeowner to first withdraw his homestead amount from the sales proceeds before the judgment creditor receives any funds.

The exemption in bankruptcy sales

For an individual who files a bankruptcy petition, any sale of the individual's home during the bankruptcy, whether voluntary or court ordered, is considered a **forced sale** entitled to the automatic homestead exemption. Thus, a bankruptcy petitioner who voluntarily sells his home (even if the sale is against the bankruptcy court's order) is still entitled to an automatic homestead exemption on the proceeds of the sale. [**In re Reed** (9th Cir. 1991) 940 F2d 1317]

Consider a homeowner whose home is in foreclosure under a lender's first trust deed. The homeowner did not file a declaration of homestead prior to the recording of the judgment lien against the property.

At the trustee's sale, a bid in excess of the loan leaves funds to be disbursed to junior lienholders.

Since **foreclosure** under a power-of-sale provision is a **voluntary sale** by private agreement (trust deed provisions), not a forced sale by a judgment creditor that triggers use of the automatic homestead exemption, the automatic homestead exemption does not protect the homeowner's equity on a foreclosure sale. Thus, the homeowner whose home is lost to foreclosure exposes any excess proceeds from the trustee's sale to the creditor's lien, unless a declaration of homestead was recorded prior to recording the creditor's abstract of judgment. [**Spencer** v. **Lowery** (1991) 235 CA3d 1636]

Editor's note — A homeowner in foreclosure will receive his automatic homestead exemption if he files a bankruptcy petition before the foreclosure is completed. In a bankruptcy proceeding, all sales are considered forced sales. Thus, the dollar amount of the equity covered by the automatic exemption is protected from the claims of involuntary creditors. [In re Reed, supra]

Additionally, the creditor holding a judgment lien (a recorded abstract of judgment) can simply wait until the equity in the home increases, due to inflation, appreciation or loan reduction, and then begin a forced sale once the value of the home exceeds the amount of the homestead exemption. Thus, the homeowner who relies solely on the automatic homestead exemption to protect his equity is imprisoned in his own home unless he files a bankruptcy petition since he cannot voluntarily sell and avoid the judgment lien.

Although a sufficient net equity may not exist to allow the judgment creditor to force a sale of the home, the homeowner may not use a *quiet title action* based on an automatic homestead exemption to remove the lien, unlike a declared homestead.

Declared homestead allows resale

A recorded declaration of homestead, in contrast to an automatic homestead exemption, allows a California homeowner to take the offensive against his creditors. Used as a sword, the declaration of homestead coupled with a quiet title action allows the homeowner to **sever the liens** attached to his title.

Unlike the automatic homestead exemption, judgment liens **do not attach** to the exempt homestead amount in the equity under a declared homestead if the homestead declaration is recorded prior to the recording of the creditor's abstract of judgment. [CCP §704.950(a)]

Judgment liens do, however, attach to any equity exceeding the amount of the declared homestead exemption and all liens and encumbrances on the property at the time the abstract of judgment is recorded. [CCP §704.950(c)]

With prior planning, priority of the declaration can be accomplished by the homeowner. While it takes the creditor several months to obtain and record an abstract of judgment, a declaration of homestead can be prepared and recorded on readily available forms in a matter of minutes. [See **first tueday** Form 448]

Once recorded, a declaration of homestead lasts until:

- the homestead owner records a declaration of **abandonment of the homestead**; or

- the homestead owner records a **new declaration** of homestead on another residence. [CCP §§704.980, 704.990]

If a homeowner wishes to **sell his declared homestead** that has become clouded with a creditor's lien, the homeowner may either:

- negotiate a release of the lien with the creditor [See Chapter 12]; or

- clear title to the home through a quiet title action based on the priority of his declaration of homestead.

Clearing title of a lien

A *quiet title* action determines the priorities of the creditor's lien and the recorded homestead on title. If the homeowner demonstrates the homestead declaration is valid and was recorded prior to the creditor's lien, the title will be cleared of the lien, provided no equity remains after the homestead amount. [Viotti, *supra*]

Judgment creditors junior to a declared homestead where no excess equity exists soon realize their futility in litigation. Thus, they are generally receptive to a negotiated release. Consequently, the homeowner can usually "buy" a partial (or full) release from the creditor — typically for less than the costs of a **quiet title** action. [See Chapter 12; and **first tuesday** Form 409]

After title is cleared and the homeowner sells his property, he has six months to reinvest the homestead proceeds in another home. If the proceeds are reinvested in a new residence within six months, the new residence may then be declared a homestead by recording a homestead declaration within six months after the purchase.

When the homeowner records a new homestead declaration on his replacement residence, the recording *relates back* to the time the prior homestead was recorded. This leaves no gap for the creditor's lien to gain priority over the homestead declaration on the new residence. [CCP §704.960]

If the homestead equity exemption has increased after the creditor recorded his abstract of judgment, the amount of exemption the property owner is entitled to in his **new residence** is the amount that was in effect when the abstract of judgment was recorded, not the current increased amount.

However, if the homeowner has not invested the proceeds of the sale in a new homestead after six months, and the proceeds are still in the State of California, the proceeds of the homestead sale can be attached by the judgment creditor.

An alternative to vesting title in the judgment debtor's name is to use a title holding arrangement, such as a corporation or limited liability company (LLC) created by the homeowner to hold title. Thus, the abstract of judgment against the homeowner will not automatically attach to the title held by these entities.

The homestead exemption and CIDs

Consider the a prospective buyer of separate interest in a common interest development (CID). When entering into the purchase agreement, the buyer agrees to the CID association's covenants, conditions and restrictions (CC&Rs), which include a clause limiting the owner's ability to claim a homestead exemption senior to any judgment obtained by the association.

The buyer, now an owner, fails to pay the association's assessment fees, and the association obtains a judgment against the owner for the unpaid assessment. The association claims the clause in the CC&Rs agreed to by the owner bars the homestead exemption from taking a senior position over the association's judgment. Since the owner initially agreed to the clause in the CC&Rs, it acts as a **voluntary lien** on his separate interest, and is thus unprotected by the homestead exemption.

However, *a foreclosure* on any assessment lien obtained by the association is considered an **involuntary lien** that is always senior to the owner's homestead exemption. [CCP §703.010(b)]

SECTION E

Assuming
The Loan

Chapter 14

Taking over a due-on-sale trust deed

This chapter identifies the ownership activities that trigger the due-on-sale clause in a trust deed, and the negotiations necessary with the lender to avoid a call or recast of the loan on a sale.

Events triggering the call provision

An existing first trust deed encumbering a one-to-four unit residential parcel of real estate contains a due-on clause.

An investor in small residential units becomes aware of the property since a Notice of Default (NOD) has been recorded commencing a foreclosure. The investor contacts the owner who occupies the property as his residence.

The investor submits an equity purchase (EP) offer to the owner that calls for the investor to:

- make a lump-sum **cash payment** for the owner's equity;

- **acquire title** to the property *subject to* the existing first trust deed lien that is in foreclosure; and

- **reinstate**, negotiate a short payoff or later **refinance** the trust deed loan.

The owner-in-foreclosure accepts the offer and escrow is opened.

Following expiration of the five-business-day seller cancellation period, escrow closes. The EP investor takes possession intending to fix up the property and immediately:

- resell the property in a cash or installment (carryback) sale; or

- exchange it by acquiring replacement property for a continuing reinvestment in real estate.

The lender discovers the transfer and *calls the loan due*, giving the EP investor 30 days to pay the loan off or make other arrangements with the lender — or it will start another foreclosure (for failure to pay on the call).

If the lender enforces the call by refusing to allow the EP investor to assume the loan, the EP investor will need to refinance the property unless he can promptly resell the property to a new buyer for cash or cash to a new loan. The worst scenario: all fails for the EP investor and the lender proceeds to foreclosure based on the unsatisfied call.

Editor's note — A grant deed sale of encumbered property is not the only transfer that triggers the due-on clause. The due-on clause is triggered on **the transfer of any interest** *in the real estate, except:*

- *leases for a current term no longer than three years and without a purchase option; and*

- *intra-family transfers of single-family, owner-occupied residential property on the death of an owner or an encumbrance for equity financing. [12 Code of Federal Regulations §§591.2(b), 591.5(b)(1)]*

Thus, regardless of whether the transaction is labelled a lease-option, AITD or land sales contract, the EP investor has triggered the lender's right to call the loan on taking possession.

Economic recessions and recoveries

In times of stable or falling interest rates, lenders, when requested, usually permit assumptions of loans at the existing note rate, unless a prepayment penalty clause exists. Lenders have no financial incentive to recast loans, or call and re-lend the funds at a lower rate.

However, in times of steadily rising rates, with rates exceeding the note rate on the loan, lenders seize any event that triggers the due-on clause as an opportunity to increase the interest yield on their portfolio. Once the due-on clause is triggered, the lender requires the loan to be recast at current market rates as a condition for allowing an assumption, lease or further encumbrance of the property.

Thus, real estate ownership encumbered by due-on trust deeds become increasingly difficult to transfer during periods when interest rates rise. Lender due-on interference is virtually guaranteed since the interference results in an increase in the lender's portfolio yield, which permits them to remain solvent in spite of their self-inflicted plight.

However, the *inhibiting effect* on buyers who are required to assume the existing financing at higher interest rates has an adverse economic effect on real estate sales, as well as the availability of private junior financing and long-term leasing. Ultimately, as rates and lender interference rise, many buyers, equity lenders and tenants are driven out of the market, which further depresses property values.

Meanwhile, owners are faced with the prospect of watching the value of their property fall below the remaining balance on their loans, leaving owners with no equity in the property. It is a vicious cycle, the upshot of which is a dramatic increase in loan foreclosures.

Due-on interference has been an obscure issue for the 25-year period (1982 through 2007) after *automatic enforcement of the due-on clause* became federal law. During this period, mortgage rates declined from 15% to 6%, buyers earned more money as employee productivity rose, their standard of living increased as inflation dropped and mortgage money became more plentiful due to reduced government and corporate borrowing. When these virtuous conditions change and interest rates rise on fixed-rate 30-year real estate loans, the due-on issue will no longer be obscure.

Check the trust deed provisions

In 1982, the Federal Depository Institutions Act created due-on-sale interference rights for lenders, including:

- *a right to call* the loan automatically; or

- a *right to recast* the loan terms and conditions.

Thus, a due-on-sale clause became fully enforceable by any real estate lender or carryback seller regardless of *impairment* of the security or the buyer's *creditworthiness* standards previously required to call a loan under the due-on clause. [12 CFR §591.5(b)(5)]

The EP investor's first step in analyzing the financing encumbering a property is to request and review a copy of the trust deed of record. The document is acquired from a title company, usually part of a title profile they provide as a customer service.

Examining the trust deed allows the EP investor to determine whether a due-on-sale clause exists.

If a due-on-sale clause does not exist, the loan is **fully assumable**. In which case, the EP investor can order a beneficiary statement from the lender through escrow and close without further contact or concern for lender interference with the sale. Payments are tendered to the lender after closing.

The EP investor need not be concerned with negotiating an assumption and note modification with the lender who does not have a due-on clause in the trust deed, or paying any fees to the lender except the statutory amount for their preparation of a beneficiary statement.

Without a due-on-sale clause, the lender has no right to demand a change in the interest rate or payment schedule, a shortening of the loan period or any other change in the original loan terms.

While the owner-in-foreclosure may want a buyer-seller subject-to assumption agreement, the lender cannot interfere with a subject-to purchase without a due-on clause. [See **first tuesday** Forms 431 and 432]

However, most trust deeds today contain due-on clauses due to the adhesion by all lenders (and thereby for consumers) to the use of unmodified standardized forms, a result of secondary money market requirements for the resale of trust deed loans.

Depending on the lender, these loans may be *assumed* — usually recast with a few modifications — or *called*, forcing the EP investor to refinance or close a resale of the property within four to five months.

Assumptions under the due-on-clause

Whether the lender will allow an assumption, and on what terms, depends on a number of general economic factors.

When current interest rates are substantially the same or lower than the interest rate on the loan, or the lender is merely servicing a loan that he previously sold, the lender will likely be willing to negotiate an assumption with the EP investor — waiving its due-on rights for a price, an exaction called an *assumption fee*.

However, if current rates are much higher than the note rate, the lender is more likely to refuse the assumption, or if an assumption is allowed, to demand an increase in the interest rate and payments, with points and assumption fees.

When a junior trust deed exists, the assumption and modification of the first trust deed raises the entirely separate and resolvable issue of subordination.

A junior trust deed holder exists

Lender assumptions usually involve material modification of the loan (by increased or variable interest and payments, shortened due date, introduction of prepayment penalties, etc.).

Consider the position of a lender who holds a note secured by a first trust deed on a parcel of real estate. The property is also encumbered by a second trust deed. The first trust deed lender enters into a modification of the trust deed note by extending the due date, raising the interest rate and increasing the amount of principal due. The second trust deed holder does not consent to the modification.

Later, a note secured by a second trust deed on the property becomes delinquent. The second trust deed holder initiates judicial foreclosure proceedings, and claims the first trust deed lost its priority since the senior lienholder substantially modified the terms of the trust deed note.

The senior trust deed holder claims only the modified portion of the note loses priority since only the modifications impair the secured position of the second.

Can the second trust deed holder entirely avoid the first trust deed?

No! Only the modified portion of the note secured by the first trust deed is unenforceable against the second trust deed holder since the second trust deed remained unimpaired in the same position as when the second trust deed lien was recorded. [**Lennar Northeast Partners** v. **Buice** (1996) 49 CA4th 1576]

Now consider a seller who carries back a second trust deed on the sale of property **without the consent** of the holder of the first trust deed to waive enforcement of its due-on clause.

The first trust deed lender learns of the sale and calls the loan. To avoid the call, the buyer assumes the first trust deed loan and the note's due date is shortened. The carryback seller then claims his second trust deed now has priority over the entire amount of the modified loan since the modification substantially impairs the carryback seller's security by increasing the potential for default.

The lender claims its trust deed retains priority since the lender owes the carryback seller no duty to obtain the seller's consent to a modification.

Here, the modification of the senior loan without the consent of the junior carryback seller does not result in a change in trust deed priorities since the seller sold and accepted as security a second trust deed without the lender's written consent, events triggering the due-on clause. [**Friery** v. **Sutter Buttes Savings Bank** (1998) 61 CA4th 869]

When negotiating with any existing second trust deed holder to waive its due-on-sale rights and allow an assumption, the EP investor should also negotiate for the second's consent to any modification of the first should the first trust deed lender demand one.

The assumption offer

Before bringing the loan current, the EP investor should consider negotiating with the lender, preferably before closing, for the most favorable assumption terms available. The lender must be made aware an assumption is considered a trade-off — the investor will bring the loan current and keep it current. Possibly, the investor will allow the lender to recast the loan to the current market rate of interest, all in exchange for the lender agreeing not to call the loan on the EP transaction.

If the investor intends to assume the loan, the EP agreement between the investor and the seller must set out, as specifically as possible, the parameters of the assumption and modification agreement (recast) to be negotiated with the lender. Then, if the terms demanded by the lender are excessive, the investor may cancel the EP transaction.

Terms for **recasting** a loan include numerous items such as:

- interest rate adjustment on the loan;

- amortization period for the loan;

- monthly payments to amortize the loan; and

- the fees to be paid for assuming the loan. [See **first tueday**Form 156 §4]

Wording for the loan assumption parameters to be included in an assignment addendum attached to the purchase agreement can be seen in **first tuesday** Form 401-2.

If the terms of the assumption and modification of the note are not included in the EP agreement, the seller-in-foreclosure may be able to enforce the purchase agreement if the buyer wants to cancel the sale and the lender's terms and conditions are reasonable. [**Kadner** v. **Shields** (1971) 20 CA3d 251; Calif. Civil Code §3390]

Also, by being as specific as possible about the assumption terms to be obtained from the lender, the EP investor limits the rates the seller-in-foreclosure can force him to accept to close the transaction.

Contacting the lender

On opening escrow, the EP investor should promptly contact the lender to begin assumption negotiations — while the loan is delinquent and reportable to government agencies by the lender. Escrow should immediately request the beneficiary statement.

Of course, the assumption terms demanded by the lender will depend on a combination of the current market rates, the lender's seniority and the creditworthiness of the EP investor.

If current interest rates are higher than the note rate on the loan, most lenders will want to raise the interest rate on the loan to the current market level. At the very least, expect the lender to demand up-front fees, including points and assumption fees. "Buy-down" points are sometimes demanded to lower interest rates and provide the lender with current earnings (and a less valuable loan).

On the other hand, if current market rates are at levels below the note rate, the EP investor is in a prime position to negotiate for more favorable terms.

Because the lender is interested in maintaining its high yield loans, the lender will be more willing to waive or redraft provisions in the note and trust deed, such as the prepayment penalty or variable interest rate, or even eliminate or modify the due-on-sale provision.

Before approving the assumption, the lender may also ask the EP investor to provide credit information and an appraisal of the property to ensure its value has not deteriorated to an unacceptable level.

Once the assumption terms are settled, the EP investor must make sure the terms are confirmed in writing. The assumption agreement should be signed and delivered to escrow, together with any subordination agreements from junior trust deed holders to be delivered to the lender and the title company on closing.

In negotiating an assumption/waiver of the due-on rights with the lender, the EP investor may never rely on the lender's oral promises. The lender's promise to waive its due-on rights is not enforceable unless in writing. [CC §1624]

If the modification demanded by the lender on the assumption does not fall within the loan assumption parameters spelled out in the EP agreement, the EP investor may:

- assume the loan at the lender's rate, thereby waiving his contingency;

- close the transaction by taking title subject to the loan without a formal assumption;

- negotiate a cash-to-new-loan arrangement with the seller, and obtain new financing; or

- cancel the transaction based on the assumption/modification demands exceeding the limitation in the purchase agreement.

Waiver by conduct

While a lender's promise to waive its due-on-sale clause must be in writing to be enforceable, a lender can also waive its due-on rights by its conduct.

For example, an investor purchases property subject to an existing loan and without a formal assumption with the lender.

A beneficiary statement is ordered by escrow, but the lender is not informed when the actual transfer occurs. However, the lender later becomes aware of the transfer, but does not call the loan.

The lender continues to accept several monthly payments from the investor after its discovery of the transfer of ownership to the investor.

Later, interest rates climb and the lender calls the loan based on the sale. The EP investor refuses to pay off the loan and the lender begins foreclosure. The EP investor seeks to stop the foreclosure, claiming the lender waived its due-on rights by accepting payments after it became aware of the transfer.

Can the lender call the loan and foreclose on the property?

No! The lender has, by its conduct, *waived* its due-on-sale rights regarding the transaction. The lender failed to take steps to call the loan, or if it called the loan, it failed to act on the call, while continuing to accept several monthly payments from the investor after becoming aware of the transfer. [**Rubin** v. **Los Angeles Federal Savings & Loan Association** (1984) 159 CA3d 292]

Chapter 15

FHA and VA loan assumptions

This chapter reviews Federal Housing Administration (FHA) and Veterans Administration (VA) enforcement of assumption regulations controlling loans they have insured.

Avoiding fees and investor prohibitions

An investor wants to locate single family residences (SFRs) to purchase and hold long-term as rentals. He is aware of publicity about high foreclosure rates among government-insured, low-cost housing. Specifically, he is interested in inexpensive homes with fixed-rate loans insured by the Federal Housing Administration that are in foreclosure (FHA).

The investor is looking to **take over** existing fixed-rate financing rather than obtain new financing to fund his purchase of the SFRs.

The investor knows the trust deed FHA uses for loans insured by the Department of Housing and Urban Development (HUD) contains a *due-on-sale clause*. The purpose for originally including the provision was to call loans taken over by investors to reduce the number of defaults on FHA loans. Investor-owners generally have a high default rate compared to owner-occupants.

However, the investor is advised that before the lender can *call* an FHA-insured loan on the sale of the secured property subject to the loan, the lender must first obtain HUD's approval. In practice, HUD does not grant the lender the right-to-call a loan if the buyer is credit worthy. Thus, lenders and servicing agents are limited to using the due-on clause to induce an investor to assume the loan, typically accomplished by contacting the seller prior to the close of escrow. The objective of the lender when interfering is to demand and receive a fee of one-half point or more on the sale. These earnings are received in exchange for the lender simply changing the name of the owner in their records and sending payment coupons to the new owner.

FHA-insured loans and investors

Prudent long-term investors seek out the more desperate seller's who are in default on loan payments. They pay little or no money down to acquire and convert the property to a rental unit. The investment approach of high repute is "price, time and location."

However, some investors are short-term day trader types who only intend to immediately flip the property after buying it, without investing any additional capital. In doing so, they often do not make even one payment to the lender. These investors occasionally collect and keep rent, called *rent skimming*, or *equity skimming* if done on a scale of five or more units. **Rent and equity skimming** are crimes under federal and state law. [12 United States Code §1709-2; Calif. Civil Code §§890 et seq.]

In response to the activities of rent-skimming investors in the 1980s, the HUD's initial reaction was to establish a policy prohibiting investor assumptions of FHA insured loans on SFRs.

Thus, the existence of a due-on clause in FHA secured loans purports to restrict the sale of the secured property to qualified owner-occupants only. [HUD Mortgagee Letter 89-31]

Additionally, before an **owner-occupant** can assume a loan (and pay the lender an assumption fee), he must be **creditworthy**. The creditworthy test and assumption fees on the sale of the secured property remain in effect during the entire life of the loan, not merely for a period of a few years. [Mortgagee Letter 89-31]

However, in spite of the HUD-published due-on enforcement policy, the servicing lender cannot call the loan on a subject-to transfer to an investor unless they have received *prior approval* from HUD. As a matter of practice, HUD has not authorized a call when an investor acquires the property, unless the investor defaults on the loan payments.

Closing subject to an FHA loan

Investors having the financial ability and willingness to make payments on a Federal Housing Administration (FHA) insured loan encumbering property they have agreed to purchase should obtain a beneficiary statement from the lender. The statement is ordered out by escrow and, when received, reviewed by the investor to confirm the seller-in-foreclosure's representation about the loan's condition.

The investor then closes escrow, taking over but not formally assuming the loan with the lender or servicing agent, by either:

- cashing out the seller's equity; or

- combining cash and a note carried back by the seller to pay for the seller's equity.

The seller's risk of FHA recourse

When a seller permits anyone, including an investor, to take title subject-to his Federal Housing Administration (FHA) insured loan, the seller remains exposed to the recourse liability inherent in the FHA insurance plan.

The downside risk for a seller on a sale subject to an FHA-insured loan is his continuing **personal liability** for any loss the FHA may incur due to a deficiency in the property value at the time of a foreclosure. This deficiency in the property value might occur due to declining prices occurring long after the investor acquires title.

If the subject-to investor fails to make payments on the FHA loan, and the property's value becomes insufficient to satisfy the remaining loan balance, Housing and Urban Development (HUD) has the right to collect a deficiency from the original borrower.

The right to pursue the original borrower for any deficiency belongs to HUD, not the lender. The lender has been paid in full under the FHA loan guarantee program.

Borrowers under programs insured by the FHA or Veterans Administration (VA) do not receive California **anti-deficiency protection** for losses sustained by these federal agencies on their loan insurance programs. The federal statutory right to collect losses suffered by the HUD loan insurance program preempts state law to the contrary. [**Carter** v. **Derwinski** (9th Cir. 1993) 987 F2d 611]

Thus, the seller, on a transfer of title subject to an FHA insured loan, should consider entering into an *assumption agreement* with the investor. Further, the agreement can be secured by a performance trust deed carried back on the property. [See **first tuesday** Forms 432 and 451]

With an assumption by the investor secured by a trust deed on the property, when the investor does not perform on the **assumption agreement** by making payments on the loan when they become due, the seller may call all amounts due on the defaulted loan and foreclose to protect his interests.

Release of liability

To be released from liability for any deficiency on a Federal Housing Administration (FHA)-insured loan taken over by an investor, the seller must obtain a formal *release of liability* from the Housing and Urban Development (HUD) as part of the assumption package demanded by the lender.

A **release of liability** is granted by the lender, not HUD, on a sale when the buyer takes over the loan if:

- the seller requests a release from personal liability;

- the prospective buyer is creditworthy;

- the prospective buyer assumes the loan; and

- the lender uses an FHA-approved form to release the seller from personal liability. [HUD Form 92210.1; 24 Code of Federal Regulations §203.510(a)]

If the conditions for a release of liability exist, but the seller does not request the release from personal liability, the seller remains liable to the FHA for any losses due to a default occurring within five years after the sale. [12 USC §1709(r)]

However, after five years pass from the time the property is sold subject to the loan, the seller is released from personal liability if:

- the investor assumes the loan with the lender;

- the loan is not in default at the end of the five-year period; and

- the seller requests the release of liability from the lender. [24 CFR §203.510(b)]

Many owners sell their homes subject-to FHA-insured loans knowing full well the risks of a deficiency. However, sellers generally believe future appreciation and HUD's recent refusal to pursue collection of losses as part of their policy to expand home ownership minimize any real risk of a value-deficiency exposure. After all, HUD goes to great lengths to encourage homeownership, frequently ignoring their own risk reduction guidelines. The pursuit of deficiencies would absolutely chill that objective.

In economically depressed parts of the country, property is conveyed subject-to FHA-insured loans as a way to attract buyers. These transfers tend to decrease the level of foreclosures against homeowners who can no longer afford to own their home and are unable to otherwise find a buyer who will occupy the property.

Conversely, a demand by the seller for a substitution of liability and the lender's counter-productive assumption fees tend to drive potential investors away. Thus, the price of homes is driven down, adversely effecting the level of foreclosures.

FHA inactivity on a sale

Any hesitation a seller-in-foreclosure may have about selling a single family residence (SFR) subject-to a Federal Housing Administration (FHA)-insured loan is put at ease by the Housing and Urban Development's (HUD's) internal policy not to collect deficiencies against owners who made loan payments in good faith.

After foreclosure by a lender, the FHA pays the lender for any loan losses under their mortgage insurance policy (MIP) or acquires the property by paying off the loan. If acquired, the FHA resells the properties to offset its losses. FHA then sends collection letters but does not otherwise contact the homeowner.

Sellers who receive cash for their entire equity occasionally ignore the loan assumption provision and lender threats. Thus, they close escrow, transferring their title subject to the FHA-insured loan.

Yet, HUD, with its shadow of a no-investor policy, severely cripples a defaulting seller's ability to sell his home and financially right himself.

If HUD's no-investor policy were enforced, it would tend to increase the number of FHA repossessions during recessionary periods, an undesirable effect for all parties involved.

Thus, buying a residence subject-to an FHA-insured loan, regardless of when the loan was originated, will likely continue without government interference and lender assumption threats, so long as the loan is brought current and kept current.

Assuming a VA loan

The Veterans Administration (VA) loan assumption policy is entirely different from the HUD/FHA assumption policy. The HUD has a long-standing policy of encouraging homeownership throughout America. VA is narrowly focused on loans made to veterans who want to acquire a principal residence without a down payment — nothing more.

An investor buying property secured by a VA-guaranteed loan may take over the loan if:

- the loan is **current**;

- the investor **assumes** the loan; and

- the investor is **creditworthy**. [38 USC §§3713(a), 3714(a)(1)]

For an investor to assume a VA loan, a fee of .5% of the loan balance is to be paid to the VA by the investor. [38 USC §3729(b)]

The VA **assumption fee** is to be paid to the lender on closing the sale with the investor. The lender has 15 days to forward the fee to the VA or the lender will face late charges. [38 CFR §36.4312(e)(2)]

Additionally, the lender can charge and retain an assumption fee of $300, plus the costs of a credit report, unless the maximum amount for an assumption fee allowed under state law is less. [38 CFR §36.4312(d)(8)]

While no statutory rule exists in California for calculating assumption fees, the fees should reflect actual out-of-pocket costs incurred by the lender for processing the assumption.

When an assumption application is approved by the lender, the VA borrower is released from further liability to the VA under the mortgage insurance program, including liability for losses caused by the investor's default in payments. [38 CFR §36.4323(h)]

However, the veteran who is released by the VA is not also released by the lender from further liabilities for the loan. For instance, the veteran who **refinances** his home with a VA insured loan has liability under the loan for any deficiency in the property value beyond the limited amount of VA mortgage insurance. For the lender to collect from the seller on a recourse loan, the lender would have to judicially foreclose and wait for one year after the foreclosure sale to take possession of the property.

The veteran exposed to the risk of refinancing liability and concerned about it should consider negotiating and entering into a *novation agreement* with the lender to be relieved of liability for a potential deficiency. Liability to a lender for a VA-insured loan used to refinance a property is different from the mortgage insurance liability the veteran has with the VA.

A **novation agreement** requires the consent by three parties — the investor, seller and lender — to release the seller from further liability to the lender even though the seller has been released from mortgage insurance liability by the VA under a substitution of liability.

If the lender refuses to allow the investor to assume the loan, the VA may review the findings and determine whether the investor is entitled to assume the loan.

If the veteran is unable to make payments on his VA-insured loan, but finds a qualified investor to assume the loan, the VA may require the lender to agree to the loan assumption since it is in the best interest of the VA. [38 USC §3714(a)(4)(B)]

However, neither the lender nor the VA must release the seller from liability on the loan when the assumption is granted to avoid foreclosure. [38 CFR §36.4323(h)]

If the VA refuses to allow the investor to assume the loan, and the veteran borrower sells the property nonetheless, the lender may call the loan and demand payment of the remaining principal and interest without prior approval from the VA. [38 USC §3714(a)(4)(C)]

Also, the lender may later call the VA insured loan if the veteran borrower sells his residence and fails to notify the lender of the sale. [38 USC §3714(b)]

However, when a lender becomes aware the veteran borrower sold the property secured by the VA-insured loan and then the lender fails to notify the VA, the lender, not the seller-in-foreclosure, will be liable for any VA losses on the loan. As a result, VA is advised whenever an investor takes title to a property and makes payments. [38 USC §§3714(c)(1), 3714(c)(2)]

Chapter 16

Assumptions: formal and subject-to

This article explores the takeover of an existing loan by an investor on his purchase of a homeowner's residence during the period it is in foreclosure.

A loan takeover by an EP investor

On the sale of a parcel of real estate, any existing financing encumbering the property can remain of record and be taken over by the buyer under one of four procedures:

- a **formal assumption** between the lender and the buyer;

- a **subject-to assumption** between the seller and the buyer;

- a **subject-to transfer** of ownership without an assumption agreement of any type; and

- a **novation** on the loan between the lender, seller and buyer.

Consider a seller of his personal residence that is encumbered by a first trust deed in foreclosure. The seller enters into an equity purchase (EP) agreement and escrow instructions that provide for an investor to **take title subject-to** the existing first trust deed loan. [See **first tuesday** Form 156 §4]

The investor plans to close escrow on the transfer without entering into a written assumption agreement with the lender, often called a *formal assumption*. The investor intends to negotiate with the lender after closing and before he brings the loan current to determine whether the lender will call the loan or demand an assumption and modification of loan terms. If negotiations are unsuccessful, the EP investor can refinance with another lender.

The interest rate on the seller's existing loan is at or above current market levels. The experience of the investor and his broker indicates the lender will not call the loan and demand a payoff or assumption under the circumstances. If it calls the loan, the investor reasons the lender will lose either its servicing fees or its high portfolio yield on the loan, and will still have an uncured delinquency, depending on whether the lender is servicing the loan for another lender or owns the loan.

A beneficiary statement is requested by escrow. The lender properly complies with the request by sending a statement of the loan condition to escrow within 21 days of its receipt of the request, as required. [Calif. Civil Code §2943(e)(3); see Chapter 18]

However, the lender unilaterally **instructs escrow** not to close until the investor has been approved by the lender and has assumed the loan since the lender's trust deed contains a due-on clause.

Can the lender interfere with the closing of a subject-to transaction when the investor and seller do not also instruct escrow to process a lender approval or loan assumption?

No! Escrow instructions for the sale of property subject to the existing loan are entirely between the investor, seller and escrow. The lender has no legal right to interfere with the transaction to prevent the closing — it is not a party to the escrow.

More importantly, escrow has no authority from its principals to follow any lender instructions attached to the beneficiary statement. The lender's remedy is limited to calling the loan under its due-on clause in the trust deed after the subject-to transaction is closed, if the lender chooses to do so. [**Moss** v. **Minor Properties, Inc.** (1968) 262 CA2d 847]

Neither a subject-to transfer nor a formal assumption impose any RESPA or TILA Regulation Z required disclosures on the lender when their loan is taken over by an investor. The loan is no longer a *personal-use loan*. As always, lenders will protest in an effort to induce a loan modification at high rates and the collection of assumption fees. During tough economic times, loan officers are forced to pay their way. [12 Code of Federal Regulations §226.20(b)(1)]

The subject-to transaction

A subject-to transaction is initially structured by filling out the appropriate financing provision in a purchase agreement form. The subject-to provision provides for entry of the principal amount of the loan and the terms for its payment, applying the amount to the purchase price the investor will pay for the property. The financing provision states the investor is to take title to the property subject to the existing loan. [See **first tuesday** Form 156 §§4 and 5]

The seller's representation of the terms of the loan is confirmed by the investor on receipt of the lender's **beneficiary statement** by escrow. The investor can rely on the beneficiary statement for future payment schedules, interest rates and loan balances in spite of the lender's attempts to stipulate escrow's use of the beneficiary statement on the investor's assumption of the loan. [CC §2943(d)(1)]

Some investors instruct escrow not to request a beneficiary statement, fearing the request may cause the lender to **call or modify** the loan after escrow closes. The seller's most recent loan payment receipt or annual loan statement might then be used as the source of loan information. However, the investor must be aware the lender is not bound by the content of the payment statements but is bound by the content of the beneficiary statement. [See Chapter 18]

Some investors acquire their ownership rights to property by entering into **unrecorded sales agreements** with the seller, such as lease-option agreements (not a leaseback arrangement) or land sales contracts. Thus, the seller and investor completely avoid conveyances, escrow, title insurance and most other customary (and expensive) transfer activities until they can either work out an assumption or originate new financing.

However, unrecorded sales transactions do trigger due-on clauses and property reassessments, as well as create risks of loss inherent in an unrecorded transaction and leave room for misunderstandings about who owns the property (the buyer does).

During periods when current market interest rates are comparable to or lower than the note rate on an existing loan:

- a **beneficiary statement** should be ordered to confirm the loan amount and loan terms;

- the change of ownership conveyance should be **recorded and insured**; and

- the conveyance should promptly be brought to the **lender's attention** so the lender will be barred from calling the loan months later should interest rates rise causing the lender to claim the transfer went undisclosed.

Conversely, during periods of rising or high interest rates, as compared to the note rate on an existing loan, the lender is often not notified of a subject-to sales transaction. Notice of the transaction would allow the lender to gain financially from a call or recast of the loan at the expense of the seller or the investor.

However, the lender can enforce its due-on clause and call the loan on its *future discovery* of any sale, regardless of how the sale was structured. Also, on a later discovery of the transfer, any brokers, attorneys or accountants assisting in the sale whose **primary objective** in negotiating the sales transaction was to induce the investor and seller to avoid the due-on clause may be liable to the lender (in tort) for any *retroactive interest differential* (RID) lost by the lender based on market rates at the time of the transfer. A *hold* *harmless agreement* from the seller or the investor would be appropriate for providing indemnity to the agents and brokers negotiating the undisclosed transaction. [See Chapter 21]

The seller of property, which was sold either subject-to or on an assumption of the existing loan, should be concerned about his liability for the loan after it is taken over by the investor. Seller liability initially depends on whether the loan is a *recourse* or a *nonrecourse loan*. However, the seller is liable for the lender's loss resulting from its error on a beneficiary statement or a payoff demand, up to the value of the property.

Nonrecourse debt

A seller is not liable for a deficiency in property value on the foreclosure of a *purchase-money* loan previously taken over by a buyer under any procedure. The loan is a nonrecourse debt subject to *anti-deficiency* laws.

Purchase-money loans secured by real estate include:

- seller carryback financing on the sale of any type of real estate that becomes the sole security for the carryback note;

- a loan or debt that funded or financed the purchase of an owner-occupied, one-to-four unit residential property, also called a *purchase-assist loan*. [Calif. Code of Civil Procedure §580b]; and

- a loan made for the construction of an owner-occupied, single family residence (SFR), and perhaps a loan made to improve the structure (the legal status of dwelling improvement loans remains uncertain).

A trust deed lender on a default in a **purchase-money** loan may only resort to the property by foreclosing to recover the balance due. [CCP §580b]

Even if the property has insufficient remaining value to satisfy the balance of the purchase-money loan on foreclosure, the lender cannot hold the original borrower (seller) or an assuming buyer personally liable for any deficiency in the property value, unless:

- the buyer inflicts *waste* on the property; and

- the lender *underbids* to provide for the judicial recovery of the dollar amount of the waste.

On the take-over of a purchase-money loan by an investor, the loan retains its original nonrecourse purchase-money characteristics, regardless of whether the investor takes title subject-to or assumes the loan, or a novation occurs.[**Jackson** v. **Taylor** (1969) 272 CA2d 1]

Thus, an investor who takes over a purchase-money loan under any procedure is entitled to the anti-deficiency protection imbedded in the loan. In contrast, **purchase-assist** financing originated by a non-occupying investor on any type of residential property, including one-to-four unit residential property, would be a recourse loan, not a *purchase-money loan*.

However, the Federal Housing Administration (FHA) and the Veterans Administration (VA) have recourse to the borrower for losses under their mortgage insurance programs on a foreclosure and resale of the property. [See Chapter 15]

Recourse real estate loans

Recourse loans are all loans except those classified as **purchase-money loans** as reviewed above.

Consider an investor who takes title to property subject to an existing home equity loan, a recourse (liability) loan. The loan proceeds were not used to purchase or improve the seller's residence.

The investor defaults on the loan and the lender initiates and completes a judicial foreclosure (not a trustee's sale) on the property. The fair market value of the property at the time of the judicial foreclosure sale is insufficient to fully satisfy the loan, resulting in a deficiency.

The lender now seeks a money judgment against the seller for the amount of the deficiency in the property's value since the fair market value bid at the judicial foreclosure sale did not fully satisfy the loan amount. The seller claims he is not responsible for the loan since it was taken over by the investor.

Is the seller liable for the deficiency on the recourse loan after the investor takes title to the secured property subject to the existing loan?

Yes! When property is sold and its title is conveyed to a buyer **subject-to** an existing recourse loan, the seller remains liable for any deficiency on the recourse loan should the buyer fail to pay. [**Braun** v. **Crew** (1920) 183 C 728]

Further, unless the buyer enters into an **assumption agreement** with either the seller or the lender, the buyer is not liable to either the seller or the lender for a drop in the property's value below the loan balance (unless the buyer damages the property resulting in a decrease in its value, called *waste*). [**Cornelison** v. **Kornbluth** (1975) 15 C3d 590; CC §2929]

However, if the subject-to investor and the lender later enter into an assumption agreement that includes a significant modification of the terms of the recourse loan without the seller's consent, the seller cannot be held liable for the loan. [Braun, *supra*; CC §2819]

Buyer-seller assumption

A seller can reduce his risk of loss when a buyer takes over a **recourse loan** by including a provision in the purchase agreement that requires the buyer to enter into an **assumption agreement** with the seller, called a *subject-to assumption*.

A subject-to assumption agreement is not to be confused with a so-called *formal assumption* entered into between the buyer and the lender.

The subject-to assumption, initially agreed to in the purchase agreement and documented in es-

crow, is a promise given by the buyer to the seller to perform all the terms of the loan taken over by the buyer on the sale. [See Form 431 accompanying this chapter]

The subject-to assumption agreement gives the seller the right to be held harmless — *indemnified* — by the buyer for the amount of any deficiency judgment a recourse lender might be awarded against the seller in a judicial foreclosure. To be enforceable by the seller, the assumption agreement must be in writing. [CC §1624]

Although the buyer's promise to pay the loan under a subject-to assumption is given to the seller, the buyer also becomes liable to the recourse lender under the legal doctrines of *equitable subrogation* and *third-party beneficiaries*. [Braun, *supra*; see Form 431 §6]

Even though the buyer, upon entering into any type of assumption agreement, takes over the primary responsibility for the recourse loan, the seller remains **secondarily liable** to the lender. The seller's risk of loss arises when the buyer fails to pay the recourse loan and the market value remaining in the property is insufficient to cover the loan amount. [**Everts** v. **Matteson** (1942) 21 C2d 437]

To avoid the delay in pursuing reimbursement from the buyer for any loss covered by the subject-to assumption, purchase agreement provisions calling for the buyer to enter into an assumption agreement with the seller may also call for the investor to secure the assumption agreement by a **performance trust deed** carried back by the seller as a lien on the property sold. [See **first tuesday** Forms 432 and 451]

With a recorded trust deed held by the seller to secure the subject-to assumption agreement, any default by the investor on the loan allows the seller to:

- demand the investor to tender the entire balance remaining due on the assumed loan, subject to the investor's right to reinstate the delinquencies; and

ASSUMPTION AGREEMENT
Unsecured and Subrogated

DATE: _____, 20_____, at _____, California.

Items left blank or unchecked are not applicable.

FACTS:

1. This assumption agreement is entered into by

  1.1 _____, as the Buyer,

  1.2 and _____, as the Seller,

  1.3 regarding Buyer's acquisition of real estate referred to as _____
  _____.

2. FIRST TRUST DEED NOTE:

  2.1 Buyer is acquiring title to the real estate subject to a first trust deed dated _____,

  2.2 executed by _____, as the Trustor,

  2.3 in which _____ is the Beneficiary,

  2.4 recorded on _____, as Instrument No._____, in the Official Records

  of _____ County, California, and

  2.5 given to secure a promissory note of the same date for the principal sum of $_____.

3. SECOND TRUST DEED NOTE:

  3.1 Buyer is acquiring title to the real estate subject to a second trust deed dated _____,

  3.2 executed by _____, as the Trustor,

  3.3 in which _____ is the Beneficiary,

  3.4 recorded on _____, as Instrument No._____, in the Official Records

  of _____ County, California, and

  3.5 given to secure a promissory note of the same date for the principal sum of $_____.

AGREEMENT:

4. Seller hereby assigns and delegates to Buyer all rights and obligations in the above note(s) and trust deed(s).

5. Buyer hereby assumes and agrees to timely pay the debt evidenced by the above promissory note(s) and to perform all of Trustor's obligations under the trust deed(s) securing the note(s).

6. This agreement is made for the benefit of the Beneficiary(ies) of the trust deed(s) securing the note(s).

7. Should Buyer or Buyer's successors default in the performance of this agreement, the whole sum of the principal and interest on the assumed indebtedness(es) shall become immediately due at the option of the holder of this assumption agreement.

  7.1 On default, Seller shall become subrogated to the interest of Beneficiary under the defaulted note and trust deed.

8. In any action to enforce this agreement, the prevailing party shall receive attorney fees.

I agree to the terms stated above.	I agree to the terms stated above.
Date:_____, 20_____	Date:_____, 20_____
Seller: _____	Buyer: _____
Seller: _____	Buyer: _____

- proceed with foreclosure under the performance trust deed to recover the property and cure the default on the loan assumed by the investor.

A **subject-to assumption**, like any subject-to transaction, does not alter the lender's right to enforce its *due-on clause* on discovery of the unconsented-to conveyance, unless the lender has waived its due-on rights by failing to call the loan after acquiring knowledge of the transfer of ownership or to act on a prior call made. [See chapter 14]

Novation

Consider an EP investor who is willing to cash out a seller-in-foreclosure's equity and assume an existing recourse loan with a lender. However, the seller is unwilling to sell the property and remain liable for the loan after closing when he no longer has an interest in the property and is unable to protect himself.

Can the sale be closed without the seller remaining liable on the recourse loan assumed by the investor?

Yes! The lender can enter into an agreement with both the investor and the seller providing for both the investor's **assumption** of the loan and a **release** of the seller's liability, an agreement called a *novation* or *substitution of liability*. The lender typically charges a fee and may demand a modification of the loan terms if the interest rate on the loan is below current market rates.

On a formal investor-lender assumption of a loan secured by an owner-occupied, one-to-four unit residential property, the lender is required to **release the seller from liability** for the loan assumed by the investor. [12 CFR §591.5(b)(4)]

A **novation agreement** is comparable to the existing lender originating a new loan with the investor, except the trust deed executed by the seller remains of record and the note remains unpaid.

Thus, the lender under a novation agreement (or a formal assumption) will review the investor's credit status, probably demand a modification of the interest rate to current levels, and charge an assumption fee. So the lender receives all the benefits it would have received on a new-loan origination made to the investor.

However, any fees or increase in the interest rate received by the lender on the loan, called *portfolio yield*, defeats most of the advantages an investor and seller have when the investor takes title subject to the seller's existing loan.

Welcome to economic Darwinism.

SECTION F

Escrow

Chapter 17

Opening escrow

This chapter explains the equity purchase (EP) investor's use of checklists and pre-printed instructions to better prepare for opening and closing an escrow.

The process for closing the sale

Escrow is a process employed to facilitate the closing of a real estate transaction entered into between two parties, such as a EP investor and a seller-in-foreclosure, who have agreed to the transfer of real estate, typically under a primary underlying agreement, e.g., a purchase agreement.

An **escrow consists of**:

- **one person**, such as a seller of real estate, who delivers written instruments (or money when he is the buyer) to an escrow company for the purpose of the person fully performing his obligations owed another person under an agreement they previously entered into for the sale, financing or leasing of real estate; and

- the **escrow company**, who delivers the written instruments (or money) to the other person, such as the EP investor, on the occurrence of a specified event or the performance of prescribed conditions, such as the issuance of title insurance. [Calif. Financial Code §17003(a)]

For an individual to engage in the business of acting as an **escrow agent**, he must himself be licensed and employed by a corporation also licensed by the California Commissioner of Corporations, unless exempt.

Individuals exempt from the escrow licensing requirements include:

- a licensed real estate broker, either individual or corporate, who represents a party to a transaction (an owner, buyer, lender or tenant) in which the broker will perform escrow services;

- a licensed attorney who is not actively engaged in conducting (holding himself out as) an escrow agency;

- a bank, trust company, savings and loan association (thrift) or insurance company; and

- a title insurance company whose principal business is preparing abstracts or making searches of title used for issuing title insurance policies.

Duties of an escrow officer include:

- collecting necessary documents, such as appraisals, disclosure statements and title reports called for in escrow instructions;

- preparing documents necessary for conveyancing, encumbering and evidencing the creation of debts required for escrow to close;

- calculating prorations and adjustments; and

- disbursing funds or transferring documents when all conditions for their release have been met.

Opening escrow

Consider an investor and seller-in-foreclosure who enter into a equity purchase (EP) agreement for the sale of the seller's one-to-four unit principal residence. As agreed, escrow now needs to be opened to handle the closing of the transaction. [See **first tuesday** Form 156 §13.1]

SALES ESCROW WORKSHEET
For Use on Seller-Occupied SFR Properties

DATE: _____, 20_____, at _____, California.

BY: _____

1. PARTIES, PROPERTY AND PRICE:

1.1   Date escrow to close _____

1.2   Property address _____

_____

Parcel number_____

City_____ County _____, California.

1.3   Price $_____

Down payment $_____

Initial deposit into escrow $_____

Loan amount on closing $_____

1.4   Seller's name _____

Address _____

_____

Phone _____ Fax _____ Email _____

Seller's Broker_____

1.5   Buyer's Name _____

Address _____

_____

Phone _____ Fax _____ Email _____

Buyer's Broker _____

2. LIENS RECORD:

	First Trust Deed	Second Trust Deed
Original amount	$_____	$_____
Current balance	$_____	$_____
Interest rate	_____% ☐ ARM	_____% ☐ ARM
	Type_____	Type_____
Monthly payments	$_____	$_____
Due date	_____	_____
Assumed or reconveyed	_____	_____
Loan number	_____	_____

Lender(s) name and address(es) _____

_____

2.1   Bond or assessment lien balance of $_____, payable $_____ annually, including

interest at the rate of _____%.

District Name _____

Address _____

_____

Phone _____ Fax _____ Email _____

2.2   New Trust Deed loan in amount of $_____, payable approximately $_____

monthly, including interest at the annual rate of _____% ☐ fixed; ☐ ARM.

Loan charges to be paid by _____.

2.3   Seller Carryback Note and Trust Deed $_____ payable $_____ monthly, or more, including annual interest of _____%, all due _____ years from close. First payment due _____, 20_____.

☐ Contract collection clause [See **ft** Form 442 §3]

☐ 90-day balloon payment notice provision (mandatory on one-to-four residential units) [See **ft** Form 418-3]

☐ Late charge of $_____ after _____ days [See **ft** Form 418-1]

☐ Prepayment penalty [See **ft** Form 418-2]

☐ Due-on-sale clause

☐ All-inclusive Note and Trust Deed addendum [See **ft** Form 442 or 443]

☐ Tax reporting service charge to be paid by _____

☐ Request for Notice of Default/Delinquency on senior Trust Deed [See **ft** Form 412]

3. DISCLOSURES CHECKED ARE YET TO BE MADE TO BUYERS:

3.1   Lead-based paint disclosure for pre-1978 residences — right to inspect/waiver. [See **ft** Form 313]

☐ Buyer's receipt   ☐ Seller's compliance

☐ Buyer's Broker acknowledgement   ☐ Listing Broker acknowledgement

3.2   Condition of Property — Transfer Disclosure Statement (TDS). [See **ft** Form 304]

☐ Buyer's receipt   ☐ Seller's compliance

☐ Buyer's Broker visual inspection   ☐ Listing Broker visual inspection

a.   Environmental Hazards Guide for Homeowners and Buyers.

     ☐ Buyer's receipt

b.   Home Energy/Rating Information Booklet.

     ☐ Buyer's receipt   ☐ Seller's compliance report

     ☐ Buyer's Broker acknowledgment   ☐ Listing Broker acknowledgment

3.3   Natural Hazard Disclosure Statement — three-day right to cancel. [See **ft** Form 314]

☐ Buyer's Receipt

a.   Homeowner's Guide to Earthquake Safety (pre-1960 housing, woodframe, no slab). [See **ft** Forms 315 and 316]

     ☐ Buyer's receipt   ☐ Seller's city compliance report

b.   Commercial Guide to Earthquake Safety for pre-1975 housing (unreinforced masonry, woodframe roof or floors).

     ☐ Buyer's receipt   ☐ Seller's city compliance

     ☐ Buyer's Broker acknowledgment   ☐ Listing Broker acknowledgment

3.4   Mello-Roos bond conditions — Notice of Special Tax [District _____].

☐ Buyer's receipt

3.5   Criminal activity and security statement. [See **ft** Form 319]

☐ Buyer's receipt   ☐ Seller's compliance

3.6   Certificates for

☐ Well Water   ☐ Septic System

☐ Buyer's approval   ☐ Seller's compliance

3.7   Tax withholding disclosures. [See **ft** Forms 301 and 301-1]

☐ Seller's compliance   ☐ State   ☐ Federal   ☐ Escrow's Receipt

3.8   Homeowners' association (HOA) documentation: articles, by-laws, CC&Rs, current and approved/additional assessments and unpaid assessments, fines, charges on Seller, unenforceable age restrictions, notice of Owner's violation, list and status of property defects, operating budget, operating rules, CPA's financial statements, insurance policy summary, notice of litigation, and collection and lien enforcement policies.

☐ Buyer's receipt   ☐ Seller's compliance

3.9   Financial Disclosure Statement — For Entering into a Seller Carryback Note. [See **ft** Form 300]

☐ Buyer's receipt   ☐ Seller's receipt

☐ Buyer's Broker acknowledgment   ☐ Listing Broker acknowledgment

3.10   Estimated closing statement — approved prior to closing. [See **ft** Form 402]

☐ Buyer's approval   ☐ Seller's approval

3.11 Ordinance Compliance — Local Option Disclosure: city occupancy report, water conservation, retrofit. [See **ft** Form 307]

☐ Buyer's receipt   ☐ Seller's compliance

☐ Buyer's Broker acknowledgment   ☐ Listing Broker acknowledgement

3.12 Property operating data. [See **ft** Form 352]

☐ Buyer's receipt   ☐ Seller's compliance

4. SELLER COMPLIANCE:

4.1 ☐ Termite report and clearance

4.2 ☐ Water heater strapping/bracing installed

4.3 ☐ Smoke detector installed/operative

4.4 ☐ Home warranty policy

insurer _____

coverage _____

4.5 ☐ Payoff demand

☐ Seller's approval [See **ft** Form 429-2]

4.6 ☐ Beneficiary Statement approval by Buyer [See **ft** Form 429]

4.7 ☐ Bill of sale on personal property sold [See **ft** Form 434]

4.8 Holdover Occupancy Agreement [See **ft** Form 272]

☐ Buyer's receipt   ☐ Seller's receipt

4.9 ☐ Release of Recorded Instrument [See **ft** Form 409]

4.10 ☐ _____

_____

5. BUYER COMPLIANCE:

5.1 ☐ Preliminary title report approval   ☐ Buyer's receipt

5.2 New financing approval.

☐ Buyer's receipt   ☐ Seller's receipt

5.3 Interim Occupancy Agreement (pre-closing occupancy). [See **ft** Form 271]

☐ Buyer's compliance   ☐ Seller's compliance

5.4 Submission of credit application for carryback note. [See **ft** Form 302]

☐ Seller approval   ☐ Buyer's compliance

5.5 ☐ Beneficiary statement on loan takeover or assumption

☐ Buyer's approval

5.6 ☐ Fire/hazard insurance agent_____

☐ Carryback Seller as loss payee

5.7 ☐ Appraisal of property's fair market value

☐ Buyer's approval

5.8 ☐ Home inspector's report [See **ft** Form 269]

☐ Buyer's approval

5.9 ☐ Final pre-closing walk-through inspection [See **ft** Form 270]

☐ Buyer's approval   ☐ Seller's compliance

5.10 ☐ _____

_____

6. PRO RATES, ADJUSTMENTS AND MISC. INSTRUCTIONS:

6.1 Impound account on loan takeover to be:

☐ Charged to Buyer and credited to Seller.

☐ Transferred without adjustments.

6.2 Pro rates and credits from ☐ date of closing, or☐ other date _____:

☐ Property taxes and Mello-Roos type bonds   ☐ Rents/Security deposits

☐ Balance/Interest on loan takeover   ☐ Association assessments

6.3 ☐ _____

_____

7. TITLE POLICY:

7.1   Seller's vesting _____

7.2   Buyer's vesting _____

Taking title as:
- ☐ Joint tenants
- ☐ Separate property

☐ Community property with right of survivorship
☐ Community property   ☐ Tenants in common
☐ An individual   ☐ An unmarried person

7.3   Title company _____

7.4   Title policy _____

- ☐ ALTA
- ☐ ALTA-R
- ☐ Joint protection

☐ CLTA
☐ Homeowners(s) (one-to-four units)
☐ Lenders

☐ Abstract
☐ Binder
☐ Owners (other than on-to-four units)

Premium to be paid by _____

7.5   Other title conditions _____

_____

_____

8. BROKERAGE FEES: ☐ in mutual instructions   ☐ in supplemental Seller instructions

$_____ to _____ paid by _____

$_____ to _____ paid by _____

Agent: _____ Date:_____, 20_____

FORM 403   01-08   ©2008 **first tuesday**, P.O. BOX 20069, RIVERSIDE, CA 92516 (800) 794-0494

In modern real estate practice, **opening escrow** simply means establishing a depository for the deed, the money and other items, collectively called *instruments*. These deposits accompany instructions signed by all necessary parties authorizing escrow to transfer or hand those items to particular parties or others on closing.

Before accepting any instruments as an escrow holder for a transaction, the escrow officer will need to be informed, i.e., *instructions dictated*, by an agent of one of the parties (or a party himself) regarding precisely when and under what circumstances the documents and monies deposited with escrow are to change hands. Escrow then prepares (drafts) instructions that are signed by the principals to the escrow transaction to authorize escrow to accept and deliver the deposited instruments.

Any number of details (preparation, receipt and transfer of monies and documents) must be attended to by the escrow holder before the trans-

action can be completed, called a *closing or settlement*.

As a checklist for "going to escrow," a worksheet helps to organize the collection of facts, data and supporting papers the escrow officer will need to prepare instructions and clear the conditions to be met to close escrow. [See Form 403 accompanying this chapter]

The documents work together

Modern real estate sales transactions depend on both the purchase agreement and the escrow instructions working in tandem to close a transaction.

Both the purchase agreement and the escrow instructions are *contracts* regarding interests in real estate. To be enforceable under the Statute of Frauds, both documents must be **in writing**. [Calif. Civil Code §1624; Calif. Code of Civil Procedure §1971]

A purchase agreement sets forth the sales price and terms of payment, together with conditions to be met before closing.

Escrow instructions constitute an additional agreement between the EP investor and seller-in-foreclosure that includes an escrow company. Instructions do not replace the purchase agreement, but are merely directives with which an escrow agrees to comply to carry out the terms of the purchase agreement by coordinating a closing on behalf of both the EP investor and the seller-in-foreclosure.

However, escrow instructions occasionally add exactness and completeness that provide the enforceability sometimes lacking in purchase agreements prepared by brokers or their agents, usually the failure of a signed and delivered acceptance.

The purchase agreement is the primary underlying document in a real estate sales transaction and is considered the original contract. All further agreements, including the escrow instructions, must comply with the primary document, unless **intended to modify** the original agreement.

When agents negotiate a transaction, they and their brokers are responsible for ensuring the escrow instructions, whether prepared or dictated by themselves or others, conform to the purchase agreement.

To provide for a smoother, timely closing, the person dictating instructions needs to collect and hand escrow, at his earliest opportunity, all of the information the escrow officer needs to prepare the instructions and documents. The person dictating instructions should use a **checklist** to mark off the items and information escrow might need to process and close the transaction.

The escrow officer will prepare the instructions from information provided to the officer. These activities of dictating, reviewing and conforming instructions to the purchase agreement become the responsibility of the investor and seller-in-foreclosure when no agent is involved.

Of note, an escrow officer does not have an obligation to notify the parties of any suspicious fact or circumstance detected by the officer before close of escrow, unless the fact **affects closing**. However, as is the policy of many an escrow officer selected by the agent (or investor) to handle the closing, the officer will alert the agent (or investor) to potential problems that lie outside the escrow instructions that have been brought to the attention or observed by the escrow officer. [**Lee** v. **Title Insurance and Trust Company** (1968) 264 CA2d 160]

To avoid confusion when dictating instructions, the broker must consider the type of transaction (sale, exchange, loan or lease) that is being escrowed, the dates scheduled for the elimination of any contingencies the escrow officer must await before taking further steps, and the date scheduled for close of escrow.

If the escrow instructions drafted and signed are vague or incomplete on any point, the underlying purchase agreement must be reviewed by the agents and the parties before dictating amended or supplemental instructions. The **terms of the purchase agreement supersede** any inconsistencies between the purchase agreement and the escrow instructions, unless a modification of the original purchase agreement is intended and so stated in the instructions.

If the point in dispute is not addressed in the purchase agreement, then it is not part of the contract and must, if agreeable, be added to the escrow instructions by amendment.

Naturally, amended instructions adding terms that are new or modifications of provisions in the purchase agreement should note they modify the purchase agreement.

Escrow instructions that **modify** the intentions stated or implied in the purchase agreement must be **written, signed and returned** to escrow by both parties. Proposed modifications signed by some but not all parties are **not binding on a party** who has not agreed to them.

ESCROW INSTRUCTIONS
Buyer and Seller Instructions

Items left blank or unchecked are not applicable.

Escrow number _____ Dated _____, 20 _____

Escrow/Brokerage company _____

Licensed by the Department of _____, State of California, license # _____

Escrow officer _____

Address _____

_____

Phone number _____ Fax _____

Buyer _____

Seller _____

TERMS OF SALE: (for escrow use only)

$_____ TOTAL Consideration Seller to receive from Buyer

$_____ Assessment Bond paid with property taxes

$_____ 1st Trust Deed of Record

$_____ 2nd Trust Deed of Record

$_____ Trust Deed to record

$_____ Trust Deed to record

$_____ Cash through Escrow

$_____ Other Consideration_____

1. **You, the escrow officer, are authorized and instructed as follows:**

   1.1 Buyer deposits herewith the sum of $_____.

   1.2 On or before _____, 20_____, the date set for closing, Buyer will deposit with You on your request the additional sum of $_____, to make a total deposit of $_____.

   1.3 Buyer will deliver to You prior to the date set for closing any additional funds and instruments required which You request.

   1.4 You may thereafter use these funds and instruments until such time as You have received written instruction not to do so. Brokers are authorized to extend any performance date up to one month.

   1.5 Close of escrow is the date instruments are recorded.

2. Upon the use of these funds and instruments, You are to obtain the following policy of title insurance, with the usual title company exceptions, in the following checked type and form:

   Title to be vested in Buyer or Assignee free of encumbrances other than those set forth herein. Buyer's interest in title to be insured under a policy issued by_____
   as a(n) ☐ Homeowner(s) policy (one-to-four units), ☐ Residential ALTA-R policy (vacant or improved residential parcel), ☐ Owner's policy (other than one-to-four units), ☐ Joint Protection policy (also naming the Carryback Seller or Purchase-assist Lender), or ☐ Binder (to insure resale or refinance within two years).
   Endorsements _____

   _____

   2.1 With title insurance in the amount of $_____ covering the following described real property, commonly known as _____
   and legally described as _____

   _____

   _____

   _____

   _____,

   2.2 Showing title vested in _____

   2.3 Subject to the following only:

   a. All General and Special taxes for the _____ fiscal year, including any special district taxes or personal property taxes collected with the ad valorem taxes.

   b. Assessments and Bonds with an unpaid balance of $_____.

   c. Any covenants, conditions, restrictions, reservations, rights, right of ways and easements of record, or in deed to record, and EXCEPTIONS of water, minerals, oil, gas, and kindred substances, on or under said real property, now of record, or in deed to record.

   d. First encumbrance now of record with an unpaid balance of $_____, payable $_____ monthly, including interest of _____% per annum. ☐ ARM

   e. Second encumbrance now of record with an unpaid balance of $_____, payable $_____ monthly, including interest of _____% per annum, all due and payable _____, 20_____.

   f. Deed of Trust to record in the amount of $_____.
Execution of loan documents under §2.3f or §2.3g shall be Buyer's approval of their terms. Should Seller carry back under §2.3h, You are to obtain Seller's written approval of the loan terms for any Deed of Trust to record.

   g. Deed of Trust to record in the amount of $_____.

   h. Purchase money Deed of Trust with Assignment of Rents on standard form, executed by Buyer securing a note for $_____ in favor of Seller as their interests appear on the preliminary title report, with interest at _____% per annum from close of escrow, principal and interest payable in installments of $_____, or more, each on the same day of every calendar month, beginning one month from ☐ close of escrow, or ☐ _____, 20_____, and continuing until _____.

You, as escrow holder, are instructed to prepare the note and Deed of Trust and insert the correct principal amount and correct first payment date, interest accrual date and due date as soon as they can be determined. The address for deliver of note payments is _____
_____.

3. You are to obtain at Seller's expense beneficiary statements on the Deed(s) of Trust (or mortgage) now of record (§2.3d and §2.3e above). If the principal balances shown by the statements are more or less than the amount shown above, You are to make adjustments as checked below:

   ☐ cash through escrow, ☐ total consideration, or ☐ purchase-money Deed of Trust.

   3.1 You are to deliver to Buyer for Buyer's approval prior to close of escrow a copy of the beneficiary statement for each Deed of Trust to remain of record on closing.

   3.2 You are to deliver to Seller prior to close of escrow, any payoff demand necessary to eliminate encumbrances so You can comply with conditions in §2.3 for title insurance.

4. You are to obtain at Seller's expense a UCC-3 clearance on the following described personal property
_____
_____
_____

and cause title thereto to be vested in Buyer subject to the following UCC-1 financing statements:

   a. A UCC-1 obligation in the approximate amount of $_____, payable $_____ per month, including an annual percentage rate of _____%, all due and payable _____, 20_____.

   b A UCC-1 form in favor of Seller at Buyer's expense as additional security for any note carried back under §2.3h above.

5. Prior to close of escrow, Buyer is to hand You a sufficient hazard insurance policy. In the event Seller carries back under §2.3h above, then Seller is to be named as additional loss payee. The policy is to be in an amount sufficient to cover all lien balances or the coverage demanded by the new lender if greater in amount.

6. ☐ Prior to the close of escrow and at Seller's expense, Seller to hand You a structural pest control clearance on the subject property.

7. ☐ Prior to close of escrow and at Seller's expense, You are to obtain a one-year policy of homeowner's warranty issued by _____, in favor of Buyer, covering _____.

8. Prior to the close of escrow and at Seller's expense, You are to obtain from the homeowners' association (HOA) of any common interest development which includes the described property the following checked item(s) for Buyer's approval:

   8.1 ☐ A statement of condition of assessments;

   8.2 ☐ Copies of the association's articles, bylaws, CC&Rs, collection and lien enforcement policies, operating budget, operating rules, CPA's financial review, insurance policy summary and any age restriction statement;

   8.3 ☐ Copies from the association of any notice to Seller of CC&R violations, any list of construction defects, and any assessment charges not yet payable.

9. ☐ You are authorized and instructed to prepare assignments for all existing lease/rental agreements.

10. The following checked prorations and adjustments shall be computed by You on a monthly basis of 30 days as of ☐ close of escrow, or ☐ _____, 20_____, on which date Buyer is to be treated as the owner for the entire day:

    a. ☐ Taxes, based on latest tax statement available and Seller warrants that no reassessment or reassessment activity has since occurred

    b. ☐ Hazard (fire) insurance premium

    c. ☐ Interest on existing note(s) and Deed(s) of Trust

    d. ☐ Rents and deposits based on rental statement handed to You and approved by Buyer and Seller prior to close of escrow

    e. ☐ Impounds, under §2.3d or §2.3e above, together with an assignment of these impounds to Buyer through escrow

    f. ☐ Association assessments for any common interest development which includes the property

    g. ☐ _____

  10.1 You are to account for the above prorations and adjustments into the item checked below:
    ☐ cash through escrow, ☐ total consideration, or ☐ purchase-money Deed of Trust.

11. You are to promptly obtain and hand Buyer a preliminary title report on the property from title company for Buyer's approval or disapproval and cancellation of this transaction within _____ days of receipt by Buyer or Buyer's Broker of the report.

12. The Grant Deed to state the tax statements are to be mailed to _____
_____
  at _____.

13. Escrow is herewith handed a purchase agreement dated _____, 20_____ and (a) counteroffer(s) dated _____, 20_____ and _____, 20_____, entered into by Buyer and Seller regarding the sale of the property which authorizes and instructs escrow to act on the provisions of the agreement as mutual escrow instructions to close this transaction.

  13.1 Any inconsistencies between the provisions in the purchase agreement and provisions in the instructions prepared by escrow shall be controlled by the instructions prepared by escrow.

14. The close of escrow and disbursement of funds can be affected based on the form of the deposit with escrow. Funds deposited in cash or by electronic payment allow for closing and disbursement on or after the business day of deposit with the escrow's financial institution. Funds deposited by cashier's check allow for closing and disbursement on or after two business days after deposit with the escrow's financial institution. All other forms of deposit cannot be disbursed and thus, the closing cannot occur until the funds are made available to escrow by the escrow's financial institution.

15. Buyer is required to withhold 10% of each Seller's share of the sales price for payment of Seller's federal income taxes on this transaction, unless Seller meets one of the following conditions:

  15.1 Each Seller provides Buyer with their taxpayer identification number and declares under penalty of perjury to be a citizen of the United States or a resident alien [ft Form 301];

  15.2 Buyer declares under penalty of perjury the property will be used as their residence and the sales price is $300,000 or less [ft Form 301]; or

  15.3 Seller requests and obtains a withholding certificate from the Internal Revenue Service (IRS) authorizing a reduced amount or no amount be withheld.

16. Buyer is required to withhold $3\frac{1}{3}$% of each Seller's share of the sales price for payment of Seller's California income taxes on this transaction, unless one of the following exemptions exists:

  16.1 Seller executes a real estate withholding certificate, FTB form 593-C, declaring the sale is exempt due to:

    a. The property sold is or was last used as Seller's principal residence;

    b. The property sold was the decedent's principal residence;

    c. The property was sold as part of an IRC §1031 exchange;

    d. The property was taken by involuntary conversion and will be replaced under IRC §1033; or

    e. The property was sold at a taxable loss.

  16.2 Buyer is also exempt from withholding $3\frac{1}{3}$% of Seller's share of the sales price if:

    a. The property was sold for less than $100,000;

    b. Buyer is acquiring the property by a deed-in-lieu of foreclosure; or

    c. Seller is a bank acting as a trustee under an agreement other than a Deed of Trust.

16.3 On an installment sale, Buyer may agree to withhold on each payment on the carryback note and thus defer withholding. [FTB Forms 593-I and 597]

17. In the event You become involved in litigation between Buyer and Seller arising out of this transaction, Buyer and Seller shall pay a reasonable fee for attorney services which You may be required to incur.

18. You are authorized to use Seller's instruments when You hold and can deliver to Seller the money and instruments to be delivered to Seller under these instructions.

18.1 You are authorized to pay and charge Seller for the following checked item(s):

a. ☐ Bonds, assessments, taxes and other liens of record to show title as called for.

b. ☐ Documentary transfer taxes as required.

c. ☐ Brokerage fees: $_____ to _____
   $_____ to _____
   $_____ to _____

d. ☐ Transaction coordinator's fees:
   $_____ to _____
   $_____ to _____

e. ☐ Title insurance premium on the policy to be issued to Buyer.

f. ☐ Costs of recording Seller's Grant Deed.

g. ☐ Escrow fees for your services and any charges incurred by escrow on Seller's behalf.

h. ☐ Payables submitted to escrow for payment by Seller or Seller's Broker.

i. ☐ Attorney fees: $_____ to _____

j. ☐ _____

19. You are authorized to pay and charge Buyer for the following checked item(s):

a. ☐ Escrow fees for your services and any charges incurred by escrow on Buyer's behalf.

b. ☐ Costs of and lender's charges for recording or assuming any Deed of Trust, including a policy of title insurance for any new lender.

c. ☐ Attorney fees: $_____ to _____

d. ☐ Brokerage fees: $_____ to _____

e. ☐ Title insurance premium on the policy to be issued to Buyer.

f. ☐ _____

20. _____
_____
_____
_____
_____
_____
_____
_____

I hereby agree to perform all acts called for above to be performed by **Seller.**	I hereby agree to perform all acts called for above to be performed by **Buyer.**
Date:_____, 20_____	Date:_____, 20_____
Seller: _____	Buyer: _____
Seller: _____	Buyer: _____
Signature: _____	Signature: _____
Signature: _____	Signature: _____
Address: _____	Address: _____
_____	_____
Phone: _____	Phone: _____
Fax: _____	Fax: _____
Email:_____	Email:_____

FORM 401   02-05   ©2008 **first tuesday**, P.O. BOX 20069, RIVERSIDE, CA 92516 (800) 794-0494

If, before closing escrow, an agent discovers any aspect of the escrow instructions that is in conflict with the intentions expressed in the purchase agreement or the expectations of the EP investor or seller-in-foreclosure, the agent is duty-bound to immediately bring these discrepancies to the attention of the escrow officer and his client. On notification of an error in instructions or a need for clarification, the escrow officer must hold up the close of escrow until the discrepancy is clarified and corrective escrow instructions have been prepared, signed by the investor and seller, and returned to escrow. [**Diaz v. United California Bank** (1977) 71 CA3d 161]

Required escrow disclosures

All written escrow instructions signed by an EP investor and seller-in-foreclosure must contain a statement, in not less than 10-point type, setting forth the licensee's name and the name of the state agency issuing the license or granting the authority for the person conducting the escrow to operate.

In addition, all escrow transactions for the purchase of real estate where a **policy of title insurance** will not be issued to the buyer must include an **advisory notice**, prepared in a separate docu-

ment and signed by the buyer, regarding the need for title insurance. [CC §1057.6; see Form 401-1 accompanying this chapter]

Finally, escrow has a duty to advise the EP investor in writing of the Franchise Tax Board requirements for withholding 3 1/3% of the price paid the seller-in-foreclosure, unless the seller-in-foreclosure certifies he is exempt from state income tax withholding. [Calif. Revenue and Taxation Code §18662(e)(3)(B); FTB Form 593C]

Use of the escrow instructions

The sales escrow instructions, **first tuesday** Form 401, contains all the typical provisions expected in a set of instructions prepared by an independent escrow company for a California sales transaction.

The instructions may be used as an addendum to the purchase agreement for the sales transaction. Both the escrow instructions and the purchase agreement are to be prepared by the agent or EP investor and signed at the same time by each party. Thus, the need to dictate instructions to the escrow officer and wait for them to be prepared and submitted to the seller and investor for signatures is avoided. [See Form 401 accompanying this chapter]

Chapter 18

Assigning your purchase rights

This chapter analyzes the assignment of the investor's purchase rights held in a property to a substitute buyer, be it an investment group or a resale buyer on a flip.

Syndicating or flipping a property

An enterprising, but undercapitalized, equity purchase (EP) investor locates a residence in foreclosure he would like to buy. However, the investor is not financially able to buy, rehabilitate and carry the property by himself.

If he can make a deal with the owner, the investor will sell or exchange his purchase rights to, respectively:

- a user who will pay cash to acquire the investor's purchase rights and become a substitute buyer — an activity called *flipping*; or

- a group of cash investors, formed by the investor as an LLC to fund the purchase price and carrying costs of on-going ownership — called *syndication*. [See Chapter 19]

On his sale of the property to a buyer (other than his investment group), the investor will either:

- **assign** his contract right to purchase the real estate to a substitute buyer and escrow will close in the name of the substitute buyer; or

- **resell** the property by entering into a separate purchase agreement and escrow instructions with the resale buyer and close concurrent with the closing of the investor's purchase escrow with the seller, a process called *double escrowing*.

Contracting to control the property

As an individual, the investor contracts to control the residence by entering into an EP agreement with the seller-in-foreclosure. Escrow is opened after the seller's five-business-day cancellation period expires.

Prior to closing, the investor will assign his purchase rights either to his investment group or another person as the substitute buyer. That buyer will perform all the remaining obligation of the buyer and close escrow. Since the assignment affects all the closing documents to be prepared by escrow, the assignment and related instructions needed to close escrow are best handled in supplemental escrow instructions. [See Form 401-2 §2 accompanying this chapter]

On receiving the assignment instructions, escrow will prepare all closing documents in the name of the substitute buyer. To close the transaction in the name of the substitute buyer, the seller will need to **cooperate** by signing the supplemental escrow instructions and the deed naming the substitute buyer as the grantee.

Assignment provision and vesting

A buyer's contract rights under a purchase agreement (and escrow instructions) to acquire a property are initially presumed to be assignable, called a *rebuttable presumption*. Thus, assignability can be restricted by a provision in the purchase agreement or escrow and is barred if the assignee's performance of the purchase agreement will differ from any personal performance promised by the original buyer. [Calif. Civil Code §1457; **Masterson** v. **Sine** (1968) 68 C2d 222]

ASSIGNMENT OF PURCHASE RIGHTS
Supplemental Escrow Instructions

DATE:_____, 20_____, at_____, California.

Items left blank or unchecked are not applicable.

To: _____
           (Escrow holder)

_____
           (Address)

_____

1. This assignment, assumption and supplemental instructions pertain to
    1.1   your escrow number _____,
    1.2   entered into by _____, as the Seller,
          and _____, as the Buyer
    1.3   dated _____, 20_____, at _____, California,
    1.4   regarding real estate referred to as _____
          _____.

2. Buyer _____, as the Assignor,
    hereby assigns to _____, as the Assignee,
    all of Assignor's interest in the following:
    2.1   the property referenced above;
    2.2   the above referenced escrow and any funds deposited by Assignor in escrow; and
    2.3   An underlying agreement pertaining to Assignor's acquisition of the property entitled:
          ☐ Purchase agreement, ☐ Purchase option, ☐ Exchange agreement, ☐ _____,
          a.   dated _____, 20_____, at_____, California,
          b.   entered into by _____, as the _____,
               and _____, as the _____.

3. Assignor, as consideration for this assignment, is to receive the sum of _____.
    3.1   Consideration is to be delivered ☐ outside of escrow, or ☐ through this escrow on the occurrence of
          (enter condition for payment) _____
          _____.

4. Assignee hereby assumes and agrees to perform all obligations of Buyer acquiring the property under your
    instructions and the above referenced underlying agreement for the acquisition of the property.

5. Assignee acknowledges receipt of the following items:
    5.1   your escrow instructions consisting of (identify each separate instruction signed by Buyer): _____
          _____
          _____
          _____
          _____
          _____;

    5.2   the underlying acquisition agreement referenced above;
    5.3   property disclosures, delivered to Assignor by the owner of the property, consisting of (identify each by its
          name and date): _____
          _____
          _____
          _____
          _____;

    5.4   property disclosures prepared by Assignor or third parties for Assignor consisting of (identify each by its
          name and date): _____
          _____
          _____.

6. You are authorized and instructed to:

    6.1 Prepare a grant deed from _____ ,

          showing the grantee vesting as _____ .

    6.2 Other _____

          _____

          _____

          _____

I agree to the terms stated above.	**I agree to the terms stated above.**
Assignor's name: _____	Assignee's name: _____
Signature: _____	Signature: _____
Assignor's name: _____	Assignee's name: _____
Signature: _____	Signature: _____

7. Seller hereby releases the original buyer(s) from all obligation under the escrow instructions and underlying acquisition agreement.

8. Seller consents to this assignment and accepts Assignee as the substitute buyer in these instructions and underlying acquisition agreement.

I agree to the terms stated above.

Date: _____ , 20 _____

Seller's name: _____

Signature: _____

Seller's name: _____

Signature: _____

FORM 401-2   10-07   ©2008 **first tuesday**, P.O. BOX 20069, RIVERSIDE, CA 92516 (800) 794-0494

When the purchase agreement states the buyer's purchase rights are assignable, the assignability presumed is not rebutted and no limitation exists to require the original buyer to close escrow in his name without assignment.

To put the seller on notice of the investor's right to assign his purchase rights to a substitute buyer who will perform under the purchase agreement and close escrow, the vesting provisions in the purchase agreement call for the conveyance of title by the seller to be insured in the name of the *buyer or assignee*. [See Figure 1 accompanying this chapter]

All this assignment discussion is important since the seller needs to cooperate in an assignment. Having agreed in the purchase agreement that title may be vested alternatively in the name of a substitute buyer, by assignment, the seller must then cooperate in good faith to convey title to the substitute buyer by signing closing instructions so escrow can close in the name of the substitute buyer. [See **first tuesday** Form 156 §13.5]

Having entered into an agreement that impresses a duty on the seller to cooperate in an assignment, the investor then:

- seeks out a substitute buyer;

- negotiates the amount he is to be paid for his purchase rights; and

- enters into an agreement for the sale of his right to buy the property under the purchase agreement and escrow instructions with the seller.

The resale by assignment

An investor, by an **assignment**, transfers his purchase rights to the substitute buyer, called the *assignee*. [See Form 401-2 §2]

The substitute buyer agrees to fully perform all of the investor's obligations under the EP agreement and escrow instructions, called an *assumption* (of liability delegated to the substitute buyer by the assignment). [See Form 401-2 §3]

Documentation of the assignment is typically handled through escrow as supplemental escrow instructions. [See Form 401-2]

On the investor's assignment of his purchase rights, the substitute buyer "steps into" the investor's position as the buyer in escrow. Having been assigned all the purchase rights, the substitute buyer may enforce the EP agreement requiring the seller to close escrow by conveying the property to the substitute buyer. [**San Francisco Hotel Co.** v. **Baior** (1961) 189 CA2d 206]

Also, the substitute buyer, on accepting the assignment, assumes all of the investor's obligations under the EP agreement. On elimination of all contingencies and other rights to cancel, the substitute buyer must perform by paying the purchase price and closing escrow on the transaction. If not, he is liable to the seller for wrongfully failing to close escrow. [**Fanning** v. **Yoland Productions, Inc.** (1957) 150 CA2d 444; CC §1589]

The substitute buyer who fails to close escrow without legal excuse, a breach, is also liable to the investor under the assumption provisions in the assignment for losses caused by the breach. This investor may suffer money losses if the seller pursues the investor for money losses or specific performance on the breach, unless a release of liability or novation was entered into by the seller and the investor at the time of the assignment. [**Bank of America National Trust and Savings Association** v. **McLaughlin** (1957) 152 CA2d Supp. 911]

A separate resale by grant deed

An investor flipping a property may not want to disclose to a substitute buyer the purchase price the investor is paying for the property. Also, the seller might refuse (wrongfully) to cooperate and close escrow with a substitute buyer following the investor's assignment of his purchase rights for a quick profit (which the seller feels he should get).

Instead of **assigning** his purchase rights under the EP agreement and escrow instructions to a substitute buyer, the investor can simply **resell** the real estate. In some counties, the resale will be additionally taxed on recording the second grant deed, a tax the assignment avoids.

On the investor's resale of the property, the investor and his perspective buyer will enter into an entirely new purchase agreement and escrow instructions, separate from the investor's contract with the seller.

In the context of a resale, the investor undertakes the duties a seller owes a buyer to make all the **disclosures** required of a seller of real estate. The investor may use the disclosures he received from the owner, noting any additional or contrary information known to him.

A **separate escrow** will be opened for the resale that will be funded by the resale buyer.

The primary purchase escrow with the seller and the separate resale escrow with the buyer will close concurrently. The closing of the resale escrow should be contingent on the close of the primary purchase escrow. The investor's net sales proceeds from his resale escrow will be the source of the funds he will use to concurrently close his purchase escrow with the seller.

Through this legitimate double escrow process, two grant deeds will be concurrently recorded — one from the seller to the investor who, in turn, will further convey the property by grant deed to the resale buyer in this variety of a flip.

Only one title insurance policy will be issued, and one set of loan assumptions or loan origination documents will be completed — all in the name of the resale buyer.

The seller in an EP transaction has a two-year right of rescission when investor misconduct exists under the EP statutes. On an **assignment** of the investor's purchase rights, the seller-in-foreclosure retains his **rescission rights** against the substitute buyer since the right to rescind arose under the contract taken over by the substitute buyer.

However, if the investor conveys the real estate to a buyer in a separate *arms-length* resale, the buyer is a **bona fide purchaser (BFP)** exempt from the seller's two-year right of rescission under equity purchase law. [See Chapter 4]

Disclosures on a resale

The EP investor offering to sell a one-to-four unit residential property must make a full disclosure of the physical, operating and title conditions, as well as the natural and environmental hazards of the property. The substitute buyer on an assignment of the EP investor's right to buy the property receives copies of the purchase agreement, escrow instructions and disclosures received by the investor from his seller.

On agreeing to the assignment, the substitute buyer acknowledges receipt of the documents delivered to him by the investor. [See Form 401-2 §5]

Consider an owner of a one-to-four unit residential property who agrees to sell the property to an investor. The investor, acting as a dealer, intends to flip the property by selling and assigning his contract position in escrow or selling the property through a separately escrowed transaction. [See **first tuesday** Form 156 §13.5]

The owner hands the investor a condition of property disclosure statement (TDS). The TDS does not disclose night-time noise conditions known to the owner, but not the investor.

The investor locates a buyer prior to closing. The buyer is handed the owner's condition of property disclosure statement, along with all the property disclosures the investor has received.

On closing escrow and occupying the residence, the buyer discovers the undisclosed noise condition. Due to the noise, the price paid for the property exceeds its value, a loss suffered by the buyer.

The buyer makes a demand on the owner who prepared and signed the TDS for the loss, not the investor.

The buyer claims he is entitled to recover the loss from the prior owner since the owner intended by including an assignment provision in his purchase agreement with the investor that his TDS be relied on by a buyer other than the investor.

The owner claims he owed no duty and incurred no obligation to the investor's buyer since the owner did not contract to sell the property to the buyer, only to the investor.

However, the owner contracted with the investor without restricting the investor's right to assign the property. Thus the owner is liable for the buyer's lost value due to the owner's nondisclosure of the noise in the TDS. The owner knew or should have known the condition of property disclosure statement would be relied on by a buyer the investor located and who acquired the investor's purchase rights by an assignment or by grant deed. [**Shapiro** v. **Sutherland** (1998) 64 CA4th 1534]

Carryback transactions

Consider an EP agreement that calls for the seller-in-foreclosure to carry back a portion of his equity in a note and trust deed.

The agreement contains an assignment clause noting title will be vested in the buyer or "assignee."

Prior to the close of escrow, the investor assigns his right to purchase the real estate to a substitute buyer. However, the seller refuses to carry back a note and trust deed executed and paid by the substitute buyer.

Must the seller extend credit to the substitute buyer in the form of a carryback note and trust deed?

Not automatically! A principal-based standard of reasonableness guideline applies to any refusal of the seller to contract or cooperate with the investor's assignment of his purchase rights to a substitute buyer unless it has been agreed a due-on clause will be in the carryback trust deed. The seller may refuse to permit the substitute buyer to undertake the **personal obligation** of executing and performing on a carryback note and trust deed if the substitute buyer, unlike the EP investor, is not equally or more creditworthy or would mismanage the property under his ownership. [**Madison** v. **Moon** (1957) 148 CA2d 135]

The carryback seller may require the substitute buyer to meet the same standards of creditworthiness (performance on the note) and property maintenance (performance under the trust deed) required of the investor.

When a purchase agreement imposes obligations on the buyer to perform activities of a *non-personal nature* only, an assignment of acquisition rights can be enforced by the substitute buyer.

For example, when a purchase agreement provides for payment **in cash** in exchange for the seller's equity in the property, which may include a loan assumption or funding by a purchase-assist loan taken out by the investor, all rights under the EP agreement may be assigned and enforced by the substitute buyer without the seller's consent. [**King** v. **Stanley** (1948) 32 C2d 584]

Nor may a seller refuse to cooperate in the investor's assignment of his purchase rights to a warehousing agent so the investor can complete a reverse IRC §1031 transaction, which the IRS calls a *parking transaction*. The warehousing agent is not a substitute buyer, but a middleman who will merely hold title and deed the property on to the investor at a later date. [**Nicholson** v. **Barab** (1991) 233 CA3d 1671]

Release of liability

When obtaining the seller's consent on assigning the purchase rights and obligations under an EP agreement to a substitute buyer, the investor should also seek a release from the seller of the investor's obligations under the EP agreement and escrow instructions. [CC §1530; see Form 401-2 §§7 and 8]

A **release and substitution agreement** requires the seller to look solely to the substitute buyer for performance of the purchase agreement and escrow, an arrangement called a *novation*. [**Gates** v. **Quong** (1906) 3 CA 443]

To comply with escrow instructions after the assignment of the investor's purchase rights, escrow prepares all closing documents in the name of the substitute buyer. Closing documents include deeds, carryback notes and trust deeds, closing instructions and statements, approvals and assumptions of any existing loans, title insurance, and clearance of any other items necessary for escrow to close.

Chapter 19

Syndicating the equity purchase

This chapter applies the syndication process to the funding of an equity purchase (EP) transaction.

Blind pool funding and property selection

The purchase of an owner-occupied residence in foreclosure is typically negotiated in the space of hours and closed in the course of a few days — requiring the availability of purchase funds at the outset of negotiations.

Consider an individual who forms small investment groups to gather funds to buy property, called a *syndicator*. To control property, he contracts in his own name to buy an owner-occupied one-to-four unit residential property in foreclosure by entering into an equity purchase (EP) agreement with the owner, called a *seller-in-foreclosure*. [See **first tuesday** Form 156]

Escrow is opened on expiration of the seller's five-business-day cancellation period without the syndicator's receipt of a cancellation notice.

The syndicator will *assign* his rights under the purchase agreement to an investment group he will form as a limited liability company (LLC) before the close of the purchase escrow. [See Chapter 18; and **first tuesday** Form 370]

During the short escrow period, the syndicator will not have sufficient time to create an investment circular, prepare the LLC documents, locate investors and fund the acquisition of the investment.

Thus, the syndicator solicits contribution commitments or receives funds from investors before locating the real estate their funds will acquire, called a *blind pool investment program*. The syndicator is said to have been given a "blank check" by the investors to later locate, analyze and acquire suitable property.

Creating a securities risk

After the group members fund the LLC, the syndicator locates the property, negotiates the purchase terms, arranges financing, closes escrow, and rehabilitates and manages the property as a rental or for immediate resale.

The blind pool arrangement is thus a **corporate security**. Here, the investors hand over their capital to the syndicator before the investment property is selected, a *risk of loss* controlled by the securities law, not the economics of the real estate market. Thus, the investors rely entirely on the investment expertise of the syndicator to later select a suitable property of sufficient value and quality for the placement of their investment funds. [**Underhill** v. **Royal** (1985) 769 F2d 1426]

Having created a **security** in the form of a blind pool investment program, the syndicator wants to:

- avoid the creation of a *public offering* under the securities statutes; and

- *minimize the risk of loss* of the cash investment by subjecting himself to making a full disclosure of the investment when the property selected for investment is acquired. [See **first tuesday** Form 365]

A closely knit group

The **blind pool** syndicator avoids regulatory activity governing corporate securities by not offering the investment program to the public, called a *nonpublic* or *private offering exemption*.

To comply with the **nonpublic exemption** rules when forming a group investment, the program must:

- include no more than 35 members, a husband and wife being one member;

- all members must have a deep-rooted, **pre-existing** personal or business relationship with the syndicator, or be **sophisticated investors** with prior experience in similar investments;

- each member agrees he is purchasing his interest in the LLC for his own account and not for resale; and

- no member is solicited by *advertisement*. [Calif. Corporations Code §25102(f)]

The blind pool syndicator who fails to comply with all elements of the *private offering exemption* must qualify and obtain a securities permit from the Department of Corporation before accepting funds from members — no matter how the members are solicited. [**People** v. **Humphreys** (1970) 4 CA3d 693]

Assessable LLC interests

In an EP investment program, the property is generally intended to be held for immediate resale — but may be held as a rental for investment.

The members of the EP investment program do not expect to receive spendable income from rental operations during the period of ownership prior to flipping it to another buyer. Specifically, the members expect a **negative cash flow** situation until the property acquired is resold.

Also, an EP investment program may incur unforeseen rehabilitation expenses or carrying costs beyond those anticipated by the syndicator, exhausting the reserve fund initially established for ongoing LLC ownership and operating expenses.

To protect the solvency of the program, an **additional contributions** provision is included in the LLC operating agreement. The additional contributions provision enables the syndicator to periodically request additional capital contributions from the members should the EP investment program face a deficit cash flow during the ownership of the property.

Figure 1   *Excerpt from first tuesday Form 372-2 — Operating Agreement*
(Equity Purchase Transaction)

2.1   Capital Contributions: The Limited Liability Company's capital shall be: ($_____) as set forth in Exhibit "A".

    a.   Use of Contributions and Dissolution: The LLC will be funded prior to the selection and purchase of the property. Should the LLC be unsuccessful in acquiring property, the Manager may refund the capital contributed, less any expenditures made by the LLC toward the unsuccessful acquisition of property.

    b.   Additional Contributions: Additional contributions in the aggregate sum not to exceed $_____ may be required from time to time of the Class "A" member(s) on thirty (30) days' written notice from the Manager. If a member does not deliver up his share of the additional contribution within thirty (30) days of receipt of the notice, the Manager may elect to terminate the member under Section 6 of this agreement.

Use of the additional contributions provision

The EP syndicator exercises the additional contributions provision by giving written notice to the members of the amount of funds each member is to additionally contribute to cover deficits in cash flow and reserves. The members must choose to either comply with the request or face the agreed-to termination or participation limitations for failure to meet the call. [See Figure 1 accompanying this chapter]

Thus, the sanctions encourage members to make additional contributions to keep the LLC solvent.

The members have the option of rejecting the contribution request and accepting the sanctions as a consequence. The EP syndicator will not be able to force the non-contributing members to advance the additional contributions.

Each member must make a sober business decision — whether to subject his interest to termination or limitations, or to invest more to protect his original investment, sometimes considered a "good-money-after-bad-money" analysis.

But the dilemma, while troublesome, does not affect the member's limited liability status.

The additional contributions provision, triggered by the EP syndicator's call for funds, is not a promise to pay. The member has already contributed the amount required to become a member. Each member now has a choice to make:

- either increase the amount of his original contribution to the LLC; or

- risk the buy-out consequences or limitations for refusing to meet the call.

Thus, a member does not breach the LLC operating agreement by failing to come up with the additional money — he simply exercises his **option** not to make **future contributions** as agreed in the operating agreement. [See Figure 1]

Provisions for EP syndication

The EP syndicator will include provisions in the LLC *operating agreement* and disclosures in his *investment circular* (marketing package) regarding the existence and risks of the blind pool funding.

The equity purchase provisions are designed for use in California. However, no two sets of syndication circumstances are identical. The formulas and arrangements members contract for must, by necessity, vary from transaction to transaction.

Therefore, **legal counsel** is recommended to advise on the necessary adjustments to provisions to conform to the specific facts of each EP syndicator's program, and to lend experience developed by advising others on syndication programs. The operating agreement accompanying this chapter is intended for use as a basis for seeking further advice from the reader's legal counsel.

Chapter 20

Beneficiary statements and payoff demands

This chapter addresses requests made on the holder of a trust deed for a report on the current status of the secured debt or a payoff demand for reconveyance of the trust deed.

Confirming loan conditions

A *beneficiary statement* is a written disclosure made by a lender or other creditor regarding the condition of a debt owed them, usually evidenced by a note, that is secured by a trust deed lien on real estate. [See **first tueday** Form 429]

A complete **beneficiary statement** includes information and data regarding:

- the amount of the unpaid balance;

- the interest rate of the loan;

- the total of all overdue payments of principal and/or interest;

- the amounts of any periodic payments;

- the date the loan is due;

- the date to which real estate taxes and special assessments have been paid, if known;

- the amount of hazard insurance and its term and premium, if known;

- any impound balance reserve for the payment of taxes and insurance;

- the amount of any additional charges incurred by the beneficiary that have become part of the trust deed lien; and

- whether the trust deed debt can be transferred to a new owner. [Calif. Civil Code §2943(a)(2)]

On adjustable rate mortgage (ARM) notes, the beneficiary statement must list the **note rate** as variable, and reference and attach a copy of the note containing the interest rate formula.

Formulas for ARM adjustments and payment options vary extensively from note to note. Thus, the seller or buyer relying on the beneficiary statement for an ARM needs greater detail than the current interest rate and payment amount. Thus, the lender must **attach a copy** of the note to the beneficiary statement for full disclosure.

Time period for a response to request

Any *entitled person* may request, in writing, a beneficiary statement.

An **entitled person** includes:

- the *original borrower* on the note and trust deed;

- the *successor-in-interest* (new owner) to the original borrower; or

- an *authorized agent* of either, such as a real estate broker, attorney or escrow agent. [CC §2943(a)(4)]

The lender must, within 21 days of the receipt of the written request by an entitled person, prepare and deliver a beneficiary statement. [CC §§2943(b)(1), 2943(e)(6)]

Intentional failure without legal excuse to send the statement within 21 days of receipt of request results in a $300 forfeiture by the lender to the person making the request. Also, the lender is liable for all damages resulting from its intentional failure to comply. [CC §2943(e)(4)]

However, the lender's failure to timely deliver the statement must be proven to be an intentional failure, a difficult task.

*Editor's note — Previously, mere administrative failure to send the beneficiary statement within the 21-day period resulted in an automatic forfeiture of $300 by the lender. [**Anderson v. Heart Federal Savings** (1989) 208 CA3d 202]*

The request for a beneficiary statement may be made by an **entitled person** the publication of the notice of trustee's sale. [CC §§2943(b)(2), 2943(c)]

The lender may charge no more than $30 for each beneficiary statement, with the exception of loans insured by the Federal Housing Administration (FHA) or the Veterans Administration (VA). Occasionally, the trust deed states a lesser amount that controls the beneficiary statement charge. [CC §2943(e)(6)]

Payoff demand

A *payoff demand statement* is a written demand, made by a lender, for the total dollar amount required on the date of preparation to pay off the loan as a requisite for recording a reconveyance of the property from the trust deed lien.

The **payoff demand statement** includes information and formulas to calculate the total payoff amount due after the date the demand is issued to account for and pay interest accruing on a per diem basis up to the date paid. The statement is valid for up to 30 days unless the loan terms change, such as may occur on loans with adjustable interest and payments. [CC §2943(a)(5)]

The payoff demand, as with the beneficiary statement, is required to be delivered within **21 days of receipt** of a written request from an entitled person. Additionally, and similar to the beneficiary statement, the charge for the service of preparing and delivering a payoff demand is limited to $30, unless the loan is insured by the FHA or VA. [CC §§2943(c), 2943(e)(6)]

As with the beneficiary statement, the lender's intentional failure, without legal excuse, to

timely reply results in the forfeiture of $300 and liability for any resulting money damages. [CC §2943(e)(4)]

The request for a statement

Unless an entitled person, such as an owner-in-foreclosure, **specifically requests** a beneficiary statement, a lender only needs to send a payoff demand statement. [CC §2943(e)(1)]

The request for either statement must be in writing and sent to the lender at the address given in the payment notice or payment book. [CC §2943(e)(5)]

Before delivering the beneficiary statement or payoff demand, the lender may require proof the request is being made by an entitled person, such as evidence of ownership or authority as an agent of the owner. The written request by escrow should be accompanied by the escrow's written authorization from the owner to order out a beneficiary statement. [CC §2943(e)(3)]

If a request for either a beneficiary statement or a payoff demand includes a request for a copy of the trust deed, the lender must supply a copy of the document at no extra charge. [CC §2943(e)(2)]

The statutory scheme for beneficiary statements does not require that a payoff demand include delivery of a copy of the note.

The lender may issue either the beneficiary statement or the payoff demand statement to demand the amounts necessary to pay a loan in full. [CC §2943(d)(1)]

Any **oral amendment** to either statement given by the lender must be followed up by delivery of a written amendment by the next business day. [CC §2943(d)(2)]

In addition to a beneficiary statement or a payoff demand, amended statements can also be relied on to establish payoff amounts. [CC §2943(d)(1)]

An erroneous statement or demand

Any error in the statements from a lender regarding the amount owed on a loan becomes an *unsecured obligation* of the **original borrower** after the close of escrow or completion of the trustee's sale. If the lender amends its loan statement prior to the close of escrow or the trustee's sale, the amount listed in the amended statement is valid and replaces the original amount. [CC §§2943(d)(3)(A), 2943(d)(3)(B)]

For example, an owner funds the payoff of a trust deed note by obtaining refinancing from a new lender. The payoff demand for the existing trust deed note erroneously understates the amount due. The new lender funds the amount stated in the payoff demand and the existing trust deed is reconveyed.

Later, the paid-off lender realizes the mistake in the amount of the payoff and seeks to recover the underpayment from the new lender. The paid-off lender claims the new lender is liable for the unpaid amount since it funded the payoff.

The new lender claims the real estate owner who signed the note is liable for the unpaid amount since the statutory beneficiary's payoff scheme only allows the lender to recover amounts remaining unpaid on reconveyance from the borrower obligated on the note.

Here, the lender issuing an erroneous payoff demand can only recover amounts remaining unpaid from the **original borrower**. The named borrower on the note is the sole source of recovery for amounts understated in the payoff demand. [**Freedom Financial Thrift & Loan** v. **Golden Pacific Bank** (1993) 20 CA4th 1305]

Nonrecourse debt payoff errors

A lender who makes a purchase-assist loan to a buyer of a one-to-four unit residential property he will occupy as his principal residence is barred from obtaining a money judgment for any deficiency in the value of the property to fully payoff the loan on a foreclosure. These loans are **nonrecourse loans**, called *purchase-money obligations*.

Likewise, carryback notes secured only by the property sold are nonrecourse *purchase-money* paper. Further, those who hold a purchase-money note by assignment are also barred from obtaining a deficiency judgment.

The carryback seller or lender who makes a mistake in the amount of a payoff demand or beneficiary statement issued on a nonrecourse note, is limited in its recovery to the value of the property at the time of the erroneous payoff demand.

Initially, the amount of the error becomes an unsecured purchase-money obligation of the original borrower, but the amount remains a **nonrecourse debt**. The character of the remaining unpaid debt did not change; it only became unsecured. [CC §2943(d)(3)]

Thus, the lender or carryback seller on a nonrecourse debt is limited in his recovery of the error to the difference between the amount received and the value of the property at the time of the initial payoff. [**Ghirardo** v. **Antonioli** (1996) 14 C4th 39]

Recourse debtor payoff error

The amount of an error made in a beneficiary statement or payoff demand for a **recourse debt** also becomes an unsecured obligation. However, recovery on a recourse loan is not limited to the value of the property on the date of the payoff as is the case for a nonrecourse debt. [Calif. Code of Civil Procedure §726(b)]

A lender who demands and is paid an erroneous amount on payoff of a **recourse loan** can proceed directly to a money judgment for the uncollected amount, regardless of the value of the security.

Thus, sellers of property encumbered by a recourse loan expose themselves to a continuing liability for trust deed debts they owed as original or assuming borrowers after the property is sold subject to the existing trust deed lien.

A seller originating a recourse loan is considered a *guarantor*, secondarily liable for payment of the loan if the buyer fails to pay, unless the assumption of the loan by the buyer included a significant modification in its terms to which the seller was not a party. [**Braun** v. **Crew** (1920) 183 C 728]

When the buyer later resells the property acquired from the seller by an assumption of a loan, and a mistake is made by the lender in a payoff demand or beneficiary statement on the resale resulting in an underpayment to the lender, then the **seller** who originally borrowed the funds is a guarantor of payments on the original note and is liable for the error.

Thus, a seller who originated or assumed a loan that his buyer is now assuming may feel compelled to condition the closing of the sale on a **release of liability** from the lender, called a *novation*.

The release of liability eliminates the seller's risk of "original borrower liability" for a potential future error by the lender in payoff demands or beneficiary statements. [CC §1531]

In a **novation**, as with an assumption, the buyer promises to perform the duties of the original borrower. In addition, the lender agreeing to the novation releases the seller from all liability for the debt. [See Chapter 16]

Chapter 21

Equity purchase sale-leaseback

This chapter digests the legal and tax consequences that arise due to the recharacterization of a sale-leaseback arrangement as a loan when the leaseback is coupled with a repurchase option.

A mortgage or tenancy on breach?

A homeowner defaults on loan payments secured by a trust deed on his home. The lender begins foreclosure proceedings by recording a Notice of Default (NOD).

The NOD recording is picked up by a foreclosure reporting service. The service's subscribers are then advised of the NOD. An equity purchase (EP) investor tracking NOD recordings contacts the homeowner, intending to investigate the property and submit a purchase offer.

An offer to purchase the residence is prepared and submitted to the homeowner on an EP agreement form as mandated by state law.

However, the homeowner advises the EP investor he really wants to retain possession of the residence and **buy back** the ownership when his finances pick up.

As an alternative to the EP investor's offer, the homeowner proposes a **sale/lease-option** arrangement in which:

- the investor acquires title to the property by investing only the funds needed by the owner to cure the delinquent loan payments and property taxes, and pay the annual property insurance premium and foreclosure costs;

- the seller-in-foreclosure would remain in possession under a lease with sufficient rental payments to cover the investor's costs of ownership; and

- the owner would be given an option to repurchase the residence by repaying the investor with a profit.

The EP investor refuses to go along with the owner's leaseback and option proposal. The investor claims the sale/lease-option proposal would:

- transform the investor's intended purchase into a loan transaction; and

- deprive the investor of the investment and tax benefits of owning real estate.

As a result, the investor and the owner reach a compromise, and enter into an EP agreement that provides the owner with a six-month holdover tenancy — no repurchase option included.

Has the EP investor correctly represented the legal and tax consequences of a repurchase option on a sale-leaseback as a mortgage-in-fact?

Yes! A sale-leaseback and purchase option arrangement is a *mortgage*. Thus, the EP investor has made a loan, not a purchase of the property. When an owner occupying a one-to-four unit residential property as his principal residence conveys title in exchange for retaining possession and receiving an **option to repurchase** the property and funds to cue delinquencies, a loan has been negotiated, not a sale.

The financial arrangement of the lease-option sale contains a yield (interest and principal paid as rent) and a due date (final/balloon payment of principal on exercise of option) as a condition for returning (reconveying) title. Thus, the investor becomes a lender holding title as security for repayment, not a buyer receiving the possessory rights and economic risks and benefits of an owner. [Calif. Civil Code §1695.12]

As a lender, the EP investor is not able to take depreciation or other **tax benefits** available to an owner of rental property. [**Haggard** v. **Commissioner** (9th Cir. 1956) 241 F2d 288]

An investor who receives title and concurrently gives the owner a lease coupled with an option to repurchase the property does not own the property since the grant deed conveys title as security for repayment, a *mortgage-in-fact*. Thus, the investor under a reverse lease-option, given to an owner-in-foreclosure on conveying title, must later obtain written permission from the owner before the investor may:

- encumber the property; or

- grant any interest in the property to another person. [CC §1695.6(e)]

Should the owner default on the lease, an eviction would leave the investor with title and no legal right to convey the property without the owner's approval.

Equity loan during foreclosure

Consider a seller-in-foreclosure who asks a friend to make him a loan.

The friend advances all funds necessary to cure the default under the trust deed and take the property out of foreclosure, called *reinstatement*.

As security for repayment of the friend's advance of funds, the seller-in-foreclosure conveys title to the friend. However, the seller remains in possession under a lease and option to repurchase the residence from the friend.

Later, the seller defaults on the rent due under the lease. The friend evicts the seller and sells the property to a buyer.

The seller-in-foreclosure now seeks to recover the value of his lost equity from his (former) friend. The seller claims EP law requires the seller's consent for the investor to sell the property since the transaction was a loan structured as a repurchase option entered into while the home was in foreclosure.

The friend claims EP law does not apply to him since he is not in the business of buying homes in foreclosure.

However, EP law applies to all persons whose conduct constitutes that of an EP investor, regardless of the number of EP transactions the friend completes. The friend resold the property without further written consent from the seller (even though the friend held title), in violation of equity purchase law.

The EP investor's failure to obtain the seller-in-foreclosure's written permission prior to resale of the seller's principal residence imposes liability on the EP investor for money damages for breach of the seller's repurchase (redemption) rights. The money losses collectible by the seller are based on the value of the property at the time the property is transferred without the seller's consent. [**Segura** v. **McBride** (1992) 5 CA4th 1028)

Continued occupancy

Any leaseback agreement negotiated with the seller-in-foreclosure must be reduced to a written addendum as part of the EP agreement, or by amendment prior to funding by the EP investor or conveyance of title by the seller. [CC §1695.3(f)]

The seller-in-foreclosure and EP investor might agree to any one of several occupancy arrangements:

- a sale-leaseback, typically a *holdover tenancy* for a fixed time period at which point the seller-in-foreclosure must vacate [See **first tuesday** Form 272];

- a sale-leaseback with an option to purchase as an addendum (which is a mortgage-in-fact), sometimes called a *reverse lease-option*. [See **first tuesday** Forms 161 and 550]; or

- an unexecuted purchase agreement coupled with a lease-option agreement with the seller-in-foreclosure, a formal variation on the prior arrangement. [See **first tuesday** Form 163]

In a straight leaseback, a security deposit and the first month's rent are payable to the EP investor at the closing of an EP sale since the seller-in-foreclosure will holdover for a specified time period. The seller usually prepays rent and a security deposit through escrow from his net sales proceeds.

Sale-leaseback recharacterized

Inherent in an EP sale-leaseback and option is the risk the loan transaction will be misinterpreted by the local assessor, the existing lender or the Internal Revenue Service (IRS).

Reassessment of the property occurs on execution of a sale-leaseback. [**Pacific Southwest Realty Company** v. **County of Los Angeles** (1991) 1 C4th 155]

However, if the financing scheme is brought to the attention of the assessor, a sale-leaseback intertwined with an option to repurchase is correctly recharacterized by all agencies (and the seller) as a single **financing arrangement**, rather than two consecutive sale and repurchase transactions. Thus, no change of ownership occurs, even though title is revested, and no reassessment takes place. [Calif. Revenue & Taxation Code §62(c)]

Title insurers might not issue title insurance to an investor taking title in an EP transaction unless the seller-in-foreclosure signs an estoppel affidavit declaring the EP transaction is an absolute conveyance to the EP investor and not merely security for a loan.

Thus, if the seller-in-foreclosure is given a repurchase option, the sale-leaseback is viewed as a financing arrangement, and the title company, if aware of the repurchase option, will not provide the EP investor title insurance, even though he appears as the vested owner of the property. The transaction, to be insurable, must be restructured as a note and trust deed (which would have the same financial impact).

Existing lenders view a sale-leaseback, with or without a repurchase option, as an opportunity to **call or recast** a loan under their *due-on clause —*

should they become aware of the facts. The two-step transaction (two sales) is in law a mortgage, and the transaction is a loan. If the "loan" is secured by a one-to-four unit residential property that is owner-occupied, the first trust deed lender cannot call the loan using the due-on clause.

Federal tax consequences

The **IRS** also treats sale-leasebacks as loan transactions, not a sale or a purchase, when the seller-in-foreclosure remains in possession and is given an option to repurchase title to the property. Taxwise, the sale-leaseback is a financing arrangement when:

- rental payments under a long-term lease equal an amortization of the fair market value over the term of the lease when title is to be reconveyed to the seller/tenant; or

- the final/balloon payment required to exercise a repurchase option equals principal and accrued interest that would be financially similar to the due-date payoff under a note and trust deed. [**M & W Gear Co**. v. **Commissioner** (7th Cir. 1971) 446 F2d 841]

The EP investor's tax consequences on **recharacterization** of a sale-leaseback and purchase option as a financing arrangement include:

- denial of any depreciation deductions;

- imputing of interest income reportable at 110% of the applicable federal rate (AFR) [Internal Revenue Code §1274(e)];

- reporting of would-be rental income as investment/portfolio category interest income on a loan; and

- denial of any rental operating expenses (impound for taxes and insurance premiums belonging to the seller), since the transaction is a loan.

For the EP investor to receive the tax benefits of owning real estate, he must limit the leaseback to a periodic tenancy (month-to-month) or a tenancy with a fixed date for the tenant to vacate the premises — no repurchase option allowed either way.

No repurchase options

An EP investor structuring a sale-leaseback, which does not include a repurchase option, eliminates the risk the transaction will be recharacterized as a financing arrangement if:

- the seller-in-foreclosure is given the lease in full or part exchange for his equity (or for his payment of rent); or

- the rent charged is the current fair market rate; and

- the leaseback agreement sets a "fixed" time period for the lease to terminate and possession to be transferred to the EP investor. [**Camp** v. **Matich** (1948) 87 CA2d 660]

If the seller-in-foreclosure is not given a repurchase option and remains in possession of the property after the lease expires, the EP investor can begin an unlawful detainer (UD) action without prior notice to the seller to vacate, and proceed to have the prior owner evicted. [**Ryland** v. **Appelbaum** (1924) 70 CA 268]

As in any lease, the leaseback agreement should provide for payment of increased rent if the seller-in-foreclosure does not vacate upon either the expiration of the lease or a notice to vacate used under a month-to-month rental agreement to terminate the tenancy. A reminder: The seller-in-foreclosure has defaulted on home payments. Thus, he is a serious credit risk as a tenant for the EP investor.

Chapter 22

Short payoffs on loans in foreclosure

This chapter examines the income and profit reporting for the seller-in-foreclosure when the price paid by the buyer is less than the balance due on loans encumbering the property and the loans are paid off at a discount.

The discount: income, profit or loss?

An owner whose principal residence is now in foreclosure purchased it for the price of $450,000, with a down payment of $25,000. The remaining $425,000 of the purchase price he paid was funded by a fixed-rate, purchase-assist loan covered by default insurance, called *private mortgage insurance* (PMI).

The homeowner's *cost basis* in the residence is the $450,000 price he paid, plus transactional costs he incurred on the acquisition. When he sells the property, his **cost basis** will be subtracted from the net sales price he receives, called the *price realized* by the IRS. The result is the profit or loss he will report whether he resells the property or disposes of it by foreclosure or a deed-in-lieu.

The residence was purchased at the peak of the previous real estate boom. Due to the cyclical decline in real estate values since then, the owner's residence is now worth $325,000. However, while the monthly mortgage payments have remained the same, the owner's household income has declined. All of the homeowner's **disposable income** is now consumed by payments on the loan. Thus, the owner can no longer afford to make those payments.

Editor's note — The same impact on a household's disposable income occurs for those homeowners who experience an increase in the dollar amount of monthly installments on the resetting of payments for a negative amortization ARM loan, euphemistically called a subprime loan, *while at the same time receiving normal pay raises.*

The loan balance is now $405,000, an amount far in excess of the current market value of the property.

The owner lists the residence with a broker in an attempt to sell it and get out from under the excess debt. As agreed with the broker, any purchase agreement entered into will be *subject to the lender's approval* and acceptance of the net sales proceeds as the payoff amount, called a *contingency provision*. [See Form 274 accompanying this chapter]

The broker taking the listing understands that because the fair market value (FMV) of the residence is below the outstanding debt encumbering it, he must, as additional effort required to sell the property, negotiate with the lender for a *discount* on a loan payoff demand, called a *short payoff*. If the lender agrees to accept a short payoff by discounting the amount due, the property will have gone through what has become known as a "short sale."

The income **tax issue** confronting the seller when reporting the sale of his principal residence to the IRS and the FTB is whether:

- the discount is reportable as an adjustment decreasing his cost basis, which either reduces his capital loss or creates a profit excluded from taxation by the home profit exclusion of $250,000 per homeowner; or

- the discount is reported by the seller as *discharge-of-indebtedness income* taxable at ordinary income tax rates.

The short sale and accompanying discount

A **short sale** is a sale of property that:

- generates net proceeds in an amount less than the principal balance owed on the loan(s) of record; and

- the lender(s) accepts the **seller's net proceeds** from the sale in full satisfaction of the loan(s).

The difference between the principal balance on the loan and the lesser amount of the net sale proceeds accepted by the lender in full payoff of the loan is called a *discount*, an arrangement more commonly called a *short payoff*.

If the broker is initially unable to negotiate a **short pay** (discount) with the lender, the seller will make no further payments, if he has not already ceased doing so. Thus, the lender is forced to foreclose if it fails to arrange a compromise, called a *pre-foreclosure workout*.

Some lenders require the seller to default on payments for three months before they will consider a discount to accommodate a short sale. A default is the step taken by the owner to **exercise** the "put option" he holds, a right inherent in all trust deed loans, allowing the owner to force the lender to buy the property through the foreclosure process.

The broker's ability to successfully negotiate a short payoff with the lender depends in part on the type of loan that encumbers the seller's property.

If the loan is an FHA-insured loan on an owner-occupied, single family residence, the lender may only accept a short payoff if the owner qualifies for FHA pre-foreclosure sale treatment. To qualify, the homeowner must be in default on at least three months' payments, in addition to other financial ability requirements. [HUD Mortgagee Letter 94-45]

Likewise, if the loan is a conventional loan covered by **private mortgage insurance** (PMI), the lender's willingness to negotiate a short pay will be influenced by the lender's ability to settle their claim with the private mortgage insurer to cover the lender's loss on the short payoff. Much documentation on the seller's solvency and the property's value must be produced for analysis by the lender.

The interference by short-sale coordinators

Consider the seller-in-foreclosure who owes $405,000 on the **purchase-assist** trust deed loan encumbering his residence. The property's FMV is $325,000. The original purchase price, and thus the seller's cost basis, is $450,000 (plus closing costs).

The seller has received an advertisement that implies he will incur taxes at ordinary income tax rates on any discount taken by the lender on the sale or foreclosure of the property, called *discharge-of-indebtedness income* by the Internal Revenue Service (IRS).

The ad then claims the homeowner will avoid the **tax liability** resulting from income generated by the discount on a short sale if title to the property is transferred to the person offering the service, called a *coordinator*.

The coordinator offers to take title to the real estate subject to the foreclosure and either:

- complete or arrange a short sale of the property himself; or

- allow the lender to foreclose against the coordinator for nonpayment of installments.

Does the advertisement correctly represent the homeowner's tax reporting and tax liability exposure from a short sale handled by whomever takes title subject to the loan?

No! The short sale of an owner-occupied one-to-four unit residential property encumbered by a purchase-assist or improvement loan, called a *nonrecourse loan* under California anti-deficiency law, does not trigger IRS reporting of ordinary income by the seller for the discounted and discharged portion of the loan.

SHORT SALE ADDENDUM
Loan Discount Approval

DATE: _____, 20_____, at _____, California.

Items left blank or unchecked are not applicable.

FACTS:

1. This is an addendum to the following agreement:

   ☐ Purchase agreement   ☐ Counteroffer

   ☐ Escrow instructions   ☐ _____

   1.1 ☐ of same date, or dated _____, 20_____, at _____, California,

   1.2 entered into by_____, as the Buyer,

   1.3 and_____, as the Seller,

   1.4 regarding real estate referred to as _____

   _____.

AGREEMENT:

In addition to the terms of the above referenced agreement, Buyer and Seller agree to the following:

2. Close of escrow is conditioned on Seller obtaining payoff demands at a discount from the lienholders of record in full satisfaction of all amounts owed them.

   2.1 The discounts are to be amounts which collectively allow Seller to fully perform on this agreement and escrow instructions without the need for escrow to call for funds from Seller to close escrow.

   2.2 Seller on opening escrow to promptly request payoff demands from the lienholders, directly or through escrow, and diligently assist each lienholder in their analysis of their discount and processing of their payoff demand by providing them with information and documentation on themselves and this transaction.

3. After _____, 20_____, this agreement may be terminated by either Buyer or Seller should Seller be unable to obtain written payoff demands, or consent from the lienholders, to accept Seller's proceeds from this transaction which remain after disbursement of all costs incurred by Seller in the full performance of this agreement and escrow instructions. [See **ft** Form 183]

4. Seller may accept backup offers contingent on the cancellation of this agreement.

   4.1 If backup offers are received, they will be submitted to the lienholders for payoff demands which may be accepted by the lienholders in lieu of a payoff demand on escrow complying with this agreement.

   4.2 Should lienholders submit a written payoff demand in a backup offer acceptable to Seller, Seller may terminate this agreement. [See **ft** Form 183]

5. The Seller understands a discount by a lienhold in full satisfaction of the debt owed will likely have consequences on the Seller's creditworthiness and income tax reporting, and other unforseen difficulties, including,

   5.1 The delinquencies on payments due the lienholders and the discount allowing for payment of a lesser amount then owed may be reported by the lienholder to credit reporting agencies and adversely affect the Seller in the future.

   5.2 The amount of the interest on the discount on the principal will be reported by the lienholder to the IRS as a 1099 Form receipt of income, and depending on the recourse or nonrecourse nature of the debt discounted, or whether secured by the Seller's principal residence, will be reported by the Seller as discharge of indebtedness income, part of the price realized on the sale or a reduction in cost basis.

   5.3 ☐ Seller may terminate this agreement within five days of acceptance, based on Seller's reasonable disapproval or the disapproval of tax or legal advisors to the Seller, of the consequences of this discount on Seller's credit or tax reporting, or on legal issues arising due to the discount. [See **ft** Form 183]

I agree to the terms stated above.	**I agree to the terms stated above.**
Date: _____, 20_____	Date: _____, 20_____
Buyer: _____	Seller: _____
Signature: _____	Signature: _____
Buyer: _____	Seller: _____
Signature: _____	Signature: _____

FORM 274   10-07   ©2008 **first tuesday**, P.O. BOX 20069, RIVERSIDE, CA 92516   (800) 794-0494

For reporting discounts on purchase-assist and improvement (nonrecourse) loans, the owner closing a sale of his principal residence after January 1, 2007 and on or before December 31, 2009, no longer adds the amount of the lender's discount to the price paid by the buyer to set the *price realized* on the sale — as was done in the past.

Instead, the discount on purchase-assist and improvement loans, in this case $80,000, is now deducted from the seller's cost basis ($450,000) to set an adjusted cost basis of $370,000. Thus, the sale produces a capital loss of $45,000 — the price realized ($325,000) minus the owner's adjusted cost basis ($370,000).

The tax result is congruous with the prior reporting rule: the discount is not reported as *discharge-of-indebtedness* income and produces a personal loss on the sale.

Discounts on refinancing or equity loans

The accounting for a discount on a short sale of a loan that refinanced a purchase-assist or improvement loan is very different. Consider an owner who originally purchased his principal residence for $450,000, taking out a $425,000 purchase assist loan. He later refinances the property for $525,000. The $100,000 in funds received in excess of the loan payoff is not used to purchase or improve the property. Thus, the owner's cost basis remains at $450,000 after the refinancing.

The refinancing is a *recourse* loan that carries with it different tax consequences than the owner's original purchase-assist and improvement loans that were **nonrecourse** loans.

*Editor's note — **Equity loans** and **refinancing** are always recourse loans under California's anti-deficiency law since the net proceeds do not themselves finance the owner's purchase or improvement of the one-to-four unit residence that, in whole or in part, he occupies as his principal residence. [Calif. Code of Civil Procedure §580(b)]*

The residence's current FMV is now only $325,000. Further, the owner is no longer able or willing to make his monthly mortgage payments.

The owner hires a listing agent who sells the property for $325,000 and negotiates a **short payoff** with the lender at a **discount** of $200,000.

Unlike purchase-assist and improvement (nonrecourse) loans on a principal residence, the amount of the discount on the refinancing (recourse) debt is not simply subtracted from the homeowner's cost basis to determine the tax consequences of the short sale. Instead, the portion of the refinancing exceeding the amount of the homeowner's purchase and improvement loans paid off by the refinancing ($100,000) is reported as **discharged indebtedness income**, limited to the amount of the discount.

Thus, $100,000 of the discount is taxable as discharge-of-indebtedness income at personal income rates. The additional discount amount of $100,000 remaining after first applying the $200,000 discount to the excess funds received from the refinancing of the purchase-assist and improvement loans is then excluded from income and not reported.

However, the remaining $100,000 amount of the discount excluded from income is then subtracted from the owner's cost basis ($400,000), as in the case of discounted purchase-assist and improvement loans. [26 United States Code §108(h)]

Editor's note — Had the property been sold before January 1, 2007, the entire amount of the discount ($200,000) on the recourse loan would have been reported as income and taxed at a rate of up to 35%.

Recourse loans taxed as income after 2009

The preferential tax reporting currently available for a discounted payoff of both nonrecourse and recourse loans based on the amount of purchase-assist and improvement loans will not be allowed on short sales of real estate involving *recourse loans* after December 31, 2009. No portion of the discount on a **recourse loan** will be subtracted from the owner's cost basis.

Instead the recourse loan discount will be reported as gross income, as it was reported before

January 1, 2007. Thus, the owner will not even be entitled to the 15% (capital gain) to 25% (recapture of depreciation gains) tax rate on profit for that portion of the discount representing a portion of the original purchase-assist or improvement loans. Instead, the full discount will be taxed at ordinary income rates (17% to 35% in 2007).

When a short sale occurs after December 31, 2009 on real estate encumbered by a recourse loan, the seller will incur a tax liability at **ordinary income rates** on the discount, which is labelled *discharge-of-indebtedness income*. Conversely, when a nonrecourse debt is discounted on a short sale, the seller's tax liability, if any, will still be on any profit taken on the price realized. That **price realized** will be set as the principal amount of the nonrecourse loan, without concern for the discount or the property's fair market value. [Revenue Regulations §1.1001-2(a)(2)]

For example, an owner's property is encumbered by a $400,000 trust deed loan. The loan is a **recourse debt** that exposes the owner to a deficiency judgment if the value of the secured real estate becomes less than the amount of the debt. The real estate is now worth only $300,000, $100,000 less than the loan amount, which is the deficiency. However, the owner's cost basis in the real estate is $450,000.

The owner sells the real estate on a short sale. The net amount the buyer pays for the real estate is $300,000. The lender accepts the net proceeds from the sale as a short payoff and in full satisfaction of the **recourse note**. The remaining unpaid balance of $100,000, the discount, is forgiven by cancellation of the note since the lender does not judicially foreclose as is first required to pursue a deficiency judgment against the borrower.

The owner's tax consequences, calculated based on both the sale of the property and the discount of the **recourse loan**, include:

- a **capital loss** of $150,000 ($300,000 price received from the buyer minus the $450,000 owner's cost basis); and

- **discharge-of-indebtedness income** of $100,000 ($400,000 loan amount minus $300,000 price realized and paid to the lender), reported as ordinary income.

Again, since the owner's cost basis is greater than the sales price on the sale of the owner's *principal residence*, the resulting capital loss is a **personal loss**. Since it is not a loss on property that falls within an income category due to its personal nature, it cannot be written off to offset the taxation of other income — specifically the discharge-of-indebtedness income.

Thus, after December 31, 2009, a discount on the payoff of a recourse loan encumbering a principal residence will result in taxable discharge-of-indebtedness income. Ironically, this income produced by the short sale of the principal residence cannot be offset by the capital loss produced by the same principal residence on the sale. The loss is classified as personal. [**Vukasovich** v. **Commissioner of Internal Revenue** (9th Cir. 1986) 790 F2d 1409; Internal Revenue Code §165(c)]

Discount reporting for investor-owners

The new tax reporting rules in effect until December 31, 2009 only apply to the short sale of the owner's principal residence. Discount reporting for the short sale of investor-owned property is still controlled by treasury regulations.

For an investor, the debt discharged by a discount of a loan paid off on a short sale of property other than the investor's principal residence will be a recourse loan producing discharge-of-indebtedness income, unless the investor:

- *assumed* a nonrecourse loan;

- executed a *carryback note* secured by the property when acquired; or

- executed a note containing an *exculpatory clause* releasing the investor from any personal liability.

When the discount is on any of these types of nonrecourse loans, the investor's discharged debt will be added to the price the buyer pays for the property, setting a **price realized** equal to the amount due the lender. [Rev. Reg. §1.1001-2(a)(2)]

Foreclosure on a recourse loan

Whether real estate encumbered by a recourse loan is lost to the lender in a foreclosure sale or sold to a buyer under a purchase agreement, the owner has disposed of the property. Thus, both situations should produce the same tax consequences; however, they often do not due to the amount of the lender's bid and the type of foreclosure sale.

Consider a judicial foreclosure sale of real estate encumbered by a recourse loan. The lender seeks a deficiency judgment on completion of the sale since the proceeds from the judicial foreclosure sale are insufficient to satisfy the outstanding principal balance on the recourse loan.

The investor-owner reports the amount of the lender's bid at the judicial sale (plus the amount of any liens with priority) as the *price realized* on his loss of the property through foreclosure. [**Aizawa** v. **Commissioner of Internal Revenue** (1992) 99 TC 197]

To calculate his profit or loss from the foreclosure sale, the investor subtracts his cost basis from the **price realized**, which is the high bid at the sale since the loan is recourse in nature. [Rev. Regs. §§1.1001-2(a)(2), 1.1001-2(a)(4)(ii), 1.1001-2(c) Example 8]

As long as the deficiency judgment remains unpaid, the owner will not incur any tax liability for discharge of indebtedness that is represented by the amount of the judgment. However, if the lender later cancels the deficiency judgment or allows it to expire (ten years), discount consequences apply.

An alternative of great importance to a seller, such as an investor, faced with discharge-of-indebtedness income on a recourse loan, now or after 2009, is to avoid a short sale, and thus a short payoff, by forcing the lender to foreclose and acquire the property. Lenders nearly always foreclose by a trustee's sale.

Further, lenders at a trustee's sale usually bid in the property for the amount of all monies owed them, regardless of the property's present market value. Thus, they have been fully satisfied without a discount or uncollectible amount remaining due from the owner. Thus, no discharge-of-indebtedness income.

Listing brokers take note. You are duty bound to care for and protect your client seller from known adverse consequences. Also, consider a §1031 transaction that transfers the over-encumbered property to another person who is willing to deal with the over-encumbered position in exchange for receiving some cash on the exchange.

Buying Homes in Foreclosure, 5th Edition

Instructions: Quizzes are open book. All answers are True or False.
Answer key is located on page 248.

Quiz 1 — Pages 3-33

_____1. An equity purchase (EP) transaction occurs when an owner-occupied, one-to-four unit residential property in foreclosure is acquired for investment or dealer purposes.

_____2. To be subject to equity purchase law, an investor must buy at least three owner-occupied, one-to-four unit residential properties in foreclosure.

_____3. During the seller-in-foreclosure's contract cancellation period for purchase agreements, the equity purchaser may accept a conveyance of the seller's interest in the property.

_____4. Once escrow closes, an equity purchaser's title is subject to the seller's two year right of rescission.

_____5. Delinquent interest on an existing loan that accrues before an EP investor purchases the property is an expense to the investor, even if the seller pays the interest.

_____6. Prior to December, 2007, a broker representing an EP investor when negotiating transaction was required to be bonded by a surety for any losses incurred by the seller due to the broker's conduct.

_____7. A person who, for a fee from the owner-in-foreclosure, agrees to stop or postpone the foreclosure sale is called a foreclosure consultant.

_____8. A foreclosure consultant may collect an advance fee.

_____9. On receipt of a notice of rescission from the seller in an EP transaction, the EP investor has two years to reconvey title to the seller.

_____10. The price the EP investor pays for the property in foreclosure may be considered unconscionable.

Quiz 2 — Pages 37-81

_____1. A beneficiary is not authorized by the power-of-sale provision in the trust deed to instruct the trustee to initiate a non-judicial trustee's foreclosure to sell the property described in the trust deed.

_____2. Once an NOD is recorded, the owner's right to redeem the property by a full payoff of the loan exists up to the five business days before the date of the trustee's sale.

_____3. In an equity purchase (EP) transaction, the seller is required to complete a transfer disclosure statement (TDS).

_____4. A broker's general duty to disclose all property conditions that affect the property's value can be eliminated by the broker inserting an "as-is" disclaimer in the purchase agreement.

_____5. An EP investor who discovers defects on the property after acceptance, but prior to the close of escrow, has no other remedy but to cancel the purchase agreement.

_____6. A home inspection is a physical examination of a premises to identify material defects in the condition of structure, systems, and components of the improvements on the property.

_____ 7. The use of the Natural Hazard Disclosure Statement is mandated on the sale of all property.

_____ 8. A seller-in-foreclosure who provides good faith estimates about the property's operating potential as a rental may not be held liable for inaccuracies.

_____ 9. An EP investor may rely on the preliminary title report as an accurate representation of the condition of title.

_____ 10. A binder, also called a commitment to issue, entitles the insured to title insurance coverage until a new policy is issued to a purchaser on resale of the property or a lender on a refinance.

Quiz 3 — Pages 83-116

_____ 1. The Internal Revenue Service (IRS) is authorized to negotiate with an equity purchase (EP) seller (or investor) to accept partial payment of an income tax lien in exchange for a release of the lien.

_____ 2. When a homeowner is in bankruptcy, an automatic homestead lien is not enforceable against an IRS tax lien.

_____ 3. A declaration of homestead cannot be recorded on a mobilehome that is not considered real estate.

_____ 4. The maximum homestead amount a homeowner with no dependents can qualify for is $50,000.

_____ 5. Even if a do-on-sale clause does not exist in the trust deed, the EP investor must still obtain the lender's approval to assume the loan.

_____ 6. A lender's conduct can never constitute a waiver of the lender's due-on-sale rights.

_____ 7. Borrowers under programs insured by the Federal Housing Administration (FHA) or the Veterans Administration (VA) receive anti-deficiency protection.

_____ 8. A buyer assuming a Veterans Administration (VA) loan originated on or after March 1, 1988, must pay a fee to the VA of .5% of the loan balance.

_____ 9. A seller is not personally liable for any deficiencies on non-recourse debt taken over by the EP investor.

_____ 10. When a lender enters into an agreement with both the EP investor and the seller for the investor's assumption of the loan and the seller's release of liability, the agreement is called an exculpatory agreement.

Quiz 4 — Pages 119-169

_____ 1. After the EP investor assigns his purchase rights to a substitute buyer, the substitute buyer assumes the investor's position as the buyer in escrow.

_____ 2. A substitute buyer is not subject to the seller-in-foreclosure's two-year right of rescission.

_____ 3. A release and substitution agreement requires the seller to look solely to the substitute buyer for performance of the EP agreement.

_____ 4. A blind pool investment program is a corporate security.

_____**5.** A beneficiary statement does not have to include the amount of any additional charges incurred by the beneficiary which have become part of the trust deed lien.

_____**6.** A payoff demand is a written statement of the amounts required to pay off the loan and obtain a reconveyance of the trust deed.

_____**7.** A sale-leaseback and option arrangement is considered a mortgage.

_____**8.** A seller-in-foreclosure with an option to repurchase the property may deny the EP investor permission to sell and transfer title without giving any reason.

_____**9.** A short sale is the sale of real estate for a price lower than the amount due on the loan.

_____**10.** An owner incurs a tax liability on the short sale of real estate encumbered by a nonrecourse note.

Answer References

The following are the answers to the quizzes for
Buying Homes in Foreclosure, 5th Edition
and the page numbers where they are located.

Quiz 1	Quiz 2	Quiz 3	Quiz 4
1. T 3	1. F 37	1. T 86	1. T 138
2. F 3	2. F 38	2. T 87	2. F 140
3. F 4	3. T 43	3. T 90	3. T 142
4. T 5	4. F 44	4. T 91	4. T 143
5. F 16	5. F 52	5. F 102	5. F 157
6. T 23	6. T 54	6. F 106	6. T 158
7. T 24	7. F 57	7. F 108	7. T 163
8. F 26	8. T 63	8. T 109	8. F 164
9. F 30	9. F 71	9. T 112	9. T 167
10. T 31	10. T 81	10. F 116	10. F 168

Cases

California Codes

Code of Civil Procedure

Corporations Code

Financial Code

Government Code

Federal Codes

Topical Index